# The Cambridge Program for the Social Studies Test

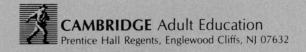

**CAMBRIDGE** Adult Education
Prentice Hall Regents, Englewood Cliffs, NJ 07632

© 1988 by Prentice Hall Regents
Published by Prentice-Hall, Inc.
A Division of Simon & Schuster
Englewood Cliffs, New Jersey 07632

Printed in the United States of America

10  9  8  7  6  5  4  3  2  1

ISBN  0-8428-8702-4

Prentice-Hall International (UK) Limited, *London*
Prentice-Hall of Australia Pty. Limited, *Sydney*
Prentice-Hall Canada Inc., *Toronto*
Prentice-Hall Hispanoamericana, S.A., *Mexico*
Prentice-Hall of India Private Limited, *New Delhi*
Prentice-Hall of Japan, Inc., *Tokyo*
Simon & Schuster Asia Pte. Ltd., *Singapore*
Editora Prentice-Hall do Brasil, Ltda., *Rio de Janeiro*

# The Cambridge GED Program

## Consulting Editors

Mary Ann Corley
Supervisor of Adult Education
Baltimore County Public Schools

Del Gratia Doss
Supervisor, Adult Basic Education
St. Louis, Missouri

Ron Froman
Administrator of Adult Education
Orange County Public Schools, Orlando, Florida

Lawrence Levin
KNILE Educational & Training Association.
Former Director ABE/ESL/HSE Services
New York City Board of Education

Noreen Lopez
Adult Educator
Illinois

Dorothy Hammond
Coordinator
New York State Writing Project

Arturo McDonald
Assistant Superintendent—Adult Education
Brownsville, Texas

Cheryl Moore
Curriculum Director, Windham School System
Texas Department of Corrections

Carrie Robinson Weir
Director, Adult Education Resource Center
Jersey City State College

Harold Wilson
Director of Adult Basic Education
Indianapolis Public Schools

Jane Zinner
Director of Grants and Curriculum
Association for California School Administrators

## Contributing Editors

Gloria Cohen, Ed.D.
Consultant, Curriculum & Gifted Education
New York Metropolitan Area

Carole Deletiner
Adult Basic Education Teacher
Formerly, New York City Technical College

Don Gerstein
Academic Educator
Wyoming State Penitentiary 1981–1986

Nathaniel Howard
Senior Training Representative
Consolidated Edison, New York City

Joan Knight
Former City-wide Supervisor of Staff Development
New York City Board of Education Adult program

Bonnie Longnion
Dean of Continuing Education
North Harris County College, Kingwood, Texas

Joe Mangano
Research Associate
State University of New York at Albany

Ada Rogers
Adult Education GED Program
Broward County, Florida, School System

Ann Rowe
Education Specialist
New York State

Elois Scott
Reading Specialist
University of Florida, Gainesville

Stephen Steurer
Correctional Academic Coordinator
Maryland State Department of Education

Dr. Jay Templin
Professor of Biology
Widener University, Delaware Campus

Jeffrey Tenzer
Auxiliary Services for High Schools
New York City

# The Cambridge GED Program

## Writers

Gary Apple
Owen Boyle
Jesse Browner
Phyllis Cohen
Carole Deletiner
Randee Falk
Don Gerstein
Peter Guthrie
Alan Hines
Jeanne James
Lois Kasper
Rachel Kranz
Gloria Levine
Amy Litt
Dennis Mendyk
Rebecca Motil
Susan Muller
Marcia Mungenast
Thomas Repensek
Ada Rogers
Ann Rowe
Richard Rozakis
Elois Scott
Sally Stepanek
Steve Steurer
Carol Stone
Lynn Tiutczenko
Robin Usyak
Kenneth Uva
Shelley Uva
Tom Walz
Willa Wolcott
Patricia Wright-Stover
Karen Wunderman

## Executive Editor

Jerry Long

## Senior Editor

Timothy Foote

## Project Editors

James Fina
Diane Maass

## Subject Editors

Jim Bedell
Diane Engel
Randee Falk
Scott Gillam
Rebecca Motil
Thomas Repensek

## Art and Design

Brian Crede Associates
Adele Scheff
Hal Keith

# Contents

# Practice

# Simulation

# Introduction

The following pages will introduce you to the Social Studies Test and to the organization of this book. You will read about ways that you can use this book to your best advantage.

## What Is the Social Studies Test?

The Social Studies Test of the GED Tests examines your ability to understand, use, analyze, and evaluate social studies material: information from the fields of history, geography, economics, political science, and behavioral science.

## What Kind of Questions Are on the Test?

When you take the test, you will read passages and answer questions that test your understanding: you will be required to restate information, summarize ideas, or identify implications of the information given in the passages you read. You will also be tested on your ability to use, analyze, and evaluate what you understand. You may read a passage that defines social studies terms and then be asked to choose examples that demonstrate the meanings of those terms. Or you may read a passage from a newspaper editorial, and be asked to distinguish facts from opinions, to recognize an assumption that the writer makes, to distinguish the author's conclusion from the supporting evidence, or identify a cause-and-effect relationship being described.

Finally, you may read a passage that presents an argument about a social studies topic and then be required to decide how valid the argument is. You may be asked to decide whether the data presented proves what the author says it does. You may be asked to recognize the hidden values and belief systems that are behind what the author writes.

None of the questions will test only your prior knowledge of social studies. You will not be asked to give any formulas, to name any scientists, or to remember any dates. You will be asked only to demonstrate that you can understand, use, and think critically about social studies material. The Social Studies Test consists of only multiple-choice questions.

## What Are the Reading Passages Like?

The passages you will read vary in length. Some short passages have only one question to answer; longer ones usually have several. Sometimes you will be given graphic material along with written material. For example, you might be given a map of projected changes in state populations from 1980 to 2000 and then be asked which states are expected to have the largest population increases. Or you might be given an excerpt from an article about crime and then be asked to identify the author's assumptions about the best way for society to reduce crime.

The Social Studies Test has 64 items, or questions. The content for Social Studies includes:

- History (including global issues):                                      25%
- Geography:                                                              15%
- Economics:                                                              20%
- Political Science:                                                      20%
- Behavioral Science (Anthropology, Psychology, Sociology):              20%

## What You Will Find in This Book

This book gives you a four-step preparation for taking the Social Studies Test. The four steps are as follows:

### Step One: Prediction

In this first step, you will find the Predictor Test. This test is very much like the actual Social Studies Test, but is only half as long. Taking the Predictor Test will give you an idea of what the real GED will be like. By evaluating your performance on the Predictor Test, you will get a sense of your strengths and weaknesses. This information will help you to plan your studies accordingly.

### Step Two: Instruction

The instruction section has two units. The first unit, Reading Strategies, can help you develop useful reading skills. It will help you sharpen your reading skills and will serve as a preparation for studying the second unit and taking the GED successfully. In the first unit, you will also study useful strategies for approaching graphic materials such as maps, charts, graphs, tables, and cartoons.

Unit II, Foundations in Social Studies, focuses on social studies material itself. In Unit II, you will read several lessons in each of the five content areas of social studies. Altogether, the lessons develop the foundation of concepts and facts you should have when you take the GED. Even though no social studies question on the GED tests only your prior knowledge, every question requires you to draw on your general knowledge of social studies. The purpose of Unit II is to help you organize and add to the general knowledge about social studies that you already have.

Each lesson in Unit II ends with questions based on the material in the lessons. Even though the items are usually not multiple-choice questions, they require you to use the same thinking processes that you will need to answer GED questions. The questions also give you the opportunity to practice writing. In completing this unit, you will be using the same kinds of reading and thinking skills that are required on the actual GED.

Both units of the Instruction section are divided into chapters. Each chapter in Unit I covers a different aspect of reading skill. In Unit II there is a chapter for each type of social studies covered in the test. Chapters are divided into lessons.

### Step Three: Practice

This section gives you valuable practice in answering the type of questions you will find on the actual Social Studies Test. There are two separate types of practice activity in Step Three.

- **Practice Items**  The Practice Items are GED-like questions grouped according to the content areas of social studies. For example, you will find items based on history grouped together, items based on geography grouped together, and so on. The Practice Items allow you to test your understanding of one field of social studies at a time.

- **Practice Test**  The second type of practice, the Practice Test, is structured like the actual Social Studies Test. In the Practice Test, the types of social studies vary from passage to passage, just as they do on the real test. This section gives you an opportunity to practice taking a test similar to the GED.

Each of the practice activities is made up of 64 items, the same number of questions as are on the actual Social Studies Test. You can use your results to track your progress and to give you an idea of how prepared you are to take the real test.

### Step Four: Simulation

Finally, this book offers a simulated version of the Social Studies Test. The number of questions, their level of difficulty, and the way they are organized are the same as you will find on the actual test. You will have the same amount of time to answer the questions as you will have on the actual test. Taking the Simulated Test will be useful preparation for taking the GED. It will help you find out how ready you are to take the real exam.

### The Answer Key

At the back of this book, you will find a section called Answers and Explanations. The answer key contains the answers to all the questions in the Lesson Exercises, Chapter Quizzes, Unit Tests, Practice Items, the Practice Test, and the Simulated Test. The answer key is a valuable study tool: It not only tells you the right answer, but explains why each answer is right and points out the reading skill you needed to answer each question successfully. You can benefit a great deal by consulting the answer key after completing an activity.

## Using This Book

There are many ways to use this book. Whether you are working with an instructor or alone, you can use this book to prepare for the Social Studies Test in the way that works best for you.

### Take a Glance at the Table of Contents

Before doing anything else, look over the Table of Contents and get a feel for this book. You can compare the headings in the Table of Contents with the descriptions found in the preceding pages. You might also want to leaf through the book to see what each section looks like.

### Take the Predictor Test

Next, you will probably want to take the Predictor Test. As the introduction before the test explains, there is more than one way to take this test. Decide which is best for you.

Your performance and score on the Predictor Test will be very useful to you as you work with the rest of this book. It will point out your particular strengths and weaknesses, which can help you plan your course of study.

### Beginning Your Instruction

After you have analyzed your strengths and weaknesses, you are ready to begin instruction. It would be best for you to work through Unit I before beginning Unit II, since the first unit focuses on the reading strategies you will use in the second unit.

At the beginning of Unit I you will find a Progress Chart. As you complete a lesson or chapter quiz, you can record your performance on that chart. The chart allows you to track your progress, from lesson to lesson. If you feel you are not making enough progress, you can vary your study method or ask your teacher for help.

Unit II is organized according to the subject areas found on the test: history, geography, economics, political science, and behavioral science. You may want to work through the whole unit in order, completing the first chapter before going on to the second chapter. Or, you may wish to work on two or more of the chapters at the same time. Again, there is a Progress Chart at the beginning of the unit to record your progress.

### Using the Practice Section

When you complete a chapter in Unit II, you have a choice: You may proceed to the next chapter or you can get some practice on the type of social studies you just studied. The Practice Items (pages 176–204) are grouped according to the types of social studies covered by the chapters of Unit II. You can test yourself immediately after each chapter. If you wish, you can wait until you've finished all the chapters, and then do the Practice Items. You should take the Practice Test, however, only after you have finished Units I and II.

### Try Your Best!

As you study the lessons and complete the activities and tests in this book, you should give it your best effort. To attain a passing score on the GED, you will probably need to get half or more of the items correct. To give yourself a margin for passing, try to maintain a score of at least 80 percent correct as you work through this book.

The Progress Charts will help you compare your work with this 80 percent figure. If you maintain 80 percent scores, you are probably working at a level that will allow you to do well on the GED.

# Prediction

# Introduction

Imagine that you were going to take the GED test today. How do you think you would do? In which areas would you perform best, and in which areas would you have the most trouble? The Predictor Test that follows can help you answer these questions. It is called a Predictor Test because your test results can be used to predict where your strengths and your weaknesses lie in relation to the actual Social Studies Test of the GED.

The Predictor Test is like the actual GED test in many ways. It will check your skills as you apply them to the kind of social studies passages you will find on the real test. The questions are like those on the actual test.

## How to Take the Predictor Test

The Predictor Test will be most useful to you if you take it in a manner close to the way the actual test is given. If possible, you should complete it in one sitting, with as little distraction as possible. So that you have an accurate record of your performance, write your answers neatly on a sheet of paper, or use an answer sheet provided by your teacher.

As you take the test, don't be discouraged if you find you are having difficulty with some (or even many) of the questions. The purpose of this test is to predict your overall performance on the GED and to locate your particular strengths and weaknesses. So relax. There will be plenty of opportunities to correct any weaknesses and retest them.

You may want to time yourself to see how long you take to complete the test. When you take the actual Social Studies Test, you will be given 85 minutes. The Predictor Test is about half as long as the actual test. If you finish within $42\frac{1}{2}$ minutes, you are right on target. At this stage, however, you shouldn't worry too much if it takes you longer.

When you are done, check your answers by using the answer key that begins on page 16. Put a check by each item you answered correctly.

## How to Use Your Score

At the end of the test, you will find a Performance Analysis Chart. Fill in the chart; it will help you find out which areas you are more comfortable with, and which give you the most trouble.

As you begin each chapter in the book, you may want to refer back to the Performance Analysis Chart to see how well you did in that area of the Predictor Test.

# PREDICTOR TEST

**TIME:** $42\frac{1}{2}$ minutes
**Directions:** *Choose the one best answer to each question.*

1. A *balance of trade* is the difference in value between what a country sells to other countries (exports) and what it buys from them (imports). If a country's total exports are worth more than its total imports, it has a balance of trade *surplus*. If the opposite is true, it has a balance of trade *deficit*. Countries try to have surpluses.

   The best strategy for a country that wants to achieve a balance of trade surplus would be to

   (1) decrease the value of both imports and exports
   (2) increase the value of imports and decrease the value of exports
   (3) decrease the value of imports and increase the value of exports
   (4) keep the value of imports at the same level but increase the value of exports
   (5) increase the value of both imports and exports

2. Members of both the Senate and the House of Representatives participate in lawmaking. But the two bodies have some separate responsibilities. All bills concerning spending and money matters must begin in the House. However, only the Senate can ratify treaties and confirm the president's appointments. Which of the following would have to begin in the House?

   (1) consideration of the president's proposed budget for the year
   (2) confirmation of the appointment of a federal judge
   (3) ratification of a treaty on arms control
   (4) a bill to regulate interstate commerce
   (5) a bill about school prayer

*Items 3 and 4 are based on the following graphs.*

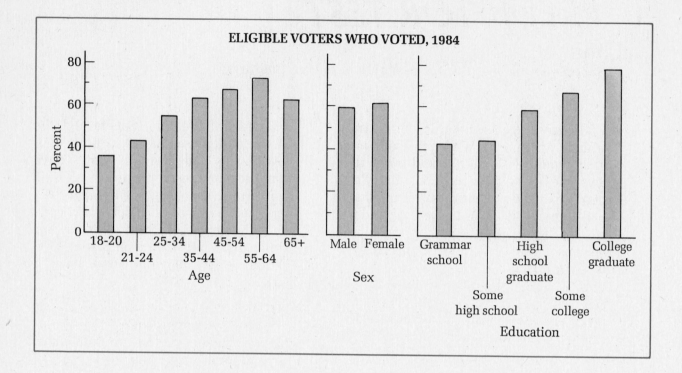

**ELIGIBLE VOTERS WHO VOTED, 1984**

3. Based on the graphs, which of the following people is LEAST likely to have voted in 1984?

(1) a 20-year-old male with a grammar-school education
(2) a 25-year-old female high-school graduate
(3) a 34-year-old male high-school graduate
(4) a 55-year-old male college graduate
(5) a 65-year-old female with some high-school education

4. Based on the graphs, a civic group that is trying to get nonvoters to register and vote should direct its efforts especially toward

(1) women
(2) high-school graduates
(3) college graduates
(4) young adults
(5) senior citizens

*Items 5 to 8* are based on the following passage.

Love is important in raising children, psychologists say, but it is not enough. Discipline is also necessary.

Discipline is not a simple matter of "dos" and "don'ts." It means setting well-defined limits for the child and allowing the child to move freely within those limits. Different parents may set different limits. That is, some will be stricter than others. This is all right. What matters is that parents don't constantly change the limits. Consistency is important.

Parents should try to strike a good balance. Authoritarian parents give their children responsibilities but few rights. Overly permissive parents give their children lots of rights but few responsibilities. Parents should avoid these extremes, giving their children both rights *and* responsibilities.

Parents' methods of disciplining are also important. Most parents use some physical punishment. Parents also discipline their children by "withdrawal of love," for example, by temporarily refusing to speak to a child. These methods of disciplining, used occasionally, are acceptable. But it is far better to emphasize praise and approval, when the child behaves well, and discussion, when there is a problem.

**5.** A father has a policy that no sweets are allowed. While standing at the grocery store checkout counter, his child spots some candy. She begins to beg, and the father, wanting to avoid a scene, buys it for her. A few days later the child asks for some bubble gum. The father becomes angry and yells at her. Which advice from the passage is he failing to follow?

(1) Children need love as well as discipline.
(2) Children need rights as well as responsibilities.
(3) Use of physical punishment should be limited.
(4) Rules should be consistent.
(5) Praise and approval can be important.

**6.** Which of the following statements best summarizes the main point of the passage?

(1) What children need most of all is discipline.
(2) Discipline of the right sort is important in raising children.
(3) Children should be given both rights and responsibilities.
(4) Discipline should include praise and discussion, not just punishment.
(5) Communication between parents and children is important.

**7.** A child who usually does well in school comes home one day with a bad report card. Based on the passage, which of the following is the best approach for a parent to take?

(1) Wait to see if the next report card shows improvement.
(2) Yell at the child and send him to his room.
(3) Discuss the report card with the child and try to find out what happened.
(4) Take the child to a Chinese restaurant and try to help the child feel better.
(5) Ignore the child, as a way of expressing anger.

**8.** Which of the following statements is NOT a recommendation of the passage?

(1) Love is important in raising a child.
(2) Discipline should be mainly a matter of "dos" and "don'ts."
(3) Discussion is important.
(4) Children need well-defined limits.
(5) Children need a certain amount of freedom.

*Item 9* is based on the following graph.

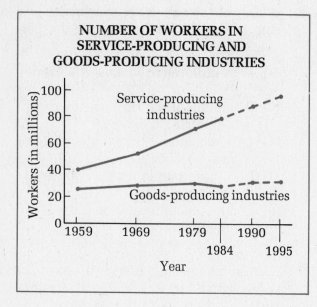

**NUMBER OF WORKERS IN SERVICE-PRODUCING AND GOODS-PRODUCING INDUSTRIES**

9. During the period shown in the graph, many women entered the labor force. Which of the following statements concerning these new members of the labor force is best supported by the graph?

   **(1)** Many women went into the service-producing industries.
   **(2)** Many women went into the goods-producing industries.
   **(3)** Many women went into low-paying careers.
   **(4)** Many women suffered periods of unemployment.
   **(5)** Many women had to retrain because of changes in the economy.

*Items 10 to 12* are based on the following information.

In the course of its history, the United States has pursued a number of different goals in dealing with other countries. Listed below are several of these foreign policy goals, with brief descriptions of each.

**[1] Isolationism:** avoiding close military, political, and economic relationships with other countries

**[2] Imperialism:** adding territory by means of force; acquiring an empire

**[3] Intervention:** using diplomatic and/or military means to support U.S. political and/or business interests abroad

**[4] Alliances:** pursuing military and economic partnerships with other countries or groups of countries

**[5] Détente:** trying to relax tensions with potentially hostile countries in order to preserve peace

10. In his last speech as president, George Washington advised his country to steer clear of all political entanglements with other nations. This advice was followed. The main foreign policy goal in the earliest years of this country was

   **(1)** isolationism
   **(2)** imperialism
   **(3)** intervention
   **(4)** alliances
   **(5)** détente

**11.** President Taft encouraged American businessmen to invest in the countries of Central America and the Caribbean. When disturbances broke out in the Central American country of Nicaragua in 1912, Taft sent in the U.S. Marines to protect American lives and property. The foreign policy goal Taft was emphasizing was

**(1)** isolationism
**(2)** imperialism
**(3)** intervention
**(4)** alliances
**(5)** détente

**12.** In 1949 the United States, Canada, and ten Western European nations signed the North Atlantic Pact. The pact said that if any of the nations signing were to be attacked, the other nations would come to its defense. In signing the North Atlantic Pact, the United States was pursuing a foreign policy goal of

**(1)** isolationism
**(2)** imperialism
**(3)** intervention
**(4)** alliances
**(5)** détente

*Items 13 to 14 are based on the following passage.*

Around the world there are millions of people who go hungry. The problem of hunger is especially serious in many of the developing countries of Africa, Asia, and Latin America.

The reason for hunger often isn't insufficient food production. Many countries that in the past weren't producing enough have now greatly increased their crop yields, thanks to new agricultural technologies. Yet people continue to go hungry. Often the reason for hunger is poverty. People are simply too poor to buy the food they need. Or sometimes the reason is distribution. That is, people who need food may live in regions that are very difficult to transport large supplies of food to—especially if a country lacks modern transportation networks.

**13.** Based on the passage, to solve the problem of hunger in the long run, governments should take steps to

**(1)** improve the agricultural technologies used
**(2)** obtain more food aid from abroad
**(3)** increase their food exports
**(4)** increase their food imports
**(5)** raise the incomes of poor people

**14.** Based on the passage, which of the following is a geographical factor that contributes to the problem of hunger?

**(1)** poor soils
**(2)** poor climates
**(3)** mountains and other land barriers
**(4)** lack of natural resources
**(5)** lack of modern technology

Item 15 is based on the following cartoon.

**15.** Which statement best expresses the main idea of the cartoon?

(1) Despite attempts at reform, democracy in the Soviet Union remains an illusion.

(2) Soviet citizens will finally be given an opportunity to choose between two candidates for office.

(3) The Soviets now have a democracy similar to Western democracies.

(4) Recent reforms in voting procedures have led to greater political tolerance in the Soviet Union.

(5) The Soviet Union still does not use voting machines in general elections.

*Items 16 to 18* are based on the following passage.

Blue-collar workers have always made up a large part of the membership of labor unions. For many years the number of jobs for blue-collar workers grew steadily. Today, however, there is a declining need for blue-collar workers. Many unions are suffering as a result.

Union leaders and members often blame the problem on tough foreign competition. Because Americans are buying more foreign goods, they say, U.S. factories are being forced to shut down. But this is only part of the explanation. More important has been the shift toward high technology in factories and offices. Because of this shift, the makeup of the labor force is changing. Certain kinds of jobs are being created, others are being lost. And unions will have to adjust to these changes if they are to survive.

**16.** The problem unions face that is discussed in the passage is mainly one of

**(1)** decreased membership
**(2)** employers' hostility toward unions
**(3)** anti-union legislation
**(4)** American manufacturers' inability to compete with foreign companies
**(5)** jobs going to foreign workers

**17.** Based on the passage, the most important strategy for unions today may be that of

**(1)** pushing for restrictions on imports
**(2)** taking a tougher stance when negotiating contracts with employers
**(3)** trying to unionize new sorts of workers
**(4)** opposing the use of new technology
**(5)** raising union dues

**18.** Based on the passage, which of the following unions would be LEAST likely to be experiencing problems?

**(1)** a union for textile and garment workers
**(2)** a union for teachers
**(3)** a union for machinists
**(4)** a union for auto workers
**(5)** a union for steel workers

*Items 19 to 22 refer to the following chart.*

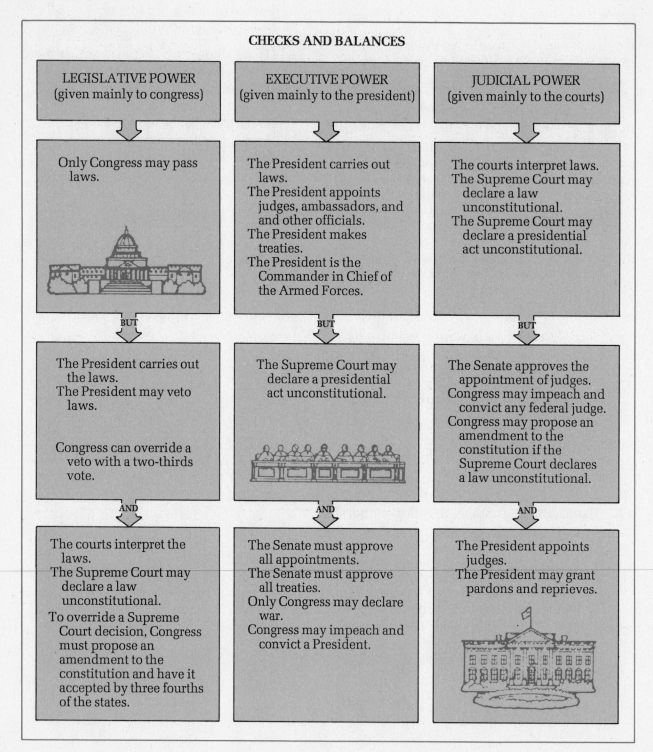

## CHECKS AND BALANCES

| LEGISLATIVE POWER (given mainly to congress) | EXECUTIVE POWER (given mainly to the president) | JUDICIAL POWER (given mainly to the courts) |
| --- | --- | --- |
| Only Congress may pass laws. | The President carries out laws. The President appoints judges, ambassadors, and and other officials. The President makes treaties. The President is the Commander in Chief of the Armed Forces. | The courts interpret laws. The Supreme Court may declare a law unconstitutional. The Supreme Court may declare a presidential act unconstitutional. |
| **BUT** | **BUT** | **BUT** |
| The President carries out the laws. The President may veto laws. Congress can override a veto with a two-thirds vote. | The Supreme Court may declare a presidential act unconstitutional. | The Senate approves the appointment of judges. Congress may impeach and convict any federal judge. Congress may propose an amendment to the constitution if the Supreme Court declares a law unconstitutional. |
| **AND** | **AND** | **AND** |
| The courts interpret the laws. The Supreme Court may declare a law unconstitutional. To override a Supreme Court decision, Congress must propose an amendment to the constitution and have it accepted by three fourths of the states. | The Senate must approve all appointments. The Senate must approve all treaties. Only Congress may declare war. Congress may impeach and convict a President. | The President appoints judges. The President may grant pardons and reprieves. |

19. According to the information in the chart, the president would NOT be able to

(1) appoint a relative as ambassador to a foreign country
(2) declare war on another country
(3) give commands to the navy during wartime
(4) make a treaty with another country
(5) carry out a law preventing terrorism

20. The main purpose of the checks and balance system is to

(1) prevent any branch of the government from becoming too powerful
(2) establish a way for the president, Congress, and the Supreme Court to work together
(3) make the Constitution adaptable to changing times
(4) make sure that all citizens are fairly represented
(5) encourage the government to be more efficient

21. Which of the following statements is NOT an example of the checks and balances system?

(1) Congress passes laws, and the courts interpret laws.
(2) The president can veto laws, and Congress can override the president's veto.
(3) The president appoints judges, and the Senate approves the appointments.
(4) The Supreme Court may declare a law unconstitutional, and Congress may then propose to amend the Constitution.
(5) The courts interpret laws, and the Supreme Court may declare a law unconstitutional.

22. In 1987 Congress passed a multibillion-dollar highway bill. This bill provided funds for new highways and bridges in many states and raised the speed limit on some rural highways to 65 mph. President Reagan vetoed the bill because he considered it too costly. In a close vote Congress overrode his veto, so that the bill became law. This bill became law because of which of the following aspects of the checks and balance system?

(1) executive power checked by legislative power
(2) executive power checked by judicial power
(3) legislative power checked by executive power
(4) legislative power checked by judicial power
(5) judicial power checked by legislative power

**23.** The problem of "groupthink" occurs in all kinds of groups—from groups advising the president of the United States to decision-making groups in corporations and smaller groups as well. Groupthink is the tendency of people in groups to become so concerned with agreeing with their leader, or with one another, that they are unable to think on their own or express criticism. Not surprisingly, bad decisions often result.

To avoid groupthink a leader might do all of the following EXCEPT

(1) encourage the group to sometimes meet without him or her
(2) get the opinion of outside experts
(3) have the group meet more often
(4) encourage those in the group to openly express their views
(5) rotate group membership, so there is always someone new

**24.** The federal government has a budget deficit. That is, it spends more money than it earns. The government *earns* money largely through taxes. Individuals and corporations are required to give the government a certain percentage of the money they earn. The government *spends* money largely on national defense and on benefit payments to individuals. Benefit payments include unemployment compensation, for workers who have lost their jobs, and social security, for workers who have reached retirement age.

Which of the following would be most likely to lessen, rather than add to, the budget deficit?

(1) More people become unemployed.
(2) More people reach retirement age.
(3) Corporations earn larger profits.
(4) A law is passed to develop an expensive new defense program.
(5) A law is passed lowering taxes.

*Item 25* is based on the following chart.

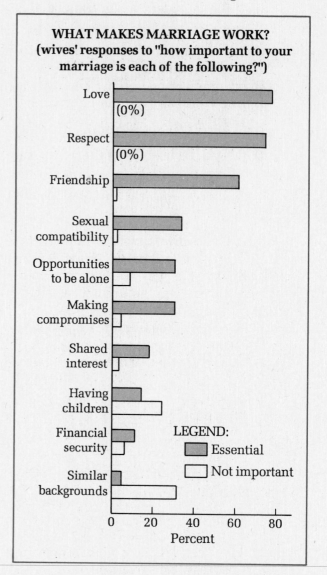

**WHAT MAKES MARRIAGE WORK?**
**(wives' responses to "how important to your marriage is each of the following?")**

LEGEND:
▨ Essential
▢ Not important

**25.** Based on the chart, which of the following circumstances would be most likely to lead to major problems in a marriage?

(1) A husband and wife come from very different backgrounds.
(2) A husband and wife find they don't have as many interests in common as they used to.
(3) A husband and wife find they don't have much feeling for each other anymore.
(4) The wife loses her job, and the family income drops significantly.
(5) Recent changes in work schedules have left a husband and wife with little chance to be alone.

*Items 26 to 30* are based on the following passage.

The initial policy of the U.S. government was to treat Native American tribes as nations, or independent governments. In keeping with this policy, Congress negotiated treaties with the tribes of the Great Plains. These treaties established large areas as permanent Native American territory. But miners and farmers traveling west wanted land. The treaties were broken.

The Plains tribes fought fiercely against white settlers and the U.S. Army. The whites, however, had better weapons and, with the coming of the railroad and the telegraph, better transportation and communication. Also, the whites exterminated the buffalo, on which the Indians depended for food and other necessities. By the 1880s, most of the Plains tribes had been forced onto two large reservations. Once this happened, their power to wage war was severely limited.

The Dawes Act of 1887 divided reservations into farms and promised U.S. citizenship to Native Americans if they became farmers and gave up their tribal practices. The act was an attempt to help the Native Americans. But it was also an attempt to make them change their way of life. By and large the act was a failure. In the 1920s and 1930s the U.S. Congress, recognizing that Native Americans wanted to preserve their own way of life, passed some new laws. From now on, U.S. citizenship would be automatic. No conditions would be attached. The tribes were to be encouraged to govern themselves.

**26.** Which of the following was NOT a factor leading to the defeat of the Plains tribes?

   **(1)** The U.S. Army had superior weapons.
   **(2)** The U.S. Army was better able to transport its men.
   **(3)** The U.S. Army divisions had better means of communicating vital information to one another than did the Native Americans.
   **(4)** Many Native Americans became farmers and gave up their tribal practices.
   **(5)** The buffalo herds were killed.

**27.** According to the passage, fighting between the Plains tribes and the soldiers virtually came to an end once

   **(1)** the U.S. government began negotiating treaties
   **(2)** the Native Americans were forced onto reservations
   **(3)** miners and farmers settled the Great Plains
   **(4)** railroads were built across the plains
   **(5)** the Native Americans agreed to change their way of life

**28.** According to the passage, why did the Dawes Act fail?

   **(1)** The tribes had been forced onto reservations.
   **(2)** Previous treaties had been broken.
   **(3)** The Native Americans wanted to keep their own culture and way of life.
   **(4)** The Native Americans didn't want to become U.S. citizens.
   **(5)** The Native Americans weren't interested in farming.

**29.** The U.S. government has had a number of policies toward the Native Americans. Based on the passage, one similarity between its earliest and most recent policies is that both

   **(1)** encourage the Native Americans to farm the land
   **(2)** encourage the Native Americans to live on reservations
   **(3)** treat the tribe as a unit of government for the Native Americans
   **(4)** attempt to destroy the Native Americans' way of life
   **(5)** emphasize the integration of Native Americans into the larger society

*Item 30 is on the following page.*

**30.** Which of the following statements best desribes what has happened over time to the Native American way of life?

    **(1)** When the plains were settled and the buffalo exterminated, the Native American way of life was ended.

    **(2)** When the Native Americans were forced onto reservations, their way of life was destroyed.

    **(3)** Over time, the Native Americans became farmers and abandoned their way of life.

    **(4)** The settlement of the Great Plains had no effect on the Native American way of life.

    **(5)** Despite some changes, the Native Americans have preserved their way of life.

*Items 31 to 32 are based on the following graphs.*

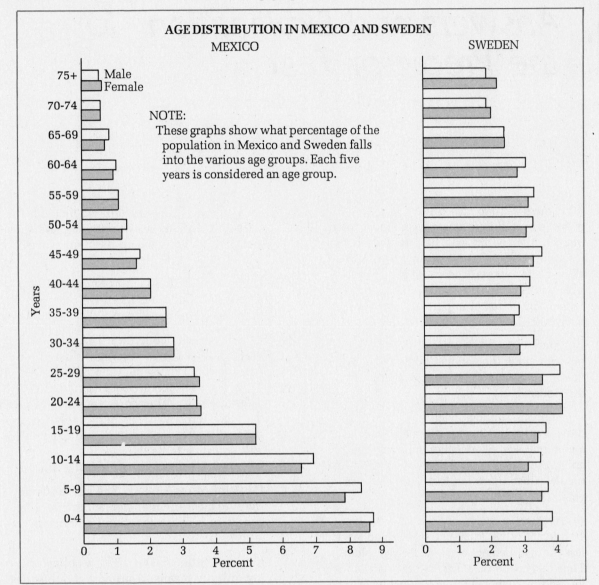

31. Which statement most accurately compares the age distribution of Mexico and Sweden?

    (1) Mexico and Sweden have similar patterns of age distribution.
    (2) Mexico's population is more evenly distributed in terms of age than Sweden's.
    (3) Overall, Mexico has a younger population than Sweden.
    (4) Overall, Sweden has a younger population than Mexico.
    (5) Mexico has a larger proportion of both very old people and very young people than Sweden does.

32. Which one of the following conclusions is best supported by the graphs?

    (1) Mexico is a larger country than Sweden.
    (2) Mexico has more people living in larger cities than Sweden does.
    (3) Mexico has better medical care than Sweden.
    (4) Mexico's standard of living will improve more rapidly than Sweden's.
    (5) Mexico's population will grow at a faster rate than Sweden's.

    Answers are on pages 16–18.

# Answers and Explanations for the Predictor Test

1. **(3)** *Analysis/Economics.* Since a surplus is possible only if exports are worth more than imports, the country will have to decrease the value of its imports and increase the value of its exports. Choice (4) is also a possible strategy, but it will not be as effective because the value of imports doesn't go down.

2. **(1)** *Comprehension/Political Science.* As a money matter, the national budget the president proposes must first be considered in the House.

3. **(1)** *Analysis/Political Science.* In each of the three graphs, the 20-year-old male who has a grammar-school education falls into the group that voted least. Therefore, of the people described, he is the least likely to have voted.

4. **(4)** *Application/Political Science.* Less than 40 percent of 18- to 20-year-olds voted (and less than 45 percent of 21- to 24-year-olds). The civic group would therefore be most interested in changing the voting habits of young adults.

5. **(4)** *Analysis/Behavioral Science.* By sometimes breaking his policy on sweets and other times insisting on it, the father is failing to apply rules consistently.

6. **(2)** *Comprehension/Behavioral Science.* The passage is basically talking about children's need for discipline and about the kind of discipline children need. Choice (1) in fact contradicts the passage, which opens by saying that both love and discipline are important. The other incorrect choices, although in keeping with the passage, are each discussed in only part of it.

7. **(3)** *Application/Behavioral Science.* The passage mentions the importance of discussion in situations where problems have arisen.

8. **(2)** *Evaluation/Behavioral Science.* The passage specifically says that discipline is more than just "dos" and "don'ts."

9. **(1)** *Evaluation/Economics.* The number of workers in goods-producing industries remained about the same. The number of workers in service-producing industries increased greatly. Therefore, people entering the labor force were far more likely to have gone into service-producing industries. This will continue to be the case, as shown by the graph's projections (the dotted lines).

10. **(1)** *Application/History.* The emphasis on steering clear of entanglements with other countries is characteristic of a policy of isolationism.

11. **(3)** *Application/History.* Taft's policy of using military means to support U.S. business interests in Central America was an example of intervention.

12. **(4)** *Application/History.* In signing the North Atlantic Pact, the United States was pursuing a foreign policy goal of alliances, in this case of alliance for defense purposes.

13. **(5)** *Evaluation/Geography.* Poverty is a major reason for hunger. Therefore, to really deal with hunger, the incomes of the very poor must somehow be raised.

14. **(3)** *Analysis/Geography.* People in developing countries sometimes go hungry because they live in areas that are difficult to transport food to. Mountains and other land barriers are geographical factors that create such difficulties. Choices (1), (2), and (4) are geographical factors, but are not relevant to the passage. Choice (5) is not a geographical factor.

15. **(1)** *Comprehension/Political Science.* Note that the two figures in the second ballot are identical (and that they're identical to the figure in the first ballot). This is the cartoonist's way of saying that democracy in the Soviet Union remains an illusion.

16. **(1)** *Comprehension/Economics.* Since many labor union members are blue-collar workers and the number of blue-collar jobs is going down, unions are facing a problem of decreasing membership.

17. **(3)** *Analysis/Economics.* Jobs that have typically been "union jobs" are being lost. New kinds of jobs are becoming important. Therefore, to remain healthy, unions must try to unionize workers in jobs that are new jobs or that have existed but haven't typically been union jobs.

18. **(2)** *Application/Economics.* Union membership has declined mainly in fields where blue-collar jobs predominated and high technology has changed the kinds of jobs available. These characteristics are not true of the teaching field.

19. **(2)** *Application/Political Science.* The chart shows that although the president is commander in chief of the armed forces, only Congress may declare a war.

20. **(1)** *Evaluation/Political Science.* The chart shows that each of the three branches of government "checks," or limits, the powers of the other branches. This arrangement therefore serves to prevent any branch from becoming too powerful.

21. **(5)** *Comprehension/Political Science.* As the chart makes clear, checks and balances are *between* branches of government. All the examples with the exception of Choice (5) involve two branches. Choice (5) involves only the judicial branch.

22. **(1)** *Analysis/Political Science.* This example actually involves two checks. The veto of the bill was an executive check on legislative power. The bill became law, however, because the veto was overridden by Congress. Therefore it became law because of a legislative check on executive power.

23. **(3)** *Evaluation/Behavioral Science.* More frequent meetings, by increasing group contact, would, if anything, *encourage* groupthink. All the other choices would discourage groupthink, either by bringing in outside views or by helping those in the group form and express their own opinions.

24. **(3)** *Analysis/Economics.* Corporations pay the government a certain percentage of the money they earn. So if they make larger profits, the government earns more money. This would lessen the budget deficit. All the other choices would add to the deficit.

25. **(3)** *Analysis/Behavioral Science.* According to the chart, most wives view love, respect, and friendship as the most important elements of their marriage. They view other factors, such as financial security and shared interests, as being much less important. Therefore, changes in the way a husband and wife felt about each other would be most likely to cause problems in a marriage.

26. **(4)** *Comprehension/History.* The passage does not state that many Native Americans became farmers and gave up their way of life. In fact, the opposite is implied. Therefore, this could not be a reason for the Native American's defeat. All the other choices are mentioned in the passage.

27. **(2)** *Comprehension/History.* The passage explains that once the Native Americans had been forced onto reservations, they could no longer put up an effective resistance. None of the other choices are mentioned in this connection.

28. **(3)** *Analysis/History.* The passage states that the Dawes Act was in part an attempt to make the Native Americans change their way of life. It also states that the act failed and that the laws replacing it were based on the recognition that the Native Americans wanted to keep their way of life. From this it can be concluded that the Dawes Act failed because it went against the Native Americans' desire to preserve their culture.

29. **(3)** *Analysis/History.* The U.S. government's earliest policy was to treat the tribes as governments and therefore make treaties with them. Its most recent policy, shaped by the acts of the 1920s and 1930s, is to recognize the importance of the tribes and to encourage tribal self-government. In both cases, the tribe is being treated as a unit of government.

30. **(5)** *Evaluation/History.* The passage describes a situation in which the Native American way of life has changed but endured. The other choices, which indicate either no change or complete change, are incorrect.

31. **(3)** *Analysis/Geography.* Mexico has a large percentage of its population concentrated in the younger age groups (0–4, 5–9, 10–14, etc.). Sweden does not. Therefore, Mexico's population is overall younger than Sweden's.

32. **(5)** *Evaluation/Geography.* The graphs show that Mexico has a younger population than Sweden. This means that a greater percentage of Mexico's population is at the age of having children or will be reaching that age. As a greater percentage of its population will be having children, Mexico will experience faster population growth than Sweden. None of the other choices are supported by the graphs.

# PREDICTOR TEST
# Performance Analysis Chart

**Directions:** Circle the number of each item that you got correct on the Predictor Test. Count how many items you got correct in each row; count how many items you got correct in each column. Write the amount correct per row and column as the numerator in the fraction in the appropriate "Total Correct" box. (The denominators represent the total number of items in the row or column.) Write the grand total correct over the denominator, **32,** at the lower right corner of the chart. (For example, if you got 28 items correct, write *28* so that the fraction reads *28/***32.**) Item numbers in color represent items based on graphic material.

| Item Type | History (page 85) | Geography (page 103) | Economics (page 112) | Political Science (page 125) | Behavioral Science (page 137) | TOTAL CORRECT |
|---|---|---|---|---|---|---|
| Comprehension (page 34) | 26, 27 | | 16 | 2, 15, 21 | 6 | /7 |
| Application (page 43) | 10, 11, 12 | | 18 | 4, 19 | 7 | /7 |
| Analysis (page 51) | 28, 29 | 14, 31 | 1, 17, 24 | 3, 22 | 5, 25 | /11 |
| Evaluation (page 61) | 30 | 13, 32 | 9 | 20 | 8, 23 | /7 |
| TOTAL CORRECT | /8 | /4 | /6 | /8 | /6 | /32 |

*The page numbers in parentheses indicate where in this book you can find the beginning of specific instruction about the various fields of social studies and about the types of questions you encountered in the Predictor Test.*

# Instruction

# Introduction

This section of the book contains lessons and exercises that can help you learn the things you need to know to pass the Social Studies Test.

The Instruction section is divided into two units. Unit I, Reading Strategies, will help you improve your skills at reading effectively. Unit II, Foundations in Social Studies, can help you organize and increase your general knowledge of Social Studies, and show you how to apply your reading skills to information about social studies presented in either written or graphic format.

The units are divided into chapters, which are in turn divided into individual lessons. There are many exercises and quizzes, so you will have several opportunities to apply and test your understanding of the material you study. A progress chart at the beginning of each unit will make it easy for you to keep track of your work and record your performance on each lesson.

# Reading Strategies

In this unit, you will learn important strategies for reading. When you take the Social Studies Test, you will be asked to read passages and then answer questions based on them. The better you understand the passages you read, the better you will perform on the test. The strategies you will study in this unit will help you to understand passages you read better.

Questions on the Social Studies Test ask you to demonstrate that you understand what you read and that you can read critically. This unit will help you develop strategies for (1) determining how a question based on a social studies passage requires you to think and (2) answering questions effectively.

Unit I ends with a Unit Test that will check your understanding and ability to use the reading strategies. You should complete Unit I before going on to Unit II.

# UNIT I PROGRESS CHART
# Reading Strategies

**Directions:** Use the following chart to keep track of your work. When you complete a lesson and have checked your answers to the items in the exercise, circle the number of questions you answered correctly. When you complete a Chapter Quiz, record your score on the appropriate line. The numbers in color represent scores at a level of 80 percent or better.

| *Lesson* | *Page* | | |
|---|---|---|---|
| | | CHAPTER 1: **A Strategy for Reading** | |
| 1 | 25 | Previewing Test Items | **1 2 3** |
| 2 | 28 | Questioning As You Read Test Items | **1 2 3** |
| 3 | 29 | The Four Levels of Questions | **1 2 3** |
| | 32 | Chapter 1 Quiz | **1 2 3 4 5 6 7 8 9 10** |
| | | CHAPTER 2: **Comprehension** | |
| 1 | 34 | Restatement | **1 2 3** |
| 2 | 36 | Summarizing | **1 2 3** |
| 3 | 38 | Identifying Implications | **1 2 3** |
| | 41 | Chapter 2 Quiz | **1 2 3 4 5 6 7 8 9 10** |
| | | CHAPTER 3: **Application** | |
| 1 | 43 | Application from Passages and Graphics | **1 2 3** |
| 2 | 46 | Application from a List of Categories | **1 2 3** |
| | 49 | Chapter 3 Quiz | **1 2 3 4 5 6 7 8 9 10** |
| | | CHAPTER 4: **Analysis** | |
| 1 | 51 | Facts vs. Opinions and Hypotheses | **1 2 3** |
| 2 | 53 | Identifying Unstated Assumptions | **1 2 3** |
| 3 | 56 | Conclusions vs. Supporting Statements | **1 2 3** |
| 4 | 57 | Identifying Cause-and-Effect Relationships | **1 2 3** |
| | 59 | Chapter 4 Quiz | **1 2 3 4 5 6 7 8 9 10** |
| | | CHAPTER 5: **Evaluation** | |
| 1 | 61 | Adequacy and Appropriateness of Information | **1 2 3** |
| 2 | 63 | The Effect of Values on Beliefs and Decision Making | **1 2 3** |
| 3 | 65 | Accuracy of Facts Based on Documentation | **1 2 3** |
| 4 | 66 | Identifying Logical Fallacies in Arguments | **1 2 3** |
| | 69 | Chapter 5 Quiz | **1 2 3 4 5 6 7 8 9 10** |

# A Strategy for Reading

## Objective

In this chapter, you will

- Preview material you are about to read
- Question material as you read
- Preview and question items based on history, geography, economics, political science, and behavioral science material
- See how previewing and questioning helps you answer items on the Social Studies section of the GED

## Lesson 1    Previewing Test Items

**Why should you preview written material before you read it?**

Sometimes a TV commercial will allow you to *preview* a program. The commerical shows you the program's high points to give you an idea of what to expect.

Likewise, you probably already preview many things you read. For example, when you open a magazine, you probably flip through it before starting to read. From the table of contents, the titles of articles, and the illustrations, you get an idea of what the magazine contains.

You can also preview material that you find on a test. For example, when you see a passage or a graphic on the Social Studies Test, you should preview the material before you actually read it. Previewing the material will help you to read more actively, with more confidence. You'll have a better idea of how long the passage is, how many questions you'll have to answer about it, and what the questions will be about. Knowing these things will help you read more effectively, so that you do better on the test.

When you first approach a passage or graphic on the Social Studies Test, take a few seconds to preview it before you actually read it. Glance over it for a few seconds to get an idea of the overall format and the general topic. Here are some steps for previewing Social Studies passages and graphics:

1. Find where the directions begin and end.
2. Get a sense of how long the passage is, and how many items follow it.
3. Get a sense of the form of the passage or graphic. Is there a graph? a table? a cartoon? Is there both graphic information and written informa-

tion? Some passages take the form of a set of definitions. Then each item asks you which definition applies to a given situation, and presents you with the same set of multiple-choice answers to choose from. Is this that type of passage?

4. Pay close attention to any headings, captions, or labels. What clues do they give you?

5. What clues do you get from any words that "jump off the page"—that is, dark print, underlining, extra spacing, capitalization, repetition, or italics (slanted print)?

Use what you have just learned to preview the following item.

*Item 1* is based on the following graphs.

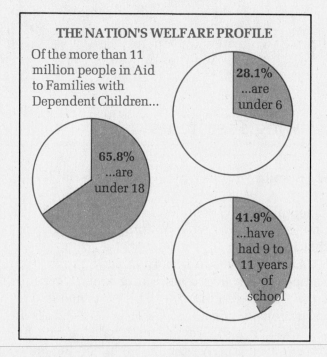

From Robert Pear, "Rewriting the Social Contract
for America's Have-Nots," *The New York Times*,
April 12, 1987, page E5. Used with permission.

**1.** Based on these graphs, which of the following is true?

    **(1)** 65.8 percent of Americans age 18 and under are on AFDC.

    **(2)** 28.1 percent of Americans under age 6 are on AFDC.

    **(3)** More than half of the people on AFDC are age 18 or under.

    **(4)** More than half of the people on AFDC are under age 6.

    **(5)** More than half of the people on AFDC have high school diplomas.

Here are some things to notice as you preview:

• You begin with the directions, "*Item 1 is . . .*"

• Choice (5) of Item 1 marks the end of the material you preview when approaching this series of graphs. Can you see at a glance how much material you will need to look at in order to answer the item? Since there is only one item, it wouldn't make sense to spend too much time on the graphs.

- In the graphs, each circle contains a number (%) shown as a shaded part of the circle. Circle graphs make it easier for you to see what portion of the whole group is being discussed.
- The title of the graphs tells you they are concerned with welfare.
- The label in the upper left-hand corner tells you that each circle refers to people on AFDC.
- The percent signs remind you that each number represents a percent of the whole, not an actual number of people.
- The captions inside the circles tell which people the shaded portions stand for, in each case.

By previewing the graphs for just a few moments, you have picked up a lot of information about them. You are now better prepared to understand the graphs, and so are more likely to complete the item correctly.

## Lesson 1    Exercise

Items 1 to 3 are about the following passage and its item.

There are five regions of differing climates in South America.

(1) Amazon Basin—the area through which the Amazon River flows; heavy rainfall averages 70 inches to 100 inches per year
(2) Coastlands—coastal areas including those that border the Caribbean Sea and the Atlantic Ocean; rainfall averages 40 inches per year
(3) Highlands—the Andes Mountains and high areas of Brazil and Guiana; the cool weather is good for growing coffee
(4) Pampas—grassy slopes; the weather is sometimes humid, sometimes dry
(5) Wastelands—desert areas; the climate supports little life

Each of the following statements describes a place in South America that is in one of the climatic regions described above. Choose the climatic region in which the place is probably found. The regions may be used more than once in the set of items, but no one question has more than one best answer.

1. The hot Atacama Desert in Chile has little water but is rich in copper. The climatic region described is the

   (1) Amazon Basin
   (2) Coastlands
   (3) Highlands
   (4) Pampas
   (5) Wastelands

1. Your preview of the material above showed you that the item about the Atacama Desert is based on a paragraph/cartoon/list of definitions. (Choose one.)

2. Suppose you were previewing the following item to see which of the definitions would apply to it. List the five choices you would keep in mind.

   Corn and wheat are grown in Argentina's most important agricultural region, a gradually sloping area where cattle and sheep also graze on the coarse grass. The climatic region described is the _____.

3. Explain why it is a good practice to preview material before reading it from start to finish.

Answers are on page 260.

## Lesson 2   Questioning As You Read Test Items

**Why should you question as you read?**

As you watch a TV commercial that previews a show, you probably wonder about the story that is behind the key scenes that are shown. You may even make guesses about the story, and then watch the show to see if your guesses were right. As you watch the show itself, you may continue to make predictions about what is going to happen. Then you keep watching, to see if your predictions were right.

Likewise, when you are previewing material on the Social Studies Test, you may make guesses and predictions as to what it will be about. If you put these guesses in the form of questions, you may read in order to answer your own questions. This questioning process helps you to read actively and effectively to gather the information you need.

### Steps in Questioning Social Studies Material

1. After you preview material, ask a question that you might find the answer to as you read.
2. Predict the answer to the question you developed.
3. Read to see your prediction was right.

Use what you have just learned to question the following passage and item:

Four of the United States' pioneering women travelers were Annie Smith Peck, Delia J. Akeley, Marguerite Harrison, and Louise Arner Boyd. Peck (1850–1935) was a mountain climber. Akeley (1875–1970) was an anthropologist. Harrison (1879–1967) was a documentary filmmaker, and Boyd (1887–1972) was an Arctic explorer.

The four women have in common that they were all

**(1)** pioneer women in colonial America
**(2)** among the first famous American women travelers
**(3)** the first women world travelers
**(4)** photographers who filmed the wonders of the Arctic
**(5)** mountain climbers who climbed the world's highest peaks

## Steps in Questioning a Specific Passage

1. Read the incomplete sentence that introduces the item and reword it into the form of a question: "How can I summarize what these four women had in common?"

2. Before you read the passage, make your own prediction. You may have noticed the capitalized word *Arctic* in your preview. You might predict that the four women all explored the Arctic.

3. Read the passage. You find that your prediction is not confirmed. The passage mentions only Boyd in regard to exploring the Arctic. The four women were all American women travelers apparently interested in the world's people and geography.

Continue to ask yourself questions as you read, as many or as few as you need to stay actively involved in gathering information. Whether your predictions are right or wrong is not important. Reading to find out more about your predictions will automatically help you to follow the passage more easily and to remember it better.

# Lesson 2 Exercise

1. The questions you ask as you read do not all have to come from the test questions. For example, after reading the first sentence of the passage about the four women travelers, what question could ask yourself?

2. Suppose you are teaching someone who is reading a textbook how to use questioning. The person says, "When I stop to make up questions, doesn't that slow down my reading speed?" What would you answer?

3. Suppose there is a GED question based on a speech. The first sentence in the speech reads: "When your friend is out of work, it is a recession, but when you are unemployed, it is a depression." What question might you ask yourself before you read the rest of the speech?

Answers are on page 260.

# Lesson 3    The Four Levels of Questions

**What are the four levels of questions on the Social Studies Test? Why should you learn to identify them?**

Just as the tasks you face in real life vary in difficulty, so do the items on the GED. There are four levels of questions on the GED: comprehension, application, analysis, and evaluation.

**Comprehension** questions, those at the lowest level, simply require you to show that you understand the material. For example, suppose you are presented with the following statements:

After Louie's first meal at the Homemade Restaurant, he developed a stomach ache that lasted all evening. He decided to give the restaurant a second chance, but he was up all night following his second repast there.

A comprehension question might be: What does the word "repast" mean? Your answer will show whether you understand the definition of "repast." Even if you had never heard the word before, there are enough clues in the passage to help you guess that it means "meal."

**Application** questions require you to understand the information you are given and to apply that understanding to a new situation. An application question based on the statements about the restaurant might be: Do you think Louie would bring his mother to the Homemade Restaurant for Mother's Day? Even though the passage does not say anything about Louie's mother, you can use what you are told about Louie's stomach problems to figure out that he probably would not risk taking his mother to the restaurant.

**Analysis** questions require that you not only understand the ideas, but also think about relationships between them, such as cause and effect. An analysis question might be: What might have caused Louie's stomach ache? Using what you are told about Louie's experience, plus your own common sense, you can speculate that the food probably made Louie sick.

**Evaluation** questions require that you judge the accuracy of information based on standards you are given. An evaluation question related to the restaurant passage might be: Which of the following statements is better supported by the evidence?

(a) Louie had food poisoning.
(b) Louie owned the restaurant.

The answer key in this book labels the level of every question.

## Abilities Measured by Each of the Four Levels of Questions

Each of the four levels of questions places different demands on your thinking. Once you recognize these demands, you will know how to read the material so that you answer the item successfully.

Comprehension questions measure the ability to restate information, summarize ideas, and identify the implications of the information given.

Application questions measure the ability to use ideas in a new situation.

Analysis questions measure the ability to distinguish facts from hypotheses or opinions, to recognize unstated assumptions, to distinguish a conclusion from supporting statements, and to identify cause-and-effect relationships.

Evaluation questions measure the ability to assess the adequacy of data to support conclusions, recognize the role that values play in beliefs, assess the accuracy of facts as determined by proof, and indicate logical fallacies in arguments.

## Lesson 3 Exercise

1.  Based on the information in this lesson, which of the following statements is true?

    **(1)** Comprehension items ask you to judge ideas.
    **(2)** Application items ask you to use information in a new situation.
    **(3)** Analysis items ask only for your understanding of the material.
    **(4)** Evaluation items ask only that you use information in a new way.
    **(5)** Application items don't require that you comprehend the material.

2.  If the following item was also based on the passage about Louie and the restaurant, which type of question would it be: comprehension, application, analysis, or evaluation?

    If Louie fell off a horse, would he probably get back on or give up riding horses?

3.  TRUE or FALSE: The reason you are encouraged to learn to identify the different levels of items on the GED Test is that the GED Test itself will require you to label each item.

    Answers are on page 260.

# Chapter 1 Quiz

1.  Change the underlined words to make the following a true statement: To preview a graph or a table, <u>you should look carefully at every word from top to bottom.</u>

2.  There are advantages to predicting an answer to a test item before you actually read the choices. List two of them.

*Items 3 and 4 are based on a preview of the following material.*

> The first amendment to the Constitution guarantees freedom of religion, freedom of speech, and freedom of the press.
> Who would be the LEAST likely to "plead the first amendment" in a legal battle?
>
> **(1)** a woman who feels she is being paid less than male coworkers
> **(2)** a news reporter who does not want to reveal his or her sources
> **(3)** a student who is in trouble for using obscenity in a speech
> **(4)** a magazine an actress is suing for damage to her reputation
> **(5)** a group wanting a textbook banned for praising a given religion

3.  In your preview, which form did you notice was used to present the information?

    **(1)** cartoon
    **(2)** list of definitions
    **(3)** graph showing changes over time
    **(4)** brief, one-sentence passage
    **(5)** long magazine article

4.  The question being asked is an evaluation question. Explain how you can identify it as one.

---

5.  Suppose you were presented with a line graph captioned, "Increasing overcrowding at Mills Prison, originally built for 1800 inmates." During your preview, you would notice the labels on each side of the graph. One side would be labeled in years and the other in _____.

*Items 6 to 9 refer to the following material.*

> In some cultures, polygyny, the marriage of one husband to two or more wives at the same time, is practiced. Polyandry, the marriage of one woman to two or more men, is much more rare.
> Which of the following is an example of polygyny?
>
> **(1)** A young woman's husband dies and she remarries.
> **(2)** A divorced woman remarries.
> **(3)** A man who already has one wife marries another woman.
> **(4)** A woman who already has one husband marries another man.
> **(5)** A widower marries his dead wife's sister.

6. In your preview, you should have noticed a clue as to how many items are based on the material. Identify the clue words and tell why they "jump off the page."

7. The questions you keep in mind as you read the short passage can include those that appear in the items as well as those that you _____.

8. Make up a question based on the first sentence of the passage. Explain whether it is answered in the second sentence.

9. What level of question is being asked?

_____

10. The strategy you have learned to use when approaching written material can be broken into five steps. Add the missing step.

   1. Glance at the form of the material and its item(s).
   2. Ask questions while reading the material.
   3. _____.
   4. Examine each of the five choices you are given.
   5. Decide on the correct answer.

Answers are on page 260.

# 2 Comprehension

## Objective

In this chapter, you will learn about the kinds of items that make up 20 percent of the Social Studies section of the GED: comprehension items. You will

- Identify comprehension items that ask you to restate, to summarize, or to identify the implications of what you have read
- Answer comprehension items in social studies that illustrate each aspect of this skill

## Lesson 1  Restatement

**Why is restatement an important comprehension skill?**

When you restate an idea, you put it in your own words, or you identify it when you see it in another form. When your friend says, "I'm tone deaf," and you reply, "You mean you can't sing?", you are checking your comprehension of your friend's statement by restating it.

### Restating Information in Paragraphs

Read the following paragraph and answer the question.

> The sales tax is now the most important source of state revenue. All states impose selective sales taxes—taxes levied only on the sale of certain consumer items such as liquor, tobacco, or gasoline. Forty-five states now have a general sales tax—a tax placed on nearly all items sold.

Which phrase best restates the definition of a sales tax as used in the passage?

(1) tax designed to raise all the revenues government needs
(2) tax added to price of every item sold
(3) tax on selected items sold
(4) luxury tax on special items sold
(5) tax levied to discourage sale of some items

Choices (1) and (2) are incorrect. Nowhere does the paragraph say the sales tax raises *all* government revenues or is added to the price of *every* item sold. Choice (3) is correct because the sales tax is imposed on *selected* items. This is a restatement of the second sentence. Choice (4) might seem correct, because the passage mentions tobacco and liquor, which are examples of luxuries. The last sentence, however, notes that nearly every state has a general sales tax on "nearly all" items sold—in other words, not just luxuries. Choice (5)—referring to taxes that discourage sales of some items—is not a restatement of anything mentioned in the passage.

### Restating Information from Graphics

Look at Figure 1. You may wish to place a marker on this page, since this graph is referred to several times in the unit.

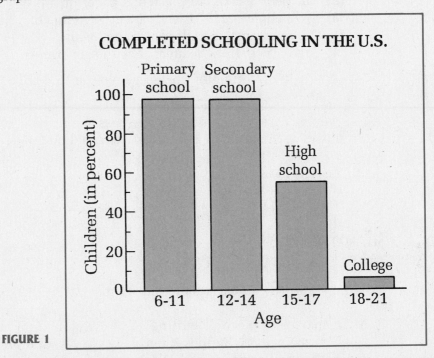

**FIGURE 1**

How would you restate the main idea of the graph in words? Note that the caption and descriptions for each part of the graph give some information about the main idea. If you combine this information with the data in the graph, you can restate the main idea of the graph: that fewer children of high school and college age complete school than do primary and secondary school-age children.

To restate the main idea of a paragraph or graphic:

1. Use clues to identify the topic. In paragraphs, repeated words are clues; in graphics, titles and captions are clues.

2. Find the most important thing said about the topic.

3. Restate that information in your own words.

4. In a multiple-choice question, choose the best restatement from the five choices.

## Lesson 1 Exercise

*Items 1 to 3 are based on the following paragraph.*

Today a republic is a form of government in which virtually all citizens have the vote, and the power of the state is limited by a constitution. As such, it is different from a democracy. The public controls the government in both cases. The republic, however, is ruled indirectly by the people through an elected assembly. In a democracy, on the other hand, the people take part directly in governing.

1. Which sentence best restates the definition of democracy in the passage?
   (1) A legislature rules the people.
   (2) The people take the place of a government.
   (3) The people play a direct part in government.
   (4) A strong elected leader rules the people.
   (5) A group of strong leaders runs the government.

2. Restate the information in the paragraph to complete this sentence. A republic is _____.

3. TRUE or FALSE: According to the passage, in both a republic and a democracy, the ultimate control is exercised by the people.

Answers are on page 261.

## Lesson 2  Summarizing

**What skills do you use when you summarize?**

A summary of a piece of writing or of a graphic is a short statement that gives its main idea. Suppose you go on a vacation and write a postcard home: "Having a great time. Went skindiving today. Will go on a picnic tomorrow." The first sentence of your postcard provides a summary. The other sentences provide supporting details of the main idea.

### Summarizing a Paragraph

Read the following paragraph and answer the question.

The destructiveness of World War II inspired 46 nations to meet in San Francisco and form a world body that would unite to "save the succeeding generations from the scourge of war." As a result of this meeting, the United Nations was founded in June 1945. Today the United Nations has its headquarters in New York. There, the General Assembly, with over 100 members, recommends courses of action. The Security Council, with 27 seats, gives the major countries a permanent place and the right to veto any proposal.

Which sentence best summarizes the paragraph?

**(1)** The destructiveness of World War II inspired nations to meet.

**(2)** The United Nations began in 1945 and is located in New York.

**(3)** The United Nations has a General Assembly with over 100 members.

**(4)** The major powers sit on the 27-seat Security Council.

**(5)** The major powers may veto any proposal.

Choice (1) gives background information, not the main idea of the paragraph, which is contained in Choice (2). Notice how Choice (2) combines information from the second and third sentences of the paragraph. Choices (3), (4), and (5), by contrast, merely restate details about the main *parts* of the United Nations as it is described in the paragraph. These choices do not make a general statement about the United Nations as does Choice (2). A good summary statement gives the best *overview* of a reading passage, even though other statements about details may also be true.

### Summarizing Information in Graphics

Look carefully at Figure 2 to figure out the main characteristics of the geography of West Germany.

**FIGURE 2**

Your summary might read: "West Germany is an industrial country that also has agriculture and natural resources." Notice how the statement combines dairying, vineyards, and farming under "agriculture." Similarly, "natural resources" include coal, oil, forests, and fishing. By generalizing and combining specific examples, you are able to come up with the main idea conveyed by the map.

To summarize the main idea of a paragraph or graphic:

1. Leave out unimportant or repetitious material.
2. Generalize from a number of specific items.
3. Combine specific items into a broader single statement.
4. Select or create a main idea that best represents the total picture.

## Lesson 2 Exercise

*Items 1 to 3 are based on the following map.*

1. In one sentence, summarize the location and nature of the major Swiss resources.

2. In one sentence, summarize the location and nature of the major Austrian resources.

3. Name the first step you took to answer Item 1.

Answers are on page 261.

## Lesson 3   Identifying Implications

**What strategies do you use to identify implications?**

To identify the implications of an idea means to recognize the idea's underlying meaning. For example, imagine that you see a small child with a smile on her face playing in the park. You infer that the child is happy. You may also infer that the child is happy because she is in the park. These are reasonable implications that you may draw from the incident.

## Identifying Implications in Social Studies Material

Always look for the underlying meaning of what you read. Read the following paragraph about black applicants to college and answer the question that follows. Think about the implications of the words *stream* and *trickle*.

> Fifteen years ago those of us who recruited talented black students for competitive colleges could depend on a small but constant stream of young men and women from the inner cities of this country . . . in good years these students represented more than 25 percent of the black population on our campuses. Now that stream of talent that flowed out of Boston, Chicago, Los Angeles and New York has become a trickle.

The word *stream* implies that the number of black students from the inner cities was

(1) steady and reliable
(2) smooth and wet
(3) powerful and strong
(4) small and sporadic
(5) irregular and unpredictable

You probably sensed that the word *stream* is not being used literally here, so Choice (2) is obviously incorrect. The writer is clearly using *stream* as a metaphor, to convey the idea of a continuing "flow" of students. Thus Choice (1) best fits the passage. This stream was still relatively small, however. Only 25 percent of the total number of black students came from inner cities. Therefore, Choice (3) is incorrect. Choices (4) and (5) are also incorrect. Both describe a trickle rather than a stream.

The same article about black college applicants concludes:

> We can still save many young people from wasted lives. In another decade we may not be able to do so. . . . If current trends continue, by the year 2000, 70 percent of all black households will be headed by women and only 30 percent of black men will be employed. The trickle of black recruits will surely dry out altogether, and the cost to the nation will be incalculable.

From David L. Evans, *Newsweek*, March 16, 1987, page 8. Used with permission.

From this conclusion you can infer that the writer believes

(1) long-term planning is necessary to save the younger generation
(2) there is no chance to save this generation of black people from failure
(3) wasted lives, high unemployment, and single-parent families lower educational achievement
(4) time is on the side of those struggling to save this generation of blacks
(5) single-parent households need not be a barrier to educational achievement

Can you give reasons from the passage why Choice (3) is correct and the other choices are incorrect?

### Strategies for Identifying Implications

When trying to identify the implications of an idea, ask yourself the following questions:

1. Do the facts given in the selection support the inferences you are making?
2. Does the implication make sense to you?
3. Can you use common sense and what you already know to support the inference you are drawing?

## Lesson 3   Exercise

*Items 1 to 3* are based on the following paragraph.

Interstate compacts are a rather common way in which states establish cooperative relations. An interstate compact is a formal agreement between states. It must be ratified by the legislatures of the states involved and approved by Congress. These compacts are frequently concerned with the construction of public facilities, the conservation of natural resources, the protection of health, and similar matters.*

1.  The paragraph implies that when states make interstate compacts

    **(1)** people in the states are more friendly
    **(2)** states' rights are protected
    **(3)** all states have uniform laws
    **(4)** cooperation between states is possible
    **(5)** state borders become more important

2.  Which statements in the paragraph led you to choose your answer to Item 1?

3.  Why are the other choices for the answer to Item 1 incorrect?

Answers are on page 261.

# Chapter 2 Quiz

1. Suppose you come to a chart on the Social Studies section of the GED with the title "Presidential Qualities Considered Important by the Public: A Comparison of 1972, 1976, and 1980." Briefly explain how you would apply what you have learned about previewing and questioning as you look at the chart.

2. Complete the following sentence: Most comprehension items on the Social Studies section of the GED will ask you to identify one of three things: a restatement, an implication, or a _____.

3. Label the following three items as to what each requires the reader to do: S = summarizes the important points; R = restate material in the passage; I = identify implications.
   (1) What can be inferred about the Bay of Pigs episode?
   (2) According to the last sentence, why did the invasion fail?
   (3) Which would be the best caption for the timeline about the Bay of Pigs incident?

*Items 4 to 7 are based on the following passage.*

The biggest challenge to businesses interested in the live-alone market is its diversity. The group includes aging baby-boomers who are unwed or divorced, mature singles over 40 who have never married, and widowed older people. More than 60 percent of those living alone are female, and more than half of such women are widows. Single men are usually much younger. About half of the live-alones are middle-income earners, but 55 percent earn under $10,000.

4. In the passage, those who live alone are examined in groups according to statistics about marriage, gender, age, and _____.

5. Briefly explain in your own words what the phrase *middle-income earners* seems to mean in the article.

6. TRUE or FALSE: The writer is implying that it is easier for businesses to gear their products toward a group of people who are similar than toward a group that contains many different types of people.

7. Locate the sentence from which it can be inferred that most people who live alone are not wealthy.

*Items 8 to 10* are based on the following graph.

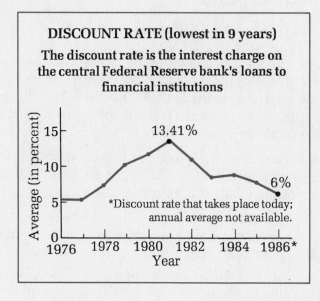

**DISCOUNT RATE (lowest in 9 years)**

**The discount rate is the interest charge on the central Federal Reserve bank's loans to financial institutions**

13.41%

6%

*Discount rate that takes place today; annual average not available.

Average (in percent)

Year

8.   Briefly describe in your own words the main idea of the graph.

9.   As shown by the graph, the discount rate in 1986 was the lowest it has been since _____.

10.   Which of the following is NOT told by the graph?

    **(1)** the definition of "discount rate"
    **(2)** the average discount rate for 1986
    **(3)** the average discount rate for 1981
    **(4)** the approximate average discount rate for 1976
    **(5)** the source for the statistics shown

Answers are on page 261.

# 3

## Application

**Objective**

In this chapter, you will learn about the kinds of items that make up 30 percent of the Social Studies section of the GED: application items. You will

- Identify application items that ask you to use ideas in a situation not already provided in a passage or graphic
- Identify a type of application item that asks you to categorize ideas according to definitions that are provided
- Answer social studies application items of both types, based on a range of subjects that you will find on the GED

## Lesson 1    Application from Passages and Graphics

How do application items differ from comprehension items?

To apply something means to use it. If you hear a weather report predicting rain, you might apply the information to your specific situation by getting out your umbrella. Similarly, application items on the Social Studies section of the GED exam test your ability to take information you are given and use it in a new situation.

### Applying Information from Passages

Read the following paragraph and answer the question.

Where have all the greenbacks gone? That's what the Federal Reserve Board wants to know after completing a study showing $136 billion in U.S. currency is missing. Believe it or not, that means 88 percent of the total supposedly in circulation is missing. Based on the study, economists have calculated that, at any one time, individuals over age 18 keep about $100 in cash and coins. Some of the rest is in company cash drawers, and another fraction is held by persons under age 18.

The explanation behind many of the missing greenbacks is most like the reason behind

- **(1)** extinction of a rare type of bird
- **(2)** loss of life savings by gambling on horses
- **(3)** destruction by fire of the contents of a house
- **(4)** disappearance of a book of stamps into a packrat's nest
- **(5)** loss of lives when a ship sinks

Choices (1), (2), (3), and (5) are incorrect because they all describe situations in which something is permanently lost, which the greenbacks are not. Choice (4) is correct because, like the greenbacks, the book of stamps is out of circulation for now, but still in existence.

Notice how important it is to comprehend what has happened to most of the missing money before you can apply the information in the passage to a new, parallel case. Notice, too, that you cannot make a prediction about the answer before you look at the choices.

## Applying Information from Graphs

Look again at Figure 1, Chapter 2, on page 35.

David L. passed each year of school without staying back until the 10th grade, when he dropped out. He is now enrolled in a GED review course and will probably have his equivalency diploma by age 25. Information about David would be included in the bar

- **(1)** on the far left only
- **(2)** to left of center only
- **(3)** to the right of center only
- **(4)** to the far left and the bar to the left of center
- **(5)** to the left of center and the bar to the right of center

To answer this question, you need to make sure you understand both the "old" and "new" situations. Then find a way to connect the two. The bar graph shows the number of children *completing* primary school, secondary school, high school, and college at various ages. Since David dropped out in the tenth grade, the implication is that he completed primary and secondary school. Since the passage says that he dropped out in tenth grade, you know he did not complete high school or college. Therefore, the two bars on the right do not apply to David; the two bars on the left do apply to him. The correct answer is (4).

Notice how you can use your own background knowledge—information that you already have—to think about an application question. For example, you know that a person who has completed tenth grade must have completed primary and secondary school, and that a person who has not completed high school and is working on a GED cannot have finished college.

You can see how important it is to read all the choices before selecting one. Also, if you make a prediction about the answer before you read the choices, you will find it easier to choose among them. Instead of possibly being confused by all the options, you will zero in on the choice most like the one you are already looking for.

To use given information in a different context:

1. Summarize for yourself both "old" and "new" information.

2. Figure out what ideas are common to both.

3. Examine all choices, predicting the answer first if you can.

4. Check each choice against the original passage or graphic by asking, does this new information parallel or fit in with the old?

## Lesson 1 Exercise

1. Fill in the blanks with a word or a phrase: Before you can answer an application question, you must first _____ the information given. It is helpful to _____ about the correct choice and to _____ all the choices before answering.

2. Identify the type of item presented by labeling each C for Comprehension or A for Application

   (a) According to the cartoon, what is the attitude of many people toward elections?

   (b) Based on the description of Indians in Puerto Rico during the 1500s, would you say their position was more like that of American whites or blacks before the Civil War?

   (c) Suppose those who support the "melting pot" theory believe that ethnic differences between immigrant minorities tend to decrease. Which of the following examples does NOT demonstrate the theory?

*Item 3 is based on the following passage.*

Much research has been done on how people in organizations such as schools and companies respond to directives, or instructions. The research indicates that individuals often conform to the "letter" of directives from higher authorities. However, individuals in organizations seldom do more than instructed unless motivated by rewards.

3. Based on the information in the passage, if you want to increase the number of minorities in your company, the most effective procedure would be to

   (1) form a study group
   (2) show departments the economic advantage of hiring minorities
   (3) appeal to department heads' sense of fair play
   (4) send a memorandum to department heads about minority hiring
   (5) hire an outside consultant

Answers are on page 261.

# Lesson 2 Application from a List of Categories

What does the "new item type" look like?

When plant lovers spot an unusual plant, they try to figure out what type of plant it is, based on how it fits into what they already know about various categories of plants. Similarly, on the GED you will be presented with items that require you to fit a new piece of information into a list of definitions or categories that you will be given. Items in this new format require that you first understand the definitions presented and then see how they apply to specific cases.

## Application of Information from a List

Read the following list of categories and answer the questions that follow.

The following are terms that can be used to describe attitudes toward people in other nations.

**(1)** Pacifism—opposition to violence of any kind

**(2)** Interventionism—favoring interference in affairs of another state

**(3)** Isolationism—declining to enter into foreign commitments

**(4)** Racism—policy of enforcing belief that one's race is superior to others

Which of the following terms best describes President Theodore Roosevelt's attitude when he vowed to send in American troops, if necessary, to collect the Venezuelan debt?

**(1)** pacifism

**(2)** interventionism

**(3)** isolationism

**(4)** racism

Which of the following terms best describes Adolf Hitler's belief that the "Aryan race" was destined to rule the world?

**(1)** pacifism

**(2)** interventionism

**(3)** isolationism

**(4)** racism

During your preview, you probably noticed that the alternatives in both items are the same. That is because both items are testing your understanding of the differences among the various policies. Notice, also, that you are not expected to know about these policies before you read the material. Success on the GED depends on careful reading of what is provided, rather than on any previous knowledge.

In the first item, the correct answer is Choice (2). Roosevelt was revealing his belief that the United States had the right to step in and influence affairs in Venezuela.

The correct choice for the second item is **(4)**. Choices **(1)** and **(3)** are contradicted by the information about Hitler. You could make a case for the fact that Hitler believed in interventionism, since he planned to take over other nations. Because the item specifically mentions his belief in "Aryan" superiority, however, Choice **(4)** is the best choice.

It is not necessary to take the time to memorize what each policy is. A more efficient strategy might be to read the "new" information about the person in the item and compare it against each piece of "old" information in the list. For example, you could ask yourself: (1) Was Roosevelt opposed to violence? No, not if he felt it was necessary. (2) Did he believe in interfering in other states' affairs? Yes, according to this statement about Venezuela. (3) Was he declining to enter into foreign commitments? Quite the contrary. (4) Did he believe his race was superior? Not necessarily. You have narrowed your choices down to (2) and (4). The best answer seems to be (2). If you are still uncertain once you have narrowed down your choices, you should make your best guess, since you are not penalized for wrong answers.

## Lesson 2   Exercise

*Items 1 to 3* are based on the following information.

Psychologists say that we resist acting on unacceptable impulses by reactions called defense mechanisms. Five types of defense mechanism are:

- Sublimation—channeling unacceptable impulses into behaviors that are acceptable, even admired
- Repression—banning dangerous or painful impulses from memory
- Reaction formation—warding off an unacceptable impulse by overemphasis of the opposite thought or behavior
- Projection—attributing your own unacceptable impulses to someone else
- Regression—coping with frustration by retreating to an earlier, more pleasant period of development

1.  A man whose father beat him severely as a child "forgets" that his father was ever anything but kind to him. Which defense mechanism is primarily operating?

    **(1)** sublimation
    **(2)** repression
    **(3)** reaction formation
    **(4)** projection
    **(5)** regression

2. A three-year-old, when scolded for a mess he made, tells his mother that it was his baby sister who made the mess. Which defense mechanism is primarily operating?

   **(1)** sublimation
   **(2)** repression
   **(3)** reaction formation
   **(4)** projection
   **(5)** regression

3. An aggressive teenager becomes a star football player. Which defense mechanism is primarily operating?

   **(1)** sublimation
   **(2)** repression
   **(3)** reaction formation
   **(4)** projection
   **(5)** regression

   Answers are on page 261.

# Chapter 3 Quiz

1.  Suppose a comprehension and an application item are both based on the same chart. If the items were compared to two steps on a ladder, which item would be the lower step?

2.  TRUE or FALSE: On the Social Studies section of the GED, you will find application items based on passages, but never on cartoons or graphs.

3.  Suppose you preview a set of items on the Social Studies section of the GED. You notice that all the items have the same five choices. Where can you look for an explanation of each of the choices?

*Items 4 to 6 are based on the following information.*

In the past, a presidential candidate's display of emotion was often seen as a sign of weakness. Now it seems that candidates think displays of emotion won't hurt and may even help their chances.

4.  Which of the following provides an example of the new trend in candidates' display of emotion? Mr. X
    (1) loses votes when he cries while defending his wife's reputation
    (2) loses votes when he is caught lying about illegal activity
    (3) gains votes when he speaks sadly about his son's fatal accident
    (4) gains votes when he promises to lower taxes
    (5) gains votes when he vows to end unemployment

5.  TRUE or FALSE: Suppose a candidate speaks in a quivering voice about how he struggled with a physical handicap. According to the article, such a revelation is less likely to hurt his political career today than it would have in the past.

6.  Create an example in which the candidate Mr. Y's display of emotion helps his chances of winning an election.

*Items 7 to 10 are based on the following cartoon.*

7. If the cartoonist had chosen another vehicle instead of a rollercoaster, which of the following would he most likely have chosen?

   **(1)** a fishing boat with its nets down
   **(2)** a sailboat in an international race
   **(3)** a rowboat gliding across a lake
   **(4)** a train hauling freight through midwestern plains
   **(5)** a truck heading out of control down a mountain

8. Suppose the cartoonist had decided to use a similar illustration to support the "domino policy." That policy holds that you can't let a small country fall into communist hands, because the other countries around it will also fall. If the small country is in South America, which rollercoaster car would probably hold the United States?

9. Briefly explain another situation where a similar cartoon could have been used with different labels.

10. Fill in the blank: To get the point of the cartoon, you have to have some comprehension about what happened to oil prices in the 1970s and 1980s. Then you apply this understanding to the picture by finding what oil prices and _____ have in common.

Answers are on page 262.

# Chapter 4

# Analysis

## Objective

In this chapter, you will learn about the kinds of items that make up 30 percent of the Social Studies section of the GED: analysis items. You will

- Distinguish facts from hypotheses or opinions
- Recognize unstated assumptions
- Distinguish conclusions from supporting statements
- Identify cause-and-effect relationships
- Answer analysis items in social studies that illustrate each aspect of this skill

## Lesson 1    Facts Versus Opinions and Hypotheses

**How can you distinguish facts from opinions or hypotheses?**

To analyze something means to look at the relationships among its parts. The cereal you eat for breakfast has been analyzed to see what nutrients it contains and how the amount of each nutrient relates to your minimum daily requirement. Analysis items on the Social Studies section of the GED assess your understanding of how separate ideas are organized within a passage or graphic.

One type of analysis item on the GED asks you to point out which of several statements are facts and which are opinions or hypotheses.

### Strategies for Telling Apart Facts, Opinions, and Hypotheses

1. Ask yourself: Is this something that can be proved by measurement or observation? If so, it is a fact.
2. Is this someone's personal interpretation of the way things are, a view that cannot be proved? If so, it is an opinion.
3. Is this an educated guess or theory developed to explain certain facts? If so, it is a hypothesis.

## Distinguishing Facts from Opinions in Passages

Read the following paragraph and answer the question.

> (1) *In the 1930s, the Great Depression left one out of every four Americans jobless,* and the Nitti family, which grew to include six children, fared no better than most. (2) *The milkman cut off the milk.* The landlord threatened to evict them. The family went on relief, and Helen stood in line for (3) *foul-smelling* (4) *but free* eggs and cheese. She hated relief. "I always felt (5) *you should take care of yourself,"* she says.

Which of the numbered, italicized phrases are facts and which are opinions?

Phrases (1), (2), and (4) are all facts. Statistics verify that one out of four were jobless during the Depression. That the milkman cut off the milk was an observable event, not a matter of judgment. It is a fact that the eggs and cheese on the relief line were free; observers could see that no money changed hands. Phrase (3), however, is an opinion. Although there might be those who would agree that the eggs and cheese were foul-smelling, there also might be those who would disagree, and neither side could prove its case. The idea, in phrase (5), that "you should take care of yourself," is an opinion that cannot be proved right or wrong.

## Distinguishing Facts from Hypotheses in Graphics

Look again at the graph about completion of schooling on page 35.

Which of the following statements is a hypothesis that might be used to explain the information shown in the graph?

**(1)** Approximately 97 percent of American children complete primary school.

**(2)** More American children complete secondary than high school.

**(3)** Approximately 55 percent of American students complete college.

**(4)** We should make an effort to see that more Americans graduate from college.

**(5)** Perhaps some students drop out of high school because they feel there are too few job training courses.

Choice (5) is the correct answer. As a hypothesis, it supplies an explanation for the facts: the reason students are dropping out is that there are not enough job training courses. Choices (1) and (2) do not explain the facts, they merely repeat them. Choice (3) repeats the "facts" incorrectly. Notice how you can check the graph to see whether Choices (1), (2), and (3) are true. That means they are not hypotheses, but facts, since only facts can be proven either right or wrong. Although Choice (4) cannot be proven, it is not a hypothesis because it does not explain anything. It merely expresses an opinion.

Remember, a statement is

• fact if it can be proven true by observation or measurement

• opinion if it is an emotional interpretation that cannot be proved

• hypothesis if it is an educated guess used to explain facts

## Lesson 1   Exercise

*Items 1 and 2 refer to the following passage.*

. . . Whether the Congressmen come from the North, East, South, or West, and no matter how many trips they may have made to Washington, they cannot help being impressed each time they see this beautiful city again. As they view the imposing Lincoln Memorial or gaze at the lofty Washington Monument, they are reminded that they are working in historic surroundings. As the new Congress assembles and prepares for the important tasks facing it, the members know that they, too, are making history.

From *American Civics* (New York: Harcourt Brace Jovanovich, 1974), page 44. Used with permission.

1.  Which of the following statements is most likely based on facts rather than on opinion?

    **(1)** Congressmen come from the North, South, East, and West.
    **(2)** Congressmen are impressed each time they see Washington.
    **(3)** Washington is a beautiful city.
    **(4)** The monuments make congressmen proud of the city's history.
    **(5)** The tasks facing the Congress are important.

2.  Give an example of an opinion from the passage.

---

3.  Label each of the following statements as a fact, an opinion, or a hypothesis.

    **(1)** Men-only clubs are a cherished tradition that should remain.
    **(2)** Men-only clubs exist because they provide a channel for unacceptable impulses toward women that might otherwise erupt in socially destructive behavior.
    **(3)** The theory that men-only clubs serve a useful function is unfair to women.

    Answers are on page 262.

# Lesson 2   Identifying Unstated Assumptions

**How can you identify an unstated assumption?**

An **assumption** is an idea that you take for granted without proof. Suppose you eat the last spoonful of ice cream based on the assumption that no one else in your family will mind. Your assumption may or may not be confirmed later.

Authors, too, make assumptions. It is very important for a reader to be able to identify unstated assumptions. Otherwise, a reader may not realize that he or she disagrees with an author's assumption. A reader who is not aware of an author's assumption may think that the author is simply "stating the facts," when the author is actually trying to persuade readers to share an opinion.

### Identifying Unstated Assumptions in Passages

Reread the article about the Depression on page 52. Which of the following can you assume Helen believed, even though the passage doesn't say so?

**(1)** She and her family were going to starve.
**(2)** Her parents were jobless.
**(3)** Sometimes you have to swallow your pride.
**(4)** The eggs and cheese did not smell good.
**(5)** Helen did not like receiving free hand-outs.

The correct answer is (3). Although Helen does not say so, she must have believed it was necessary to swallow her pride and stand on the relief lines. Choices (4) and (5) are both opinions. Since they are stated directly by Helen, they do not count as unstated assumptions. Choice (1) is an unstated assumption, but there is nothing about Helen's actions or words to show that she held this particular belief. Choice (2) is a verifiable fact.

### Identifying Unstated Assumptions in Graphics

Look at Figure 1. What is the cartoonist's assumption about how some people think?

**FIGURE 1**

Political cartoons present you with a challenge: Not only do you need to figure out the point being made, but you need to distinguish between the facts used to support the cartoonist's opinion and the assumptions behind that opinion. In the cartoon, the way the brain is labeled reveals the cartoonist's assumption: Some people tend to focus on the importance of the Nazi war criminal issue and to dismiss many other important issues as "things that don't matter." This may or may not be an accurate assumption. The cartoonist's opinion seems to be that the issue of what to do about people accused of Nazi war crimes should receive less attention, while other issues should receive more.

### Strategies to Identify an Unstated Assumption

1. Don't accept every statement at face value. Ask yourself: What is the unstated, underlying belief that I am being asked to accept?
2. Make sure that you are not confusing unstated assumptions with stated facts, opinions, or hypotheses.

## Lesson 2 Exercise

*Item 1* is based on the following passage.

Originally, each state elected one representative for every 30,000 persons living in the state. If the state's population was under 30,000, it was entitled to have one representative. In the first Congress, which met in 1789, there were 59 representatives in the House. Then, as new states joined the Union and the nation's population increased, the House steadily grew in size. To prevent the membership from growing too large, in 1929 Congress finally limited the size of the House of Representatives to 435 members.

From *American Civics* (New York: Harcourt Brace Jovanovich, 1974), page 46. Used with permission.

1.  The 1929 Congress assumed that
    **(1)** each state should have equal representation
    **(2)** if the Congress is too large, it cannot function well
    **(3)** as new states joined the Union, the House would decline in size
    **(4)** in 1789, there were 59 representatives
    **(5)** larger states should have more representatives than smaller ones

*Items 2 and 3* are based on the cartoon on page 49.

2.  The cartoonist assumes that consumers feel _____ about the drop in oil prices.

3.  Suppose you start talking with several other people who are filling up their cars with gas. You find evidence that contradicts the cartoonist's assumption concerning consumers' reactions to low oil prices. What came up during the discussion?

Answers are on page 262.

## Lesson 3   Conclusions Versus Supporting Statements

How can you tell the difference between a conclusion and a supporting statement?

A conclusion is a final statement summarizing your main idea and giving the decision or opinion that you have reached. Your conclusion is often based on several supporting details or facts that point in a particular direction. If the number of car accidents and arrests for drunken driving goes down after the drinking age is raised, you might reach the conclusion that raising the drinking age creates safer highways.

Writers, too, use supporting details such as research findings or natural observations to draw conclusions. On the GED, you will be asked to distinguish between supporting details and conclusions. To make this distinction, ask yourself: Is this one of several ideas the writer included to "make his or her case" or is it actually the case itself—the main reason for presenting the information?

### Distinguishing Conclusions from Supporting Details in Passages

Read the following passage, keeping in mind the difference between a supporting detail and a conclusion.

In Salt Lake City, the Court of Appeals ruled against individuals who blamed their cancer on nuclear weapons tests in the 1950s. Military use of the substance Agent Orange has been linked to many health problems of Vietnam War veterans. Nevertheless, in New York, courts have affirmed that risky military activities are protected against lawsuits. Even if injuries are caused through the government's misjudgment, the government cannot be sued without its consent.

What is the conclusion reached by the passage?

The conclusion is located here, as it often will be, at the end of the article. When military actions are involved, the government can only be sued when it gives its consent. Two supporting details are included to "build the case" for the conclusion: We learn that the government was protected in cases surrounding Agent Orange and in cases surrounding nuclear testing.

### Distinguishing Conclusions from Supporting Details in a Graphic

Look again at the graph about discount rates on page 42. What is the conclusion drawn about the discount rate?

Here, as in many graphics, the conclusion is found in the title: Discount rate: lowest in nine years. The rest of the graph provides the specific information about yearly discount rates necessary to be able to draw the conclusion about the nine-year trend.

Remember, supporting details are the pieces of evidence the writer uses to support the main idea. The conclusion is the main idea toward which the writer builds.

## Lesson 3 Exercise

*Items 1 to 3* are based on the following information.

If you are planning on driving in a foreign country this summer, there are some facts about insurance that you should know. In Canada, a U.S. auto insurance policy should suffice, but you will need a card from your company which guarantees that the company will meet Canadian requirements in case of an accident. Travelers to Mexico must buy a short-term tourist policy. Since countries vary in their insurance requirements, it is a good idea to find out before you travel to a particular country what that country's requirements are.

1. Which statement best states the author's conclusion?

   **(1)** Mexican and Canadian restrictions on travelers are unreasonable.
   **(2)** The passage contains information useful to travelers.
   **(3)** Travelers to Canada are often covered by their U.S. insurance.
   **(4)** Travelers to Mexico need to get tourist insurance.
   **(5)** Travelers should find out about insurance before their trip.

2. Briefly list two of the details the author uses to support his conclusion.

3. Suppose the author added the following sentence: "Travelers driving across Europe are often surprised to find out how much insurance rules vary from country to country." Is this new sentence a supporting detail or a conclusion?

Answers are on page 262.

## Lesson 4    Identifying Cause-and-Effect Relationships

**How can you tell which is the most likely explanation for a change?**

When we notice a change, or *effect*, we often look for the reason, or *cause*. If a loud sound wakes you up, you will probably get up to see what caused the sound.

One important way that authors develop their ideas is by showing how one thing causes another. You can identify causes by asking yourself: What could be behind this change? You can identify effects by asking yourself: Based on what I already know and have just learned, what changes could result from that action?

### Identifying Cause-and-Effect Relationships in Passages

Reread the passage on page 56 about suing the government. What effect might the courts' rulings have on future cases where people try to sue the government? You might predict that since the courts have established a position supporting the government in the two cases described, they will stick to this position in future cases. Thus, the earlier rulings may cause other courts to make similar rulings in the future.

## Identifying Cause-and-Effect Relationships in Graphics

Look again at the chart about completion of schooling on page 35. What could be the cause of many more children completing elementary school than high school? You probably know that the law requires young children to stay in school, but allows them to leave school once they reach a certain age. You can guess that mandatory primary school attendance is a cause of the differences shown on the graph.

Remember, when trying to establish cause-and-effect relationships, ask yourself what happened (the effect) and why it happened (the cause).

## Lesson 4   Exercise

*Items 1 to 3* are based on the passage about suits against the government on page 56.

1.  Which of the following is the most likely cause for the courts' decisions in favor of the government?

    **(1)** Agent Orange and nuclear testing did not really hurt anybody.
    **(2)** The president told the courts what to do.
    **(3)** The courts did not want to interfere with military matters.
    **(4)** Very little money was involved in the suits.
    **(5)** Very few people were involved in the suits.

2.  What effect do you think the courts' decisions might have on somebody trying to decide whether or not to sue the government in a case involving health problems caused by the use of a new weapon in the Korean War?

3.  If the Supreme Court suddenly reversed both decisions, awarding large sums of money to the people bringing the suits, what effect do you think that would have on other U.S. veterans?

Answers are on page 262.

# Chapter 4 Quiz

1. Label the following items according to whether they mainly (a) test your understanding, (b) test your ability to apply your understanding to a new situation, (c) test your ability to examine the relationships between ideas.

   **(1)** A president states, "High tariffs inevitably lead to millions of people losing their jobs." Do you think the president would vote for or against imposing a high tariff on products Japan exports here?

   **(2)** What is a likely explanation for the decline in interest rates?

   **(3)** According to the passage, what is a "tariff"?

*Items 2 to 4 are based on the following passage.*

(1) A 15-year-old vegetarian in California is protesting against having to cut up frogs in her biology class. (2) She has been told to either dissect frogs or get out of the class. (3) "Killing animals is wrong," the young woman says. (4) Her lawyers feel that First Amendment safeguards of religious beliefs should protect the girl from having to dissect frogs.

2. Restate sentence (4) in your own words.

3. Label each sentence in the passage F (fact) or O (opinion).

4. Which sentence contains the conclusion?

*Items 5 to 7 are based on the following chart.*

In a survey of 5000 American households, banks and supermarkets won higher efficiency ratings than did government institutions such as Congress or the Pentagon. The following is a chart of how U.S. households rated the efficiency of various institutions.

| Percent Saying High or Very High Efficiency | | | |
|---|---|---|---|
| Supermarkets | 51 | Business | 26 |
| Banks | 48 | The Press | 22 |
| Department Stores | 38 | Public Schools | 21 |
| Credit Card Companies | 38 | Space Agency | 19 |
| Insurance Companies | 33 | Local Transport | 17 |
| Electric Utilities | 30 | Commuter Rail | 12 |
| Police | 29 | Trade Unions | 12 |
| Airlines | 29 | Pentagon | 10 |
| Post Office | 28 | Congress | 8 |

*Source:* The Conference Board, Survey of 5000 U.S. Households, reprinted from *Newsweek*, August 4, 1986, page 4. Used with permission.

5. TRUE or FALSE: According to the chart, it is a fact that supermarkets are more efficient than Congress.

6.  What conclusion can you draw about how the Americans surveyed feel about Congress?

7.  One possible reason that many of those surveyed said that they feel supermarkets are more efficient than Congress is that _____.

*Items 8 to 10* are based on the following passage.

For many years, women's organizations in the United States struggled to win the right to vote. In the early years of the suffrage movement, women's groups were also concerned with other issues. Many of the early suffragists, for example, were also abolitionists working for an end to slavery. After the Civil War, the issue of women's rights was especially controversial, because many citizens objected to former slaves voting as well. Some suffrage leaders stopped supporting the right of Afro-Americans to vote because they believed that made their own cause unpopular. This lead to a split in the women's movement and cost it some valuable allies. Although the Fifteenth Amendment granted Afro-American men the right to vote in 1869, women's right to vote was not granted until the passage of the Nineteenth Amendment in 1920.

8.  Which of the following does the author assume but not state?

    **(1)** Women's organizations worked very hard to win the right to vote.
    **(2)** The Nineteenth Amendment was passed in 1920.
    **(3)** The split in the women's movement delayed the passage of women's suffrage.
    **(4)** Suffragists should have concentrated on only one issue.
    **(5)** The Fifteenth Amendment was more important than the Nineteenth Amendment.

9.  Label the cause (C) and the effect (E)

    **(a)** The Nineteenth Amendment was passed in 1920.
    **(b)** Women's organizations worked hard for suffrage over many years.

10. Which of the following are supporting details and which is a conclusion?

    **(a)** If there had not been a split in the women's movement, suffrage might have been won earlier.
    **(b)** The split cost the women's movement some valuable allies.
    **(c)** Women's suffrage was not won until 1920.

Answers are on pages 262–263.

## Chapter 5

# Evaluation

## Objective

In this chapter, you will learn about the kinds of items that make up 20 percent of the Social Studies section of the GED: evaluation items. You will read about and practice identifying evaluation items that ask you to

- assess whether a particular conclusion can be drawn
- recognize the role of values in decision making
- assess whether facts are accurate
- indicate logical fallacies in arguments
- answer evaluation items in social studies that illustrate each aspect of this skill

## Lesson 1   Adequacy and Appropriateness of Information

**How can you judge whether a statement is supported adequately by the evidence presented?**

To evaluate something means to judge it. When you judge whether this book has been effective in helping you prepare for the Social Studies section of the GED, you are evaluating the book. One of the standards, or mental yardsticks, you use in your evaluation might be how confident you feel about passing the test after completing this book.

Evaluation items on the GED exam test your ability to judge whether information or methods are accurate. You are often asked to use a standard provided in a passage or graphic as a yardstick against which you can judge various alternatives.

### Evaluating Adequacy of Information in Passages

Read the following passage and answer the question that follows.

A major goal of Iran's revolutionary trade policy has been to expand trade with the non-Western world. Iran's commerce minister recently reported that government figures show that Iran has successfully shifted its focus in trade away from the West toward the Islamic world. A reporter pointed out, however, that government statisticians have moved Turkey, one of Iran's largest trading partners, out of the West and into the Third World.

Which of the following statements is best supported by the evidence?

**(1)** Iran has shifted its focus away from the West.

**(2)** Iran has achieved one of its major goals.

**(3)** Western countries still serve as Iran's main trade partners.

**(4)** Statistics exaggerate how much Iran has shifted trade partners.

**(5)** Iran has not increased trade with the developing countries.

The correct answer is (4). Based on information in the passage, we can only say that Iranian figures make it look as if Iran has shifted away from Western trade partners more than it really has. Either Choice (1) or Choice (3) may be true, but we cannot tell from the passage which does not offer any statistics or facts, other than to say that Iran's "goal" is to shift its focus. However, without more evidence, we cannot say whether that goal has been reached. Likewise, the passage does not give sufficient evidence for evaluating Choices (2) and (5). There is evidence that the increase in trade with Islamic nations may not be as large as Iran says it is, but there is no evidence that the increase has not occurred.

### Evaluating Adequacy of Information in Graphics

Look again at the map of East and West Germany on page 37. Which of the following statements is NOT supported by the data provided by the map?

**(1)** West Germany has a larger population than East Germany.

**(2)** West Germany has a larger area than East Germany.

**(3)** Coal is found in both East and West Germany.

**(4)** There is more industry in West Germany than in East Germany.

**(5)** The Bohemian Forest is located in West Germany.

The correct answer is **(1)**. Choices **(2)**, **(3)**, **(4)**, and **(5)** can all be confirmed by checking the labels and symbols on the map. But the map presents no evidence about population, and we cannot assume that a country has more people just because it is physically larger.

### Assessing Adequacy and Appropriateness of Data

When trying to assess whether data is adequate or appropriate to support given hypotheses, conclusions, or generalizations, ask:

1. Is there enough information to support this statement?
2. Is the information the right kind to support this statement?

## Lesson 1   Exercise

**1.** Read the following statement and explain why the conclusion is or is not supported by the information.

Many successful people have a large vocabulary. Therefore, if I learn a thousand new words, I will be successful.

2.  Suppose an anthropologist collects the following data: Most of the people in a particular culture perform a ritual each morning. At approximately an hour before sunrise, adults and children probe their teeth with a small instrument composed of a brush attached to a stick.

    The anthropologist concludes that because this ritual takes place so early in the morning, members of this society perform the ritual to make sure that the sun comes up. Explain why or why not this conclusion is supported by the evidence.

3.  Look again at the chart on efficiency ratings on page 59.

    Which of the following statements is best supported by evidence presented in the chart?

    **(1)** People around the globe feel their governments are inefficient.
    **(2)** Most Americans spend more time in banks than in supermarkets.
    **(3)** Supermarket lines tend to be longer than post office lines.
    **(4)** Many Americans feel banks are run more efficiently than Congress.
    **(5)** Many police feel that they do their jobs better than members of congress.

    Answers are on page 263.

# Lesson 2   The Effect of Values on Beliefs and Decision Making

**Why is it important to realize how values affect a writer's beliefs?**

Each of us has a set of values, or ideals and customs, that we consider important. What we think and do is colored by those values. People who value neatness are likely to spend more time cleaning up their homes than people who do not value neatness as much.

What authors write is also colored by their values. On the GED, you will be asked to examine how particular values influence a writer's choice and treatment of a subject. Once you are aware of these values, you are in a better position to judge whether you want to accept what you are being told. Ask yourself: How does where the writer is "coming from" affect the way he or she presents information? Is the writer being objective or expressing an opinion?

## Identifying the Effect of Values on Information in Passages

Read the following letter to the editor from a news magazine.

> Don't let [anyone] intimidate you into shrinking from reporting on one of the most important stories of our time: the Soviet [murders] in Afghanistan. . . . It is . . . a campaign to exterminate another nation. The [West] holds in [its] hands the Afghan people's only chance of survival.*

*Adapted from *World Press Review*, February 1987, page 4. Used with permission.

What is the writer's viewpoint? It is clear from what is said that the writer sides with the people of Afghanistan. The use of such emotional words as *murder* and *exterminate* is intended to prevent the reader from having sympathy for the Soviet Union. The writer makes the assumption that the West has a responsibility to intervene. A Soviet soldier would probably write a letter with the opposite bias. You would need more objective evidence about the situation before you could evaluate which position is more reasonable.

### Identifying the Effect of Values on Information in Graphics

Look again at the cartoon about Nazi war criminals on page 54. It is a good idea not only to consider the cartoonist's viewpoint, but also to imagine what those on the "other side of the fence" would say. The cartoonist might feel that getting equal rights for today's women matters at least as much as punishing Nazis for crimes they committed years ago. Someone else whose relatives were killed by the Nazis might feel that punishing Nazi war criminals matters more than any other issue.

### Questions to Help Identify the Role of Values

1. What is the source I am reading?
2. What would the writer like me to believe?
3. Has the writer used facts as well as emotional appeals to support this belief?

## Lesson 2   Exercise

*Items 1 and 2 are based on the following passage.*

Teaching children to be responsible with money is a challenge for every parent. In many families, money is given out inconsistently and used to express love and power. To avoid the friction such use of money can create, establish a regular allowance for your children. Having a regular allowance helps a child learn to make decisions about how to spend money wisely.

1.  The author's views about money are NOT expressed by which statement.
    **(1)** Teaching children how to handle money is important.
    **(2)** Children are capable of spending money carefully.
    **(3)** It is not a good idea to express love with money.
    **(4)** Children should have to earn the money they are given.
    **(5)** Children should be allowed to make mistakes in what they buy.

2.  Suppose someone believes in teaching children that money has to be earned. Would the person agree with the passage?

3.  Imagine that you are a vegetarian who believes that animals have rights. Write one sentence about your opinion of fast-food hamburgers. Then write a second sentence about fast-food hamburgers from the point of view of someone who loves to eat hamburgers.

Answers are on page 263.

# Lesson 3   Accuracy of Facts Based on Documentation

**How can you tell whether the "facts" presented to you are really facts?**

Documentation is proof on paper. When you write out a check to pay for your purchases, you are often asked for documentation. You show the cashier your driver's license, a document that proves who you are.

Like customers, writers are expected to provide enough information for readers to determine whether the facts presented are accurate. When trying to assess whether facts are adequately supported by documentation, ask yourself: "Does the writer present naked facts or are the facts backed up with documentation? If so, should I believe the documentation?"

## Assessing Documentation of Facts in Passages

In order to determine the effect of the Three Mile Island nuclear accident on housing sales, which of the following would be likely to contain the best documentation?

**(1)** a memo from an Environmental Protection Agency official

**(2)** an ad paid for by a local antinuclear organization

**(3)** a 10-year sales listing kept by a local real estate sales association

**(4)** a statement by a statewide environmental study group

**(5)** a statement by a pro-nuclear lobbying group

The best answer is Choice (3). Those who sell houses keep records of the location and price of each house sold. The records reflect actual verifiable sales, not how the salespeople feel about the accident. Choices (1), (2), (4), and (5), on the other hand, all describe documents that might well reflect their writers' positive or negative reactions.

### Questions to Assess the Accuracy of Facts

1.  Are statistics, observations, or measurements of some sort provided to support the fact?

2.  If there is proof, how strong is it?

## Lesson 3 Exercise

*Items 1 to 3* are based on the following passage.

Japanese students, like American students, vary a great deal in economic background and in ability. Mixing students of differing ability in the same class and requiring all of them to cover the same material have resulted in Japan's educational success.

Two researchers carefully studied several early-grade classes in Chicago schools. Teachers placed students in three reading groups according to achievement and ability. Not surprisingly, the group that was given the fewest vocabulary words to learn learned the fewest words. If members of the "low" group had been in the "high" group, they would have learned more words. The time for teaching all American students the same rich core curriculum has come.

1.  Which of the following statements in the passage is best supported by documented evidence presented by the author?
    **(1)** Japanese students vary a great deal in ability.
    **(2)** American students vary in economic background.
    **(3)** The success of Japanese students is due to a core curriculum.
    **(4)** Students who are given fewer words to learn, learn fewer words.
    **(5)** We should start teaching a core curriculum in the U.S.

2.  The writer's case for teaching a core curriculum in the U.S. would be stronger if he included some research results from studies done on the achievement of _____ students.

3.  "If 'low' students were given more words to learn, they would learn more words." Briefly explain the kind of evidence that might have supported this statement.

Answers are on page 263.

## Lesson 4    Identifying Logical Fallacies in Arguments

**Why is it useful to be able to detect logical fallacies?**

Suppose a friend says to you, "It's true what they say about red-haired people having bad tempers. My aunt has red hair, and she has the shortest fuse of anyone I know." You could point out that your friend's reasoning is faulty. He may happen to know one bad-tempered redhead, but there may be many other sweet-tempered redheads. A fault in reasoning, or logic, is known as a *fallacy*.

A good, critical reader must be aware of misleading arguments in written material. On the GED, you will be asked to identify the fallacies, or errors, in reasoning that appear in such materials as political advertisements, editorials, and biased articles.

### Indicating Logical Fallacies in Passages

Suppose it is election time and your local newspaper carries the following advertisement, paid for by the Democratic Committee to Elect Bob White.

> Republicans represent the wealthy interest in our country. George Green is a Republican. George Green represents the wealthy interest. If you're just a working person like the rest of us, vote for Democrat Bob White.

George may indeed work to gain advantages for only the wealthy, but to come to this conclusion based on the information presented is inaccurate. The original statement is faulty. Not all Republicans represent the wealthy interest. Making a conclusion based on a faulty initial statement is like building a house on a cracked foundation. The whole house may fall down.

### Indicating Logical Fallacies Based on Graphics

Graphics, such as graphs or charts, may look impressive, but you have to examine them for logical fallacies, too. Look again at the chart showing results of the efficiency poll on page 59. Suppose the caption had read, "Efficiency in supermarkets reduces people's faith in the efficiency of Congress." This would have been a logical fallacy. You cannot conclude that efficiency in running supermarkets is the *cause* of people's belief in the inefficiency of Congress. Just because two things occur at the same time does not mean that one necessarily causes the other.

### Questions to Detect Logical Fallacies

1. Is an overgeneralization or oversimplification being made?
2. Is a false connection being drawn?
3. Is a misleading cause-effect relationship being stated?
4. Are statistics being used in a misleading way?
5. Is the original question really being answered?

## Lesson 4　Exercise

*Items 1 to 3* are based on the following passage.

Suppose you are investigating why growth in U.S. businesses lags so far behind productivity growth overseas. You learn that American businesses cut the number of blue-collar workers on their payrolls by 1.9 million between 1978 and 1985. The number of white-collar workers rose by 10 million. Productivity grew by only about 0.7 percent a year.

1. Explain why you can or cannot conclude that the decrease in the number of blue-collar workers resulted in the decline in productivity.

2. Which sentence demonstrates a generalization that is too broad?

   **(1)** Businesses paid for 1.9 million fewer blue-collar workers.
   **(2)** Businesses paid for 10 million more white-collar workers.
   **(3)** There was a 21-percent rise in white-collar employment.
   **(4)** The rise in white-collar employment outstripped productivity growth.
   **(5)** Low white-collar productivity accounts for the low output.

3. Suppose you learn that blue-collar productivity rose 13 percent between 1978 and 1984, while white-collar productivity declined by nearly 10 percent. TRUE or FALSE: It would NOT be faulty reasoning to state that "low white-collar productivity contrasted with a respectable showing by blue-collar workers."

Answers are on page 263.

# Chapter 5 Quiz

*Items 1 to 3 are based on the following passage.*

According to a recent UNESCO study, a major reason the United States is losing the import war is because of all countries studied, the U.S. is the least sensitive to other cultures. The study suggests that understanding the language and culture of another country can have a tremendous impact on the amount of business that can be conducted in that country.

1.  The passage implies that Americans

    **(1)** are losing the import war
    **(2)** think their culture is superior
    **(3)** are often unable to learn other languages
    **(4)** often do not learn the language of countries where they do business
    **(5)** are more aware of other nations' cultures than they are of the U.S.'s

2.  The author of the study probably believes that

    **(1)** U.S. residents should be more sensitive to other cultures
    **(2)** U.S. residents should be less tolerant of other cultures
    **(3)** English is the language of commerce
    **(4)** citizens of other nations should learn to speak English
    **(5)** other nations should increase their exports to the U.S.

3.  "Switzerland has the highest per person income of any country." Who would most likely have documentation to support the above statement?

    **(1)** a recent visitor to Switzerland
    **(2)** a member of the President's economic advisory council
    **(3)** a visiting friend from Switzerland

---

4.  Which of the following three test items is an evaluation item?

    **(1)** Which of the statements located in the passage about human-rights violations in Argentina is best supported by evidence?
    **(2)** Based on the passage about checks and balances, choose from the following list the situation that demonstrates checks and balances.
    **(3)** According to the passage, what are "checks and balances?"

*Items 5 and 6 are based on the following information.*

Suppose you are examining the following three pieces of written material, in an effort to better understand the Revolutionary War:

   a. A journal kept by a colonial girl between 1770 and 1780
   b. Court notes taken at the trial of Benedict Arnold
   c. A college textbook about the Revolutionary period

5.  In which case or cases do you need to consider the values of the person who wrote the material, before you accept it as true?

6.  The girl's journal is only one person's story, and might well contain opinions and distorted facts. List two questions you would ask about this girl in order to better evaluate her material.

7.  TRUE or FALSE: The "facts" given by a British author in a textbook about the American Revolution might differ from the "facts" presented by an American author in a textbook on the same topic. Explain what would make this statement true or false.

*Items 8 to 10* are based on the following passage and table.

Taxi driving is an occupation that clearly reflects the latest immigrant waves in New York. This profile was compiled from surveys of 4369 applicants for hack licenses enrolled in the New York Taxi Drivers Institute, which runs a 20-hour program that prospective cab drivers must pass to receive a license from the New York City Taxi and Limousine Commission. The surveys were conducted between October 1984 and May 1985.

| Ten Most Prominent Native Countries of Taxi Drivers | |
| --- | --- |
| **Country** | **Percent** |
| Haiti | 25 |
| Dominican Republic | 6 |
| Egypt | 5 |
| South Korea | 5 |
| Afghanistan | 4 |
| Colombia | 4 |
| India | 4 |
| Pakistan | 4 |
| Rumania | 4 |
| Soviet Union | 4 |

| | |
| --- | --- |
| Mean age | 33.5 years |
| Two or more years of college | 47% |

Source: Dr. Anne G. Morris, City University of New York, adapted from *The New York Times*, April 3, 1987. Used with permission.

8.  Which of the following two statements is better supported by the figures presented?
    a.  Taxi driving clearly reflects the latest immigrant waves in New York.
    b.  Most of the taxi drivers in New York were not born in the United States.

9.  Explain the fallacy in reasoning: Since the mean age of a taxi driver in New York is 33.5, most New York taxi drivers are about 33.5.

10. TRUE or FALSE: It is reasonable to conclude from the information given that two or more years of college are required to receive a taxi driving license in New York City. Explain your answer.

Answers are on pages 263–264.

# Unit I Test

Items 1 to 5 are based on the following passage.

Our federal government is made up of three branches—legislative, executive, and judicial. In general, the legislative body is responsible for making laws, the executive body enforces laws, and the judicial body interprets laws. A system of "checks and balances" was established to prevent any one branch from gaining too much power. For example, if the legislative branch votes to pass a bill that the executive branch feels is wrong, the President can veto the bill. Thus, the executive branch "checks" the legislative branch. On the other hand, the legislative branch can "check" the executive branch by overturning a presidential veto with a two-thirds vote.

1. Briefly explain the meaning of *checks and balances*.

2. Which of the following is an example of the power of the legislative branch being checked?
   (1) A lobbyist tries to influence legislators to pass a tax bill.
   (2) Presidential staff members try to influence legislators.
   (3) The President vetoes a tax bill passed by Congress.
   (4) The President is impeached.
   (5) The Legislature overturns the President's veto.

3. What is the basic assumption behind the system of checks and balances?
   (1) All three branches should have a say in any decision made.
   (2) If one branch became too powerful, it might abuse the power.
   (3) Two out of three branches should agree before a law is made.
   (4) Checks and balances will lead to more speedy decision making.
   (5) The President should have the ultimate authority.

4. The legislative body is responsible for making laws. Label this statement as a fact, an opinion, or a hypothesis and explain your choice.

5. Explain the fallacy in this argument: We know that the President can never become too powerful because the system of checks and balances was created in part to keep the President from becoming too powerful.

*Items 6 to 10 are based on the following table.*

This table reports the results of a poll of 1349 newspeople about which news organizations they considered most reliable.

| Ten Most Reliable News Sources | | |
|---|---|---|
| Organization | Rank | Percent of Vote |
| The New York Times | 1 | 28 |
| Associated Press | 2 | 19 |
| United Press International | 3 | 13 |
| Washington Post | 4 | 10 |
| Wall Street Journal | 5 | 9 |
| Los Angeles Times | 6 | 5 |
| Newsweek | 7 | 5 |
| Christian Science Monitor | 8 | 4 |
| Time | 9 | 4 |
| CBS News | 10 | 3 |

**Source:** Johnstone, *The Newspeople*, page 224, reprinted from Doris A. Graber, "Mass Media and American Politics," *Congressional Quarterly Press*, 1980, page 52. Used with permission.

6. In one sentence, summarize the main idea of the table.

7. The only TV network that appears among the top ten news media is
   _____.

8. Suppose that you happen to agree with 10 percent of the newspeople polled. If so, which newspaper would you consider the most reliable?

9. What is the most likely explanation for the fact that only one TV network appeared among the top ten news sources?

10. TRUE OR FALSE: There are enough data to support the conclusion that *The New York Times* is the most reliable news source. Explain your answer.

*Items 11 to 15 are based on the following passage.*

Many people think that opposition to slavery was the main cause of the Civil War. Slavery was part of the cause, but the major cause was economic. In the North the economy was built on industry, while in the South, the economy was built on agriculture. The North wanted the government to impose taxes on imported goods. The South, on the other hand, needed to import many of its goods, and thus did not want import taxes.

11. According to the article, the major cause of the Civil War was
    (1) philosophical opposition to slavery
    (2) opposition to large-scale farming
    (3) unwillingness of the South to industrialize
    (4) economic pressures put on the South by the North
    (5) unwillingness of the North to accept slavery

12. What inference can you draw about why the North wanted import taxes?

    **(1)** Without import taxes, Americans might be more likely to buy cheaper foreign goods than the North's products.

    **(2)** Without import taxes, Americans might be more likely to buy the South's industrial goods than the North's products.

    **(3)** The North wanted to make extra money on its industrial products by taxing the South for buying them.

13. Currently there is support for tariffs, or taxes on imports. How is this similar to what was happening during the period prior to the Civil War?

    **(1)** Concern for protecting U.S. workers and products still motivates support for tariffs.

    **(2)** The desire to provide the consumer with products at the lowest possible prices still motivates support for tariffs.

14. Label the supporting statement(s) (S) and the conclusion(s) (C).

    **(a)** The South made most of its money from farming.

    **(b)** The North contained many industries.

    **(c)** The North wanted tariffs, but the South did not.

    **(d)** Economic factors were the primary cause of the Civil War.

15. Explain the logical fallacy in the following argument: Since opposition to slavery was the main cause of the Civil War, the war could have been prevented if the North had not tried to force the South to abolish slavery.

Answers are on page 264.

# UNIT II

## Foundations in Social Studies

In this unit, you will study the five areas of social studies that are covered on the Social Studies Test. The lessons will give you practice at applying your reading skills to social studies materials.

The Foundations in Social Studies unit begins with a chapter that explains what social studies is. Five other chapters each cover one of the content areas of social studies that appear on the GED Test: history, geography, economics, political science, and behavioral science. The last chapter shows how the various branches of social studies interact with each other to interpret world events.

The seven chapters in Unit II are divided into lessons. Each lesson ends with an exercise that is made up of questions that require you to think the way you will have to when you take the GED. Each chapter ends with a quiz that covers or draws on the material presented in the chapter. The Unit II Test ends the unit. It has 32 items—the same amount of items as on the Predictor Test in this book. About half of the items are multiple-choice questions.

This unit will help you develop a manner of thinking that will improve your ability to understand and interpret social studies materials. Your increased ability should help you perform better on the Social Studies Test. Use the chart on the next page to record your progress as you work through the unit.

# UNIT II PROGRESS CHART
# Foundations in Social Studies

**Directions:** Use the following chart to keep track of your work. When you complete a lesson and have checked your answers to the items in the exercise, circle the number of questions you answered correctly. When you complete a Chapter Quiz, record your score on the appropriate line. The numbers in color represent scores at a level of 80 percent or better.

| Lesson | Page | | |
|---|---|---|---|
| | | **CHAPTER 1: Introduction to Social Studies** | |
| 1 | 79 | What Social Studies Is | 1 2 3 4 |
| 2 | 80 | The Social Sciences That Make Up Social Studies | 1 2 3 4 5 |
| 3 | 82 | How Social Scientists Report Information | 1 2 3 4 |
| | 83 | Chapter 1 Quiz | 1 2 3 4 5 6 7 8 9 10 |
| | | **CHAPTER 2: American History** | |
| 1 | 85 | The New World | 1 2 3 |
| 2 | 86 | From Colonists to Revolutionaries | 1 2 3 |
| 3 | 87 | Forming the American Government | 1 2 3 4 5 |
| 4 | 88 | The Growth of the United States | 1 2 3 |
| 5 | 90 | The Civil War | 1 2 3 |
| 6 | 91 | The Civil War and Reconstruction | 1 2 3 |
| 7 | 92 | The Growth of U.S. Industry | 1 2 3 |
| 8 | 94 | The United States in the First Half of the Twentieth Century | 1 2 3 |
| 9 | 95 | The United States as a World Power | 1 2 3 |
| 10 | 96 | The Cold War | 1 2 3 |
| 11 | 97 | The United States After World War II | 1 2 3 |
| 12 | 98 | The United States Today and Tomorrow | 1 2 3 |
| | 100 | Chapter 2 Quiz | 1 2 3 4 5 6 7 8 9 10 |
| | | **CHAPTER 3: Geography** | |
| 1 | 103 | Kinds of Maps | 1 2 3 4 5 |
| 2 | 105 | Climate and Weather | 1 2 3 4 |
| 3 | 106 | Resources and the Environment | 1 2 3 |
| 4 | 107 | Using the World's Resources Wisely | 1 2 3 |
| 5 | 108 | Cultural Geography | 1 2 3 |
| | 110 | Chapter 3 Quiz | 1 2 3 4 5 6 7 8 9 10 |

| Lesson | Page | | |
|---|---|---|---|
| | | **CHAPTER 4: Economics** | |
| 1 | 112 | Modern Economic Systems | 1 2 3 4 |
| 2 | 113 | The Free-Enterprise System | 1 2 3 4 5 |
| 3 | 115 | Financial Institutions | 1 2 3 4 |
| 4 | 116 | Government's Role in the Economy | 1 2 3 |
| 5 | 117 | Taxes | 1 2 3 |
| 6 | 119 | Measuring Our Economy | 1 2 3 4 5 |
| 7 | 120 | Labor and the Economy | 1 2 3 |
| 8 | 121 | International Trade | 1 2 3 4 5 |
| | 123 | Chapter 4 Quiz | 1 2 3 4 5 6 7 8 9 10 |
| | | **CHAPTER 5: Political Science** | |
| 1 | 125 | Types of Government and How They Function | 1 2 3 4 |
| 2 | 126 | The Declaration of Independence and the Articles of Confederation | 1 2 3 4 5 |
| 3 | 127 | The Constitution | 1 2 3 4 5 |
| 4 | 129 | Amendments to the Constitution | 1 2 3 4 5 |
| 5 | 130 | The Federal System— National, State, and Local Government | 1 2 3 4 |
| 6 | 131 | The United States Political Process | 1 2 3 4 |
| 7 | 132 | Government and Social Welfare | 1 2 3 |
| 8 | 133 | International Politics | 1 2 3 4 |
| | 134 | Chapter 5 Quiz | 1 2 3 4 5 6 7 8 9 10 |
| | | **CHAPTER 6: Behavioral Science** | |
| 1 | 137 | Introduction to Behavioral Science | 1 2 3 4 |
| 2 | 139 | Psychology: Subfields and Perspectives | 1 2 3 |
| 3 | 140 | The Biological Perspective and Behaviorism | 1 2 3 4 |
| 4 | 142 | The Study of Society in Sociology | 1 2 3 |

| Lesson | Page | | | Lesson | Page | | |
|---|---|---|---|---|---|---|---|
| 5 | 143 | The Study of Group Behavior | **1 2** 3 | 2 | 151 | The World Wars and Women's Liberation | **1 2** 3 |
| 6 | 144 | Introduction to Anthropology | **1 2 3** 4 | 3 | 152 | The United States Economic and Political History and School Desegregation | **1 2 3** 4 |
| 7 | 145 | The Study of Different Cultures | **1 2** 3 | 4 | 153 | Soviet Geography and the Cold War | **1 2 3** 4 |
| | 146 | Chapter 6 Quiz | **1 2 3 4 5 6 7** 8 9 10 | 5 | 155 | Famine in Africa: The Geography and the Politics | **1 2** 3 |
| | | CHAPTER 7: **Interrelationships Among the Branches of Social Studies** | | | 156 | Chapter 7 Quiz | **1 2 3 4 5 6 7** 8 9 10 |
| 1 | 149 | The Stock Market Crash: National and International Effects | **1 2** 3 | | | | |

# Introduction to Social Studies

## Objective

In this chapter you will read and answer questions about

- What social studies is
- What the social sciences are that make up social studies
- How social scientists report information

## Lesson 1    What Social Studies Is

**Why is social studies considered a complex field of study?**

As a person, you are naturally curious about other people. You may want to know why different people react to the same event in different ways. You may want to know how different events in the past have shaped the present. You may sometimes wonder why different countries have different customs and traditions. Perhaps you'd like to know more about different governments and different types of economic systems.

The answers to all of these questions can be found in social studies, which is concerned with the life, well-being, and relations of people in a **community.** The word *social* is closely related to the word **society.** A society is an organized group of people associated with each other for some common purpose. That purpose may be religious, political, cultural, scientific, or patriotic. When we talk about our entire country as one society, we are talking about a very large group of people who share many *customs* and beliefs. As a society, we share a history, a language, a political system, and an economic system.

Social studies is concerned with the study of people in society. The social studies include history, geography, economics, political science, and behavioral science.

Each one of these fields tells us something important about the societies that exist and have existed in different parts of the world. Social studies can help us understand the past and plan for the future. Social studies can help us to better understand ourselves and our world.

## Lesson 1 Exercise

1. The word *social* can be used in many ways. Explain why people are said to be social beings.

2. Listed below are a number of items. Identify the items that are customs or beliefs of the United States.

   **(a)** Thanksgiving
   **(b)** the right to vote
   **(c)** oldest sons inherit family property
   **(d)** freedom of religion
   **(e)** a belief in royalty and nobility

3. Tell if the following statement is TRUE or FALSE, and give a reason for your answer. Social studies is concerned only with societies in today's world.

4. Explain the meaning of the following statement: A society may be made up of many different small societies.

Answers are on page 265.

## Lesson 2    The Social Sciences That Make Up Social Studies

What is a *social science*?

There are five main branches of social studies. They are history, geography, economics, political science, and behavioral science.

History is the study of people and events in the past. The past may mean something as long ago as the Stone Age, or it may mean something as recent as yesterday. Every country has a history; every culture has a history; every society has a history.

Geography can be divided into two types of study. Physical geography is the study of the physical structure of Earth. Cultural geography is concerned with the way the world's **population** is distributed across the various **regions** of the world.

Economics is the social science that deals with the **production, distribution,** and **consumption** of a country's goods and services.

Political science is the study of the various types of governments that exist in the world. Sometimes different types of **governments** share some common characteristics. Some forms of government are very old; others are relatively new.

Behavioral science includes the studies of psychology, sociology, and anthropology. Psychology is the study of the mind. Sociology is concerned with the various relationships in a society. Anthropology is the study of groups of people within their cultures.

Very often, the branches of social studies overlap. For example, a study of the **American Revolution** could involve political science and economics. To understand the minds of the people who fought the Revolution, one might make use of one or more of the behavioral sciences.

## Lesson 2 Exercise

1.  Economics is concerned with all of the following EXCEPT

    **(1)** the use of a country's goods and services
    **(2)** the production of a country's goods and services
    **(3)** the distribution of a country's population across its various regions
    **(4)** the distribution of a country's goods and services
    **(5)** the regulation of wages, hours, and employment conditions

2.  In which branch of social studies would an article that compares the organization of the government of France with that of the United States be classified?

Item 3 is based on the following map.

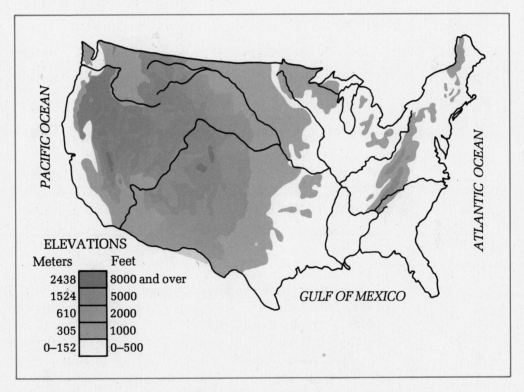

3.  Would you use this map to study physical geography or cultural geography?

4.  What features of Earth are studied by physical geographers?

5.  The branches of social studies often overlap. Explain how economic development can be influenced by such factors as geography and political science.

Answers are on page 265.

# Lesson 3    How Social Scientists Report Information

**How do social scientists report information?**

Social scientists employ many tools to present information. In economics, for example, a line graph, such as in Figure 1, may be used to show the relation between the price of automobiles and the number of cars sold.

A sociologist may use a bar graph to report statistics. The bar graph in Figure 2 gives a clear picture of the number of people engaged in manufacturing and industry over a century.

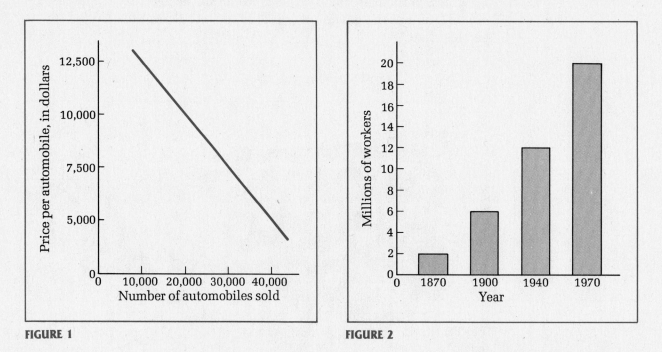

**FIGURE 1**                                          **FIGURE 2**

A circle graph shows percentages of a whole. The full circle represents 100%; a half circle is 50%; and so on. Circle graphs can be used to show product or population distribution, relative sizes of political parties and other groups, budget information, or a variety of other kinds of information.

Historians frequently use time lines to illustrate time spans between events. Maps are used to depict physical features; climate; natural resource, product, and population distribution; as well as political boundaries.

Charts and tables are frequently used to present information in an organized way. Cartoons may convey political or personal opinions.

## Lesson 3 Exercise

*Items 1 and 2 are based on Figure 1.*

1.  According to the line graph, approximately how many automobiles were sold at $10,000?

2. What can you determine about the relation between price and the number of cars sold?

*Item 3* is based on Figure 2.

3. Which one of the following conclusions can you draw based on information in the bar graph?
   (1) There was no significant population shift from rural to urban areas between 1900 and 1940.
   (2) There was a rapid growth of cities during the century before 1970.
   (3) The number of farm workers increased during the period shown on the graph.
   (4) The gross national product index fell during the period shown.
   (5) Farmers lost the market for their products during the first half of the twentieth century.

4. Of the tools of social scientists mentioned in this lesson, which one is usually used to express political or personal bias?

Answers are on page 265.

# Chapter 1 Quiz

1. Which one of the following subjects is NOT a branch of social studies?
   (1) psychology        (4) geography
   (2) history           (5) economics
   (3) biology

2. Below are lists of titles of articles and the names of some branches of social studies. Match the titles and branches.
   \_\_\_\_\_ Causes of the Civil War      **(a)** geography
   \_\_\_\_\_ Reading Maps                  **(b)** history
   \_\_\_\_\_ Consumer Tips                 **(c)** behavioral science
   \_\_\_\_\_ How Memory Works              **(d)** economics
   \_\_\_\_\_ Family Life

3. The word *social* has many forms and uses. Provide a brief explanation for its use in each of the following sentences.
   **(a)** Tom is very shy and prefers not to **socialize** with people he doesn't know well.
   **(b)** After his graduation from school, Bill joined the **Society** of Engineers.
   **(c)** A wedding is a **social** event, not a business event.

4.  Diana is writing an article on the Civil War. In which branch of the social studies does each of her topics fall?

    **(a)** lack of manufacturing in the South
    **(b)** distribution of black population
    **(c)** location of seaports and shipping centers
    **(d)** slavery in the United States

5.  Explain how a map showing the natural resources of a country would be useful in economic planning.

6.  Economics is concerned with the production, distribution, and consumption of goods and services. Based on this statement, describe some ways in which government actions can influence economics.

7.  The scientific method is an organized series of steps used by researchers to ensure objectivity and consistency in studying a problem. Why do you think anthropologists make use of the scientific method?

8.  Draw a circle graph to show the population distribution by major religions in India:

    Hindu 85%,    Buddhist 1%,    Christian 3%,    Moslem 11%

9.  The people who signed the Declaration of Independence held revolutionary ideas. In the eighteenth century most countries were ruled by monarchs who believed they ruled by divine right. The colonists believed government should get its power from the people it governs. What made the colonists' idea so revolutionary?

10. Thomas Jefferson once wrote, "I hold it, that a little rebellion, now and then, is a good thing, and as necessary in the political world as storms in the physical." What do you think the meaning of this statement is?

Answers are on pages 265–266.

# American History

## Objective

In this chapter you will read and answer questions about

- Early American history
- How the United States government was formed
- The growth of the United States
- The Civil War and Reconstruction
- The growth of industry in the United States
- Domestic issues in the United States in the twentieth century
- How the United States became a world power
- The cold war
- The United States today and tomorrow

## Lesson 1    The New World

**How did events in fifteenth-century Europe lead to the exploration and colonization of the New World?**

Three major historical developments in Europe stimulated Europeans to explore remote parts of the world. Travelers returning from the **Crusades** brought with them perfumes, spices, and other luxuries, thereby awakening interest in establishing trade with foreign lands. During the **Renaissance,** intellectual curiosity and scientific inventions such as the compass made exploration both attractive and possible. Meanwhile, the rise of monarchies and rulers who sought wealth and power led to attempts to establish colonies.

During what has come to be called the "Age of Discovery," Christopher Columbus, leading a Spanish expedition, stumbled upon the Caribbean Islands while searching for a route to Asia. English explorer John Cabot and Dutch explorer Henry Hudson also set out to find a direct route to Asia, but landed in the **New World** instead. Cabot's exploration ended in Labrador; Hudson's in New York Harbor. Amerigo Vespucci, an Italian explorer, was the first to claim discovery of a new continent. Verrazano sailed under the French flag and explored what is now Newfoundland, Maine, Massachusetts, and New York.

By the 1600s, the Spanish crown, which had sent explorers in search of gold, had established settlements in Mexico, South America, the Caribbean, and Florida. By the same time, the French had founded colonies in Canada, where the settlers engaged in hunting, trapping, and fur trading.

In 1607, England established its first permanent colony at Jamestown, Virginia to raise tobacco. Other colonies were settled by the Pilgrims, Puritans, Catholics, and Quakers who sought religious freedom in the New World.

In 1620, the group of Pilgrims sailing on the *Mayflower* drew up a document that is now regarded as the roots of American democracy. **The Mayflower Compact** was an agreement among the early settlers to govern themselves by direct democracy in what was to become Plymouth Colony in Massachusetts. By 1700 **town meetings** had been set up throughout the New England colonies. In them, individual freemen voted and enacted the laws that governed their towns. They also sent representatives to the colonial assembly.

## Lesson 1 Exercise

1. Briefly summarize Spain's role in colonizing the New World.

2. Even before the Mayflower Compact there was democratic government in a North American colony. The House of Burgesses was an elected legislature in Virginia, the first institution of representative democracy in the New World. How did the means of democratic representation in town meetings differ from that in Virginia?

3. Twentieth-century technology has made long-desired space exploration possible. Compare that condition with circumstances during the European Renaissance.

Answers are on page 266.

## Lesson 2   From Colonists to Revolutionaries

**What factors led to the Revolutionary War?**

By the 1700s, there were more than a million people living in the thirteen British colonies. The colonies fell into three groups: the **New England Colonies** of Massachusetts, New Hampshire, Rhode Island, and Connecticut; the **Middle Colonies** of New York, New Jersey, Pennsylvania, and Delaware; and the **Southern Colonies** of Maryland, Virginia, North Carolina, South Carolina, and Georgia.

In the early colonies, **individualism,** with its emphasis on initiative and free enterprise, led to rapid economic growth and prosperity. Farming was the most common occupation. In the South this was often carried out on a grand scale, on plantations. In Boston, New York, and other seaport cities, many people prospered through trading and shipping.

Until 1763, England ruled the colonies by a policy of **salutary neglect,** which, for the most part, left them to govern themselves. However, beginning in 1763, after victory in the French and Indian War, England looked to the prosperous colonies, who profited from that victory, to help pay off a huge war debt.

King George III enacted the **Stamp Act** in 1765, imposing heavy taxes on legal documents and newspapers. After strong opposition, the tax was repealed. In 1767, England taxed the colonies for tea, glass, paint, and paper. The colonists responded by dumping tea from British cargo ships into Boston Harbor, an event that came to be known as the **Boston Tea Party.** King George responded by sending troops to the colonies.

The colonists organized against the British. With the outbreak of fighting in Lexington and Concord in 1775, the **Revolutionary War** began. In 1776 the colonists issued their **Declaration of Independence** in which they objected to "taxation without representation" and declared themselves free of British rule. After seven years of war, the Americans, under General George Washington, defeated the British, and the **Treaty of Paris (1783)** was signed.

## Lesson 2 Exercise

1.  Explain how the fruit of individualism and British reaction to it after 1763 led to the Revolutionary War.

2.  What ideas about politics and economics—different from King George's ideas—brought the colonists to issue the Declaration of Independence?

3.  Why would it be unlikely for Americans today to protest taxation without representation?

Answers are on page 266.

## Lesson 3   Forming the American Government

How were the thirteen colonies united into one nation?

After the Revolutionary War, the thirteen colonies became independent states. Each state was as individualistic as its citizens, with its own government and its own local interests to protect. The states were wary of a strong, central government. They had waged a war in order to escape from one.

The first framework for a national government, the **Articles of Confederation,** adopted in 1781, provided for a "league of friendship" between the independent states. It left most of the power in the hands of the states. The central government, made up of only one house of Congress, could declare war, but it could not recruit an army. There were no central courts. Commerce between the states was difficult because states imposed taxes on goods from other states and issued separate currencies.

**Shays' Rebellion,** during which debtors, for a variety of reasons, attacked courthouses in Massachusetts, dramatized the weakness of the Articles of Confederation. The central government could not send soldiers to put down the uprising.

In 1787, a convention was held in Philadelphia to strengthen the Articles of Confederation. Instead, the 55 delegates decided to develop a new framework. The **Constitution,** which became the supreme law of the land in 1790, is the result of a series of compromises about various regional and political interests. The **Federalists** favored a strong central government and opposed the **Anti-Federalists.**

The **Connecticut Compromise** gave power to both small and large states by creating two houses in Congress. Each state would have two senators, while the number of representatives would be based on population.

The **Three-Fifths Compromise** determined that for purposes of direct taxation and representation five slaves and three free persons counted equally in determining population size.

## Lesson 3 Exercise

1. How did individualism work against national unity after the Revolutionary War?

2. In what ways did the Articles of Confederation make trade difficult between the thirteen colonies and foreign countries?

3. Before the Connecticut Compromise, there were two plans for establishing the national legislature. The Virginia Plan proposed that representation be based on population; the New Jersey Plan proposed equal representation for each state. Which plan did large states support? small states? Explain.

4. Northern and Southern states had opposite views about counting slaves as part of the population. Which group of states, before the Three-Fifths Compromise, proposed each of the following positions?

   **(a)** Count slaves for purposes of representation.
   **(b)** Don't count slaves for purposes of representation.
   **(c)** Don't count slaves for purposes of taxation.
   **(d)** Count slaves for purposes of taxation.

5. The office of president was first established by

   **(1)** the Declaration of Independence
   **(2)** the Treaty of Paris (1783)
   **(3)** the Articles of Confederation
   **(4)** the Constitution
   **(5)** George Washington

   Answers are on page 266.

## Lesson 4   The Growth of the United States

How did domestic and foreign policy shape the first fifty years of America's history?

From 1789, when George Washington was inaugurated, until Andrew Jackson was elected in 1829, most governing was in the hands of wealthy, male property owners. Only white, male property owners were allowed to vote.

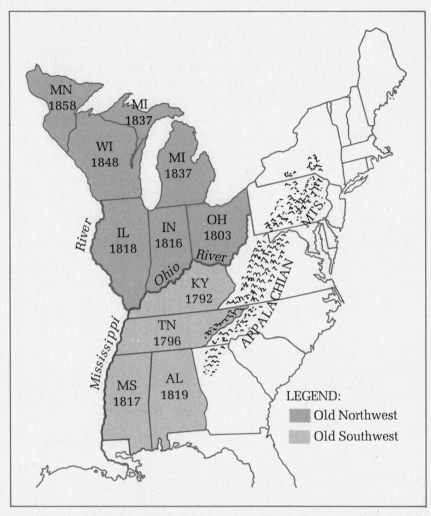

**FIGURE 1** Territorial expansion dates during the first half-century of American history. From Paul H. Roberts, *United States History Review Text,* rev. ed. (New York: AMSCO School Publications), page 148. Used with permission.

This period was characterized by **territorial expansion** (See Figure 1.), the settling of the southwestern territories, the development of industry and agriculture, a spirit of nationalism, and a policy of noninterference in European affairs.

Washington endorsed the principle of **neutralism** in foreign affairs in his *Farewell Address.* Thomas Jefferson, who became president in 1801, maintained a policy of neutrality during the wars between Great Britain and France. However, when Great Britain and France began seizing U.S. ships on the high seas, the United States went to war with Great Britain in the **War of 1812.**

Meanwhile, through a series of purchases, wars, and treaties, the United States had expanded westward. Under President Jefferson with the purchase of the **Louisiana Territory** from France, the United States nearly doubled its size. As the country grew, so did popular belief in **manifest destiny,** the belief in the expansion of the United States from the Atlantic to the Pacific oceans as part of a "divine plan."

In 1823, in order to protect national interests and to preserve neutrality, President James Monroe declared that the United States would not interfere in foreign affairs, and that Europe could not interfere with affairs of the Western Hemisphere. The **Monroe Doctrine** also warned foreign powers against establishing any new colonies on the North American continent.

As the United States grew and each new territory developed its own regional character, the shift in popular opinion from national to sectional interests was a major factor in electing Andrew Jackson president in 1828. This mood was also a factor in the series of events that led to the Civil War.

## Lesson 4 Exercise

1.  In what way was the democracy of the colonies unlike our present democracy?

2.  How were the foreign policies of Presidents Washington and Monroe similar? How did each man express this policy?

3.  One of the immediate causes for issuing the Monroe Doctrine was Russian expansion southward from Alaska. This was a threat to America's desire to expand to the Pacific. Which part of the doctrine could the United States use to halt Russian movement?

Answers are on page 266.

## Lesson 5    The Civil War

**How did sectionalism lead to the Civil War?**

The 1828 election of Andrew Jackson to the presidency saw a marked change in U.S. political philosophy. The right to vote had been extended to include all white males. Jackson appealed to the new voters by presenting himself as the first president of the "common man." He believed people were capable of governing themselves, and he opposed a strong, central government.

Earlier presidents had been wealthy property owners from Virginia and Massachusetts. Jackson, from Tennessee, was the first president to come from a Western territory. He aligned himself with the individualistic attitudes of the Western territories and with the South's advocates of states' rights.

The time of westward expansion was also the period of the **Industrial Revolution,** an era of rapid developments in industry, agriculture, and transportation. Cyrus McCormick's reaper and Eli Whitney's cotton gin had made large-scale farming possible and profitable. Cotton-growing had become the basis of the southern economy, and black slaves were the labor force that made this economy possible. Slavery was an issue that divided the North and the South. There were other regional differences that encouraged **sectionalism.**

The economy of the North was mainly industrial. Most Northerners favored a strong central government that would impose taxes on foreign goods that competed with U.S. products. They also argued for a better federal banking system for trading purposes.

The South favored strong state governments and resented the interference of the federal government, particularly with the issue of slavery.

When Abraham Lincoln, with solid support from the North and the West, was elected president in 1860, the antifederalist South saw it as a defeat. The South seceded from the United States, formed the **Confederate States of America,** and elected Jefferson Davis president. When the Confederates fired on Fort Sumter in 1861, the four-year **Civil War** began.

## Lesson 5 Exercise

1. With Jackson as president, the United States underwent a marked change in political philosophy. What were two of these important changes?

2. Economic developments that the Industrial Revolution made possible in both the North and the South provided grounds for sectional disagreement about the proper role of central government. Why did the North and the South disagree?

3. Lincoln pledged not to interfere with slavery in states where it existed. What was it, then, about Lincoln's election that prompted the South's secession?

Answers are on pages 266–267.

## Lesson 6   The Civil War and Reconstruction

**What effect did the Civil War have on the South?**

The **Confederacy** was made up of eleven southern states. The **Union** was made up of 19 free states and four slaveholding border states.

The Civil War lasted from 1861 to 1865. The Union had many advantages over the South: more factories to produce weapons, twice as many railroads, more than twice the population, and 75% of the nation's financial resources.

Most of the fighting took place in the South. The war ended with the surrender signed by Confederate General Robert E. Lee at Appomatox, Virginia, in 1865. In that same year Lincoln was assassinated. His successor, Andrew Johnson, oversaw the **Reconstruction** of the South.

Lincoln's **Emancipation Proclamation** of 1863 had freed the slaves in the eleven Confederate states. **The Civil Rights Act of 1866,** passed over Johnson's veto, had guaranteed federal enforcement of black and white equality. The **Thirteenth Amendment** ended slavery in the entire country. The **Fourteenth Amendment** to the Constitution guaranteed blacks citizenship and equal protection under the law. The **Fifteenth Amendment** gave blacks the right to vote. By 1870, all of the Southern states had agreed to these amendments and were readmitted to the Union.

Legal measures did not bring about economic and political equality for most blacks. Many became **sharecroppers** for white farmers, who in turn demanded the major share of the crops in payment for the use of the land. To prevent blacks from voting, Southern states set up literacy requirements and poll taxes. **Jim Crow Laws** legalized segregation throughout the South.

Reconstruction governments in the South were run by Northerners and Southerners who had remained loyal to the Union. They were frequently dominated by **carpetbaggers,** Northerners who had migrated to the South for economic gain. The South resented Northern interference in their affairs, and the Reconstruction, which ended in 1876, accomplished little in changing Southern politics and ways of life.

## Lesson 6 Exercise

1.  President Lincoln's reason for issuing the Emancipation Proclamation was to
    **(1)** live up to a promise he had made to voters
    **(2)** encourage the North and to weaken the South
    **(3)** demonstrate his moral opposition to slavery
    **(4)** end slavery in the United States
    **(5)** gain the black vote for his reelection

2.  Write a word or phrase that fits each definition.
    **(a)** redevelopment of the war-torn South
    **(b)** people who took advantage of the plight of the postwar South for economic gain

3.  Which of the following, according to the lesson, was NOT an advantage of the North during the Civil War?
    **(1)** larger population
    **(2)** more railroads
    **(3)** more industry
    **(4)** better generals
    **(5)** greater wealth

Answers are on page 267.

## Lesson 7    The Growth of U.S. Industry

**How did post-Civil War industrial growth affect U.S. population distribution, immigration, and living conditions?**

Industry expanded during the Civil War to meet the increased demand for guns, uniforms, and ammunition. After the war the economy became increasingly industrial.

Industrial growth was spurred by the use of electricity and by such inventions as the telephone, the electric light bulb, and the automobile.

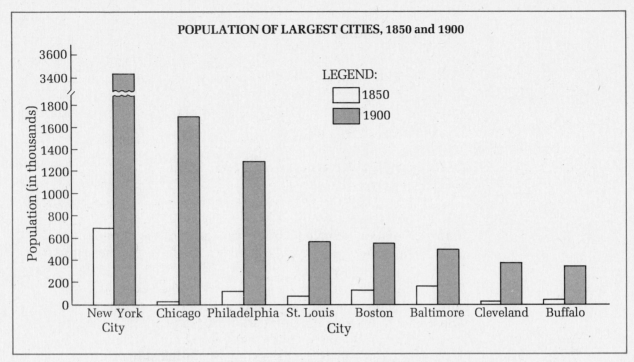

**POPULATION OF LARGEST CITIES, 1850 and 1900**

**FIGURE 2**  Population of Largest U.S. Cities, 1850 and 1900. From Teacher's Resource Handbook, *The United States: A History of the Republic,* 2nd ed. (Englewood Cliffs, N.J.: Prentice-Hall, 1984), page 257. Used with permission.

Expanding technology made it possible to obtain natural resources such as oil, iron, and coal to power factories and to produce goods.

As more factories were built, people moved to cities to work in them. In 1880, only one out of four Americans lived in urban areas. By 1900, the United States had shifted from being a country of farmers to being a country of factory workers. (See Figure 2.) By 1910, nearly half of America's population lived in cities.

Immigrants were welcomed by industrialists because they provided cheap labor for the factories. However, the huge number of people who flocked to the cities caused overcrowding. Low wages and crowded conditions bred crime, poor living conditions, and disease.

Working conditions were often as undesirable as living conditions. Long hours, lack of benefits, and poor physical surroundings were the usual lot of factory workers. As a result, the **American Federation of Labor,** the first **labor union,** was organized by Samuel Gompers in 1886. Later, the **Progressive Movement** worked to resolve some of the social problems that were growing as rapidly as industry.

## Lesson 7 Exercise

1.  What percents belong in the three blanks in these sentences? In 1880, _(a)_ of all Americans lived in rural areas; _(b)_ , in cities. By 1910, nearly _(c)_ of all Americans were urban dwellers.

2. According to the bar graph in Figure 2, which city grew the most between 1850 and 1900?

3. In what way were the goals of the Progressive Movement and the American Federation of Labor compatible?

Answers are on page 267.

## Lesson 8    The United States in the First Half of the Twentieth Century

How did the economic problems of the first part of the twentieth century change the role of the federal government in the lives of Americans?

From 1901 to 1921, the Progressive Movement brought about many political, social, and economic reforms. Child labor, unhealthy and dangerous working conditions, and impure or contaminated food and drugs were among the abuses by business the movement fought.

Laws were passed to protect consumers; **antitrust legislation** broke up and prevented **monopolies;** and child labor was abolished. Women organized and won the right to vote with the **Nineteenth Amendment** to the Constitution. **Compulsory education** was established to improve the lot of the working classes, and the **Department of Labor** was formed to protect their interests. Government policy toward the economy changed from non-interfering to regulatory.

From the end of World War I in 1918 to the **Stock Market Crash** in 1929, Americans enjoyed a period of prosperity. Business was strong and many people purchased stock in corporations. But when stock prices fell, people lost their savings. Banks went out of business in the "panic" that followed. Soon the United States was in the **Great Depression:** businesses folded and millions of people were unemployed.

Franklin D. Roosevelt was elected president in the hope that he would end the depression. Under his **New Deal** program, laws were passed to protect people's savings and to prevent banks and the stock market from failing again. Assistance programs for the elderly and the unemployed were established. The **Social Security Act** was part of the New Deal as were the **Works Progress Administration (WPA)** and the **Civilian Conservation Corps (CCC),** which employed large numbers of people in public works projects. During the New Deal, the government began to play a much more active role in the lives of Americans.

## Lesson 8 Exercise

1. In recent years some companies have been forced by law to split up into smaller companies. On what product of the Progressive Movement were those actions based?

**2.** Label each of the following definitions.

**(a)** the legislation that gave women the right to vote

**(b)** the government organization established to protect the rights of working people

**(c)** a means to improve conditions for the working class through the children

**(d)** the event that led to the introduction of the New Deal

**3.** Which of the following was not a New Deal program?

**(1)** unemployment insurance

**(2)** insurance for bank deposits

**(3)** buildup of the navy

**(4)** public works programs

**(5)** help for farmers

Answers are on page 267.

# Lesson 9   The United States as a World Power

How did the United States' policy change from isolationism to internationalism?

During the 1800s, Americans were mainly occupied with building a country and had little interest in foreign involvements. For the most part, the United States pursued a policy of **isolationism,** and kept out of international affairs.

In the 1890s, the United States became more involved with foreign countries that were sources for raw materials and new markets. America's foreign policy shifted from isolationism to **imperialism.** America wanted to gain political and economic control over other nations and territories to achieve increased wealth and power.

In 1898 America fought Spain in the **Spanish-American War** to protect trade interests in Cuba. The war, which was fought in the Carribbean and the Pacific, lasted less than a year. Spain was defeated. By the **Treaty of Paris (1898)** Cuba was freed of Spain's control, Puerto Rico and Guam were given to the United States, and the Philippines were sold to the United States. The United States had become a world power that had colonies in the Caribbean and the Pacific.

In 1914, **World War I** broke out in Europe. It became the reason for the United States to replace its policy of isolationism with one of **internationalism.** The United States remained *neutral* at first, but finally entered the war in 1917 after German submarines sank unarmed American merchant ships. America joined the **Allied Powers,** twenty-five nations including Great Britain, France, Russia, Serbia, Belgium, Japan, and Italy. The **Central Powers** were Germany, Austria-Hungary, Turkey, and Bulgaria. In 1918, Germany recognized its defeat and accepted an **armistice.** After the war, President Woodrow Wilson and leaders of European countries formed the **League of Nations** to settle international disputes. *Isolationists* in Congress voted against American participation. The League of Nations disbanded in 1946.

During the 1930s, fascist dictators rose to power in the **Axis nations:** Japan, Germany, and Italy. The United States remained neutral as the fascist powers waged war against their neighbors even though public opinion supported the Allies. Some Americans served with the armed forces of Great Britain and Canada; the United States sent supplies to the Allies. When the Japanese bombed the U.S. fleet in **Pearl Harbor** in 1941, the United States entered **World War II.**

The United States and its allies, Great Britain, France, and the Soviet Union, proclaimed victory in May 1945. The United States and Russia emerged as world powers with increasing influence on world politics.

## Lesson 9 Exercise

1. Based on information provided in the lesson, explain the difference in the quality of the United States government's neutrality before each of the two world wars.

2. Name the policies defined below.

   **(a)** a policy of not interfering in the affairs of other nations
   **(b)** a national policy directed toward gaining economic and political power over other nations

3. When the League of Nations disbanded, it transferred its properties to a new organization with goals similar to its own. What is the name of that organization which is still in existence?

Answers are on page 267.

## Lesson 10   The Cold War

**What role has the United States played in world politics since World War II?**

Clearly more internationalist after World War II, the United States joined the Allied powers to form the **United Nations (U.N.).** Like the earlier League of Nations, the U.N. was designed to promote international peace.

The Soviet Union established the Soviet bloc through its satellites, Bulgaria, Czechoslovakia, East Germany, Hungary, Poland, and Rumania. Western nations, led by the United States, began to see Soviet expansion as a threat and formed **NATO,** the **North Atlantic Treaty Organization,** to protect their interests. The **cold war** had begun.

The United States became established as the leader of the free world. In 1947, President Harry S Truman sought to contain communism with the **Truman Doctrine,** which allowed economic and military aid to countries subject to communist expansion. The United States offered economic aid to all of Europe, including the Soviet Union, through the **Marshall Plan.** Its purpose was to assist recovery from World War II destruction. Although the cold war has been mainly a clash of ideologies, there have been armed conflicts, supported by the United States and the Soviet Union, in Korea, Cuba, and Vietnam.

President John F. Kennedy saw that the poor and undeveloped nations of the **Third World** could be a target for Soviet expansion. He courted the allegiance of those countries by offering foreign aid and educational and technical assistance in the form of the **Peace Corps.** In 1963, the United States and the Soviet Union, together with about 100 nations, signed the **Limited Nuclear Test Ban Treaty** to limit nuclear weapons testing.

For the most part, the United States and the Soviet Union have maintained a policy of **détente,** or peaceful diplomacy. One of the greatest barriers to world peace, however, is the nuclear arms buildup by the superpowers and their allies.

## Lesson 10 Exercise

1. Has the Soviet Union's policy in world politics since World War II been one of imperialism or one of isolationism?

2. What label does each of the following descriptions fit?
   **(a)** the clash of ideologies between NATO and the Soviet bloc
   **(b)** countries where large portions of the population are impoverished and technology is not advanced
   **(c)** a period during international dispute when differences can be resolved through diplomatic negotiation

3. Most of NATO's members come from
   **(1)** Eastern Europe
   **(2)** Western Europe
   **(3)** North America
   **(4)** South America
   **(5)** the Soviet bloc

Answers are on page 267.

## Lesson 11    The United States After World War II

**What have some of the major issues in American domestic politics since World War II been?**

Through all the presidential administrations since World War II, economic and social reform have been central domestic issues.

President Truman (1945–1953) wanted to extend Roosevelt's New Deal through his **Fair Deal** program. A strong conservative coalition in Congress, however, defeated his efforts toward civil rights legislation, national health insurance, and federal aid to education. Truman administration social reforms included expanding Social Security, raising the minimum wage, and developing low-income housing. The **Taft-Hartley Act** placed restrictions on labor unions.

Under President Eisenhower (1953–1961) school segregation was outlawed by a Supreme Court decision and two **Civil Rights Acts** to protect voting rights were enacted. Legislation to prevent union corruption was passed, and Truman's social reforms were extended.

President Kennedy (1961–1963), during his brief term in office before his assassination, proposed some of the many social reforms President Johnson's (1963–1969) **Great Society** program achieved. At the same time, Martin Luther King helped the United States to focus its attention on many of the inequities in American society. The **Civil Rights Act of 1964** prohibited discrimination in voting, employment, and public accommodations. The **Civil Rights Act of 1968** banned discrimination in most housing sales and rentals. The **War on Poverty** and the **Medicare Act,** among other pieces of legislation, sought to improve the quality of life for Americans. Several acts protected consumers, and direct federal aid to public schools was established.

The Nixon administration (1969–1974) was characterized by its efforts to fight inflation, which affected both the United States and other countries. The energy crisis and events leading up to the president's resignation dominated the last years of the Nixon administration.

## Lesson 11 Exercise

1. President Truman issued an executive order to begin desegregation of the armed forces. What action began desegregation in schools?

2. Some observers have noted that, over the course of time, legislation has brought the issue of civil rights closer to home. Explain, by reference to the purposes of the Civil Rights Acts mentioned in the lesson, what that observation means.

3. Based on information in the lesson about federal aid to education, which of these three presidents—Truman, Eisenhower, and Johnson—was the most likely one to support a domestic policy that was "conservative when it comes to money"?

Answers are on page 267.

## Lesson 12    The United States Today and Tomorrow

**What problems do recent events suggest the United States will continue to face in the future?**

Gerald R. Ford became president after Nixon resigned, but he was defeated by Jimmy Carter in the 1976 election. Carter's most serious international

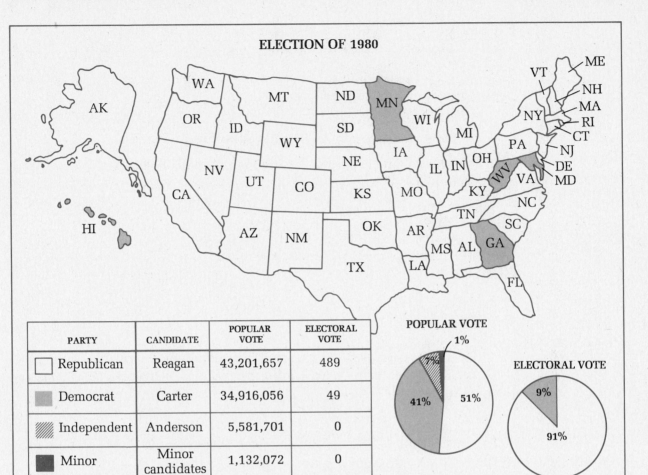

**FIGURE 3**  Results of the 1980 U.S. presidential election. From Teacher's Resource Handbook, *The United States: A History of the Republic,* 2nd ed. (Englewood Cliffs, N.J.: Prentice-Hall, 1984), page 288. Used with permission.

problem occurred in 1979 in Iran. Factions that had overthrown the Shah of Iran later seized the American embassy in Tehran and held 62 Americans hostage for more than a year. Many felt that Carter did not take a strong enough stand in handling the crisis. The chart in Figure 3 shows the result of the next election.

The Reagan administration had to deal with widespread unemployment across the country and an economic recession—an economic period of low wages and limited production similar to, but less serious than, a depression.

President Reagan's efforts to ease the recession included lowering taxes and limiting government spending. He was reelected in a landslide in 1984.

The United States continues to confront many problems that have no easy remedies: domestic and international poverty, civil rights, and inflation. Dwindling supplies of natural resources, world hunger, arms control, and terrorism are all issues that call for careful diplomacy if the world is to avoid nuclear war and to establish peace.

## Lesson 12 Exercise

1. What is the economic condition in which employment and production rates approach depression conditions?

*Items 2 to 4 are based on the information in Figure 3 on the preceding page.*

2. For how many different presidential candidates did American citizens vote in 1980?

    **(1)** one
    **(2)** two
    **(3)** three
    **(4)** four
    **(5)** more than four

3. Explain whether the 1980 election was won by a landslide popular vote or not.

4. When a candidate receives the majority of the popular votes in a state, his or her party is said to "carry" the state. Explain how it can or cannot be concluded that Anderson did not receive the majority of the popular vote in his home state.

Answers are on page 267.

# Chapter 2 Quiz

*Items 1 to 3 are based on the following quote.*

The world must be made safe for democracy. Its peace must be planted upon the tested foundations of political liberty . . . We shall fight . . . for democracy, for the right of those who submit to authority to have a voice in their own governments, for the rights and liberties of small nations.

—Woodrow Wilson (April 1917)

1. Which of the following is the best label for President Wilson's policy in April 1917?

    **(1)** imperialism
    **(2)** internationalism
    **(3)** isolationism
    **(4)** nationalism
    **(5)** neutralism

2. The quote comes from a speech to Congress that encouraged United States involvement in a war. Which war was President Wilson talking about?

3.  Which phrases in the quote state a definition for democracy?

---

4.  The United States had several motivations for fighting Spain in the Spanish-American War. Among them were (1) helping Cubans gain freedom from Spain, (2) protecting United States trade interests, and (3) retaliating for the sinking of a U.S. battleship in Havana that many blamed on Spain. Which of those three reasons best supports the idea that the United States was acting imperialistically in fighting the war?

*Items 5 to 7* are based on the following graph.

**REGIONAL SHIFT IN U.S. FOREIGN AID, 1946-1966**

|  | |
|---|---|
| Europe | 26% / 69% |
| East Asia | 16% / 27% |
| Middle East and South Asia | 8% / 24% |
| Latin America | 2% / 13% |
| Africa | 0.2% / 4% |
| Other | 4.8% / 6% |

LEGEND:
1946-1952 Total: $37.5 billion
1953-1966 Total: $84.9 billion

5.  The bulk of foreign aid spending between 1946 and 1952 was probably inspired by the
    (1) League of Nations
    (2) Marshall Plan
    (3) Monroe Doctrine
    (4) North Atlantic Treaty Organization (NATO)
    (5) Progressive Movement

6.  President Kennedy's foreign policy regarding Third World countries included financial aid. Which bar or bars on the graph report spending that includes the aid Kennedy supported?
    (1) Europe—1946 to 1952
    (2) Europe—1953 to 1966
    (3) Latin America—1946 to 1952 and 1953 to 1966
    (4) Middle East and South Asia—1946 to 1952
    (5) Middle East and South Asia—1953 to 1966

7. Which of the following is it NOT possible to determine from the graphs?
   (1) the amount of money sent to Asia from 1953 to 1966
   (2) the amount of money sent to Africa from 1953 to 1966
   (3) the total amount spent on foreign aid from 1946 to 1966
   (4) the portion of all foreign aid for "other" areas of the world from 1946 to 1966
   (5) the difference between the amounts of money sent to Latin America from 1946 to 1952 and from 1953 to 1966

*Items 8 to 10 are based on the following passage.*

There is a difference between civil rights and civil liberties. Civil rights refers strictly to freedoms that are protected from violation by private groups or individuals. Free access to housing, to schools, and to other facilities are civil rights.

Civil liberties are freedoms that are protected from violation by the government. The Bill of Rights guarantees several civil liberties, such as freedom of speech.

8. A state statute required school children to salute the flag. A certain group believed that saluting the flag violated their freedom of religion. The Supreme Court decided the statute was unconstitutional. Was the statute a violation of civil rights or of civil liberties?

9. The law requires that before the police question a suspect, they must inform the suspect of the right to remain silent, which is protected by the Fifth Amendment. Is this a protection of a civil right or of a civil liberty?

10. A court decision determined that there had been illegal discrimination when a large department store hired one person instead of another. Was the decision more likely based on the Bill of Rights or on a Civil Rights Act?

Answers are on page 268.

# Geography

> **Objective**
>
> In this chapter, you will read and answer questions about
>
> - Kinds of maps
> - Latitude and longitude
> - Climate and weather
> - Natural resources and the environment
> - Pollution
> - Cultural geography

## Lesson 1    Kinds of Maps

**What kinds of maps do *geographers* use?**

Geography is the study of the physical characteristics of the Earth and of the peoples who inhabit the Earth. The basic tool of the geographer is the map. Each of four kinds of maps gives a different kind of information.

**Political maps** are the most familiar. They show boundaries between countries, states, or regions, and the location of cities, counties, bodies of water, and sometimes historical sites. Figure 1 on the next page is a political map.

**Physical maps** show the natural features of the Earth, such as lakes, rivers, and mountains. They also show **elevation,** or how high above **sea level** a region is.

A **topographic map** is a physical map that uses **contour lines** to give you more specific details about the elevation of a region. Each contour line represents a certain distance above sea level.

**Special purpose maps** show particular features of a region such as natural resources, climate, population, or land use.

On maps and globes, imaginary lines are used to cut the Earth in half. The imaginary line that runs from east to west is called the **equator.** It divides the Northern from the Southern **Hemisphere.** The imaginary line that runs from north to south is called the **prime meridian.** It separates the Eastern from the Western Hemisphere.

Lines of **latitude** run from east to west, like the equator. They are numbered from 0° at the equator to 90° at both the northern and southern tips of the hemisphere. Lines of latitude show how far north or south from the equator a particular place is located.

Lines of **longitude** run from north to south. They are numbered from 0° at the prime meridian to 180° east or 180° west and show how far east or west of the prime meridian a place is located.

A map's **legend** tells what each of the symbols that are used in the map represents.

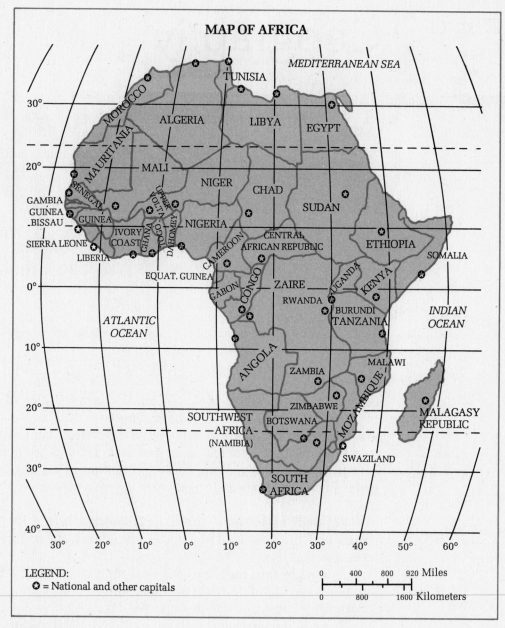

**MAP OF AFRICA**

LEGEND:
 = National and other capitals

FIGURE 1

## Lesson 1 Exercise

1.   The Aspen Walkers Club is planning a hiking trip in Canada. What kind of map will be most helpful to them in charting a route that doesn't require much climbing?

2.   According to the legend on Figure 1, about how many miles are there between the northernmost and the southernmost points on the African continent?

3. A ship sends a distress signal. What information does it radio to nearby ships so that it can be found?

4. According to Figure 1, what part of Africa is between 20° and 30°S and 10° and 20°E?

5. What type of map always names specific countries?
   **(1)** physical map
   **(2)** special-purpose map
   **(3)** topographic map
   **(4)** city map
   **(5)** political map

Answers are on page 268.

# Lesson 2   Climate and Weather

**What are the three major climates in the world?**

One of the most important features of a region is its **climate.** Climate is the topical weather pattern in a geographic area. The **weather** is the way a climate varies from day to day.

**Polar** climates are found in the very cold regions that surround the North and South poles. The ground remains frozen all year long and supports little vegetation. Polar regions are unsuitable for agriculture and are sparsely populated.

The **tropical** climate found near the equator is very hot and humid, with heavy rainfall. This produces jungles and rain forests that are thick with vegetation. Because the vegetation grows so quickly and abundantly, it is very difficult to clear away jungle and forestland for agriculture and industry. Tropical regions, too, are rather sparsely populated.

The climate of most of the rest of the world is **temperate.** In a temperate climate, a year has four seasons. Temperatures vary, but most fall within a range that is comfortable enough to grow crops for at least part of the year.

Temperate climates fall into four subcategories. The **marine** climate, which is found near seacoasts, tends to be rather humid and mild. The **continental,** or **mediterranean,** climate of inland regions usually has hot summers, mild winters, and little rainfall. The **desert** climate tends to be hot and dry, with little rainfall. The **mountain** climate, which is found at higher elevations, tends to be cool.

Because the natural resources that are needed for agriculture and industry are most accessible in temperate regions, most of the world's population is concentrated in temperate zones.

# Lesson 2 Exercise

1. What is the difference between *climate* and *weather*?

2. Why does most of the world's population live in a temperate climate?

3. Marine and mediterranean are subcategories of which climate type?

4. If you want to describe the three climate types, which of the following factors should you discuss about each?

   **(a)** weather         **(e)** population
   **(b)** temperature    **(f)** seasons
   **(c)** rainfall         **(g)** deserts
   **(d)** industry

Answers are on page 268.

# Lesson 3   Resources and the Environment

**How do natural resources determine the economy of a region?**

The development of agriculture and industry is closely related to climate and the presence of **natural resources.** Air, water, soil, minerals, vegetation, and animal life are all natural resources.

A region's economy is often determined by its natural resources. For example, many of the major cities of the world are located on major bodies of water. Before the airplane made it possible to transport goods and passengers to all parts of the world, industries depended on ships to carry **raw materials** and **manufactured goods** back and forth. Rivers provided a linkage between inland areas and the sea. They now provide the hydroelectric power for electricity in addition to transportation.

In heavily forested areas, the lumber industry provides building materials and fuel as well as a means of livelihood for those who live in the region.

Fertile soil, especially when combined with a long growing season, is the basis for a flourishing agricultural economy in other regions.

Mineral deposits may have a dramatic impact on the economy of a region. The discovery of oil in the Middle East is probably the best-known modern example.

Since the mid-twentieth century, one of our most pressing global problems has been the **environmental crisis:** the supply of natural resources is dwindling to the point that we may eventually exhaust the raw materials we need for fuels. Water pollution has seriously affected the fishing industry and our supply of drinking water. Stripping forestland and burning **fossil fuels** have caused high levels of carbon dioxide in the atmosphere, which may seriously alter the very climate we live in.

# Lesson 3 Exercise

1. How does an *environmental crisis* occur?

2. What natural resource provides hydroelectric power for electricity?

3.  During the nineteenth century, immigrants settled in towns in the upper peninsula of Michigan to work the copper and tin mines. Today, much of this area consists of "ghost towns." What might have been a cause of the loss of population?

Answers are on page 268.

# Lesson 4    Using the World's Resources Wisely

**Why should we try to protect and preserve our environment?**

Natural resources are essential for economic growth and for life itself. An environment in which the water and the air are polluted is unhealthy and unsafe for plant, animal, and human life.

Keeping air and water clean is important for many reasons. Pollution affects the ozone layer of the atmosphere. Without an ozone layer, the atmosphere of Earth would be filled with radiation.

Water has been polluted by some industries that dump **toxic** wastes into the rivers, lakes, and oceans. Water pollution, if unhampered, can lead to dead oceans that have no plant or fish life.

Air pollution is a serious problem. Exhaust from automobiles and industrial smokestacks have contributed to this problem. Air pollution can cause water pollution. Gases created by air pollution form acids in the air. These acids return in rain and pollute lakes, rivers, and oceans. Air pollution is harmful to people's health.

Government agencies, such as the Environmental Protection Agency (EPA), monitor factors that contribute to pollution. In recent years, the government has passed laws to protect the environment. The pesticide DDT was banned when it was discovered that it caused cancer in humans. New regulations limit the amount of emission from cars, trucks, and buses. Factories may no longer dump waste materials into rivers or pump chemicals into the air. Pollution is still a serious problem. It is necessary to maintain a balance between environmental needs and the needs of industry.

## Lesson 4 Exercise

1.  Which of the following is NOT an official concern of an EPA agent?
    - **(1)** clean air
    - **(2)** clean water
    - **(3)** preservation of forests
    - **(4)** preservation of historical sites
    - **(5)** noise levels

2.  Provide a brief explanation of the concept of a *balance between economic and environmental needs.*

3.  Which one of the following statements is implied in the lesson?

    **(1)** Diseases can be caused by environmental factors.

    **(2)** Water pollution is only a concern of people who live near lakes and rivers.

    **(3)** The ozone layer stops pollution from rising into the atmosphere.

    **(4)** Air pollution did not exist before the twentieth century.

    **(5)** It is not the role of government to protect the environment.

Answers are on page 268.

## Lesson 5    Cultural Geography

**What are the concerns of cultural geography?**

**Cultural geography** is a branch of the social sciences that studies the racial and **ethnic** makeups of populations and how populations are distributed among the various regions of the world.

A **race** is a group of people with similar physical characteristics that are passed on from one generation to the next. Some distinguishing characteristics include skin color, hair texture, and eye shape and color. The **Mongoloid** race, which originated in Asia, makes up 43% of the world's population. The **Caucasian** race, which originated in Europe, makes up 33% of the world's population. The **Negroid** race, which originated in Africa, makes up 24% of the world's population.

Races contain different ethnic groups. For example, the Italians and the Irish are ethnic groups within the Caucasian race. An **ethnic group** is one that shares a common language and certain customs. Racial and ethnic groups have intermixed and migrated from one region to another. People from many countries may settle in a region and later intermarry, as in the United States.

Cultural geography also studies **migration,** the movements of a people from one region to another. The movement of people into a region is called **immigration;** the movement of people out of a region is called **emigration.** Many ethnic groups emigrated from their native countries and immigrated to America in search of religious freedom, social equality, and a more prosperous life-style.

**Population density** describes the average number of people in a unit of land. Let's say that the population density of a state is 400 people per square mile. That means that, on the average, 400 people live in every square mile in the state. More people live in urban areas than in rural areas.

The population density of the world varies from country to country. Australia has a population density of 5 persons per square mile. The population density of the United States is 60 persons per square mile; in Japan, it is 793 persons per square mile.

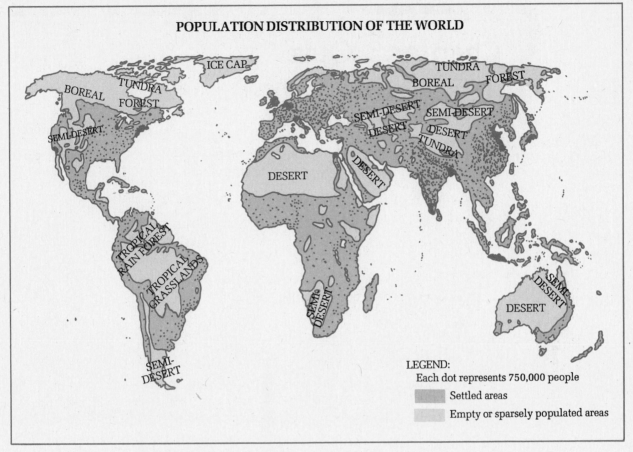

**FIGURE 2**  Population distribution of the world.

## Lesson 5 Exercise

1.  Briefly explain why America is often called the "melting pot" of the world.

2.  What type of map is Figure 2?

3.  According to Figure 2, where are the largest areas of dense population in the world?

Answers are on pages 268–269.

# Chapter 3 Quiz

1.  What is the difference between *physical geography* and *cultural geography?*

2.  Name two things that the United States government can do to protect the environment.

3.  Briefly explain the purpose of contour lines on a topographic map.

4.  Name two different ethnic groups native to Great Britain.

5.  What kinds of maps would show each of the following features?
    **(a)** cities
    **(b)** climate
    **(c)** land elevations
    **(d)** borders between countries
    **(e)** percentage of ethnic populations

6.  What is the name of the imaginary line that cuts the world in half from north to south?

7.  The Cuban Missile Crisis of 1962 brought the two superpowers, the United States and the Soviet Union, into direct conflict. One reason the United States opposed the installation of Soviet missiles in Cuba was geographic. Explain.

*Items 8 to 10 are based on the facing map.*

8.  The president of a Canadian hydroelectric company wants to build a new plant to serve the region east of Alaska. Where is a good site choice?

9.  What mineral resource can be found near the western shore of Great Bear Lake?

10. Most of Canada's mineral resources can be found in northern Canada. TRUE or FALSE?

Answers are on page 269.

## MINERAL RESOURCES AND HYDROELECTRIC PROJECTS OF CANADA

ARCTIC
OCEAN

*Great
Bear
Lake*

✪ Whitehorse

*Great
Slave
Lake*

Yellowknife ✪

ATLANTIC
OCEAN

Cape
Dorset

*Hudson
Bay*

Churchill

Schefferville

Edmonton

Vancouver

CANADIAN
SHIELD

Charlottetown

Calgary

Regina

*Steep Rock
Lake*

Laval

Victoria

Quebec

Fredericton

Halifax

Winnipeg

*Lake
Superior*

Thunder Bay
Sault Ste. Marie          Sudbury

Montreal

Ottawa
Toronto

*Lake Michigan*

Sarnia
Windsor

Hamilton

*Lake Erie*

LEGEND:

░ Coal
▲ Gold, silver
◆ Other minerals
☐ Hydroelectric projects
△ Tar sands
✪ Provincial/Territorial capitals

0      250      500 Miles

0    250    500 Kilometers

# Economics

> **Objective**
>
> In this chapter you will read and answer questions about
>
> - Economic systems
> - Free enterprise
> - Financial institutions
> - Government's role in the economy
> - Tax revenue
> - Measuring the economy
> - Labor and the economy
> - International trade

## Lesson 1 Modern Economic Systems

**What differences are there in the way businesses are owned under the three main economic systems in the world today?**

Economics is concerned with the production, distribution, and use of **goods** and **services.** Economic goods are items people pay for. Services are paid for by people, but services are not actual items. If you buy a television set, you are buying a good. If you pay for the repair of your television set, you are buying a service.

There are three major economic systems in the modern world. They are capitalism, communism, and socialism.

**Capitalism** is based on the idea that a country's economy works best when the government does not interfere in business. A capitalist system is called a **free-enterprise system** because individuals may produce what they want and as much as they want. They may charge the price they want for the product. Success in business is determined by the free marketplace.

**Communism** is based on the idea that the government owns and controls all businesses. The country's wealth and products are shared equally by all citizens. There are no wealthy people and no poor people in a **classless society.**

**Socialism** is also based on the idea of a **cooperative society** that has equal wealth for all. In most socialist countries, however, some businesses are owned by individuals. Socialist countries have tried to achieve economic equality through social welfare programs run by the government and by government ownership of major industries.

No country has an economy that is totally capitalist, communist, or socialist. Most modern countries have mixed economies that emphasize one system, but use elements of others.

## Lesson 1 Exercise

1.  Label each of the following as a good or a service: cars, clothing, repair work, machinery, tutoring, food, child care, medical care.

2.  Which one of the following would be a more drastic change in a country's economic system: (a) a change from capitalism to socialism, or (b) a change from capitalism to communism?

3.  In which type of system—capitalist, communist, or socialist—would there be the most competition in business? In which system would there be the least competition in business?

4.  Why is the study of economics classified as one part of *social* studies?

Answers are on page 269.

## Lesson 2   The Free-Enterprise System

**How does *competition* work in a free-enterprise system?**

Business can be said to be any activity in which the goal is the **exchange** of goods and services for **profit**. Businesses are organized in different ways.

Some businesses have a single owner, or **proprietor**. More than 75% of all U.S. businesses are owned by single proprietors. About 8% of U.S. businesses are **partnerships**, in which two or more people are owners and operators. A **corporation** is a business that is **licensed**, or **chartered**, by state or local governments. Corporations are owned by people who buy **shares**, or **stock**, in the business. About 17% of U.S. businesses are corporations. A corporation that owns or controls companies in many fields is called a **conglomerate**.

A free-enterprise system needs competition between businesses to survive. Companies compete to produce a better product at a lower price. To do so, companies must consider **supply** and **demand**. Supply is the amount of the product that can be sold. Demand means how many people want to buy the product. By studying both supply and demand, businesses can determine an **equilibrium point**—the price at which consumers will buy exactly the amount supplied by the producer. Too much production can lead to a **surplus** of the product and cause prices to fall. Too little production can lead to **shortages** and cause prices to rise.

Obviously, the consumer plays a major role in the free-enterprise system. Businesses try to influence consumers through advertising. Consumer protection groups work to make sure that products are safe and reliable and that advertisements are honest.

## Lesson 2 Exercise

1.  A manufacturer finds that it is supplying a product at a rate that exceeds demand for it. Describe two things the manufacturer could do to help the product reach an equilibrium point.

2.  Which type is each of the businesses described below?
    (a) The XYZ Company owns oil wells, tool plants, a refinery, a publishing house, and a paper mill.
    (b) Mary's Tea Shop is owned by Mary Walker and her sister, Helen Jones.
    (c) More than 800 people in six states own shares in Gerry's Gyms.

Item 3 is based on the following advertisement.

> *"The greatest time-saver in my kitchen!"*
>
> *That's what culinary expert Heather Heath says about* **Chop-a-Lot**, *the fabulous new, state-of-the-art food processor.*
>
> You too can make even complicated meals in no time flat! **Chop-a-Lot** grinds meat . . . mashes vegetables . . . slices, shreds, or chops any food. You can use it to make delicious bread . . . superior salads, stews, and soups . . . or even delectable dinners for a crowd! **Chop-a-Lot** is available in the finest appliance stores.

3.  The company that manufactures Chop-a-Lot probably developed the preceding ad in order to help increase
    **(1)** supply
    **(2)** demand
    **(3)** surplus
    **(4)** shortage
    **(5)** competition

4.  Give some examples of professional groups that form partnerships to provide services.

5.  What advantage does a free-enterprise system have over a strictly controlled economic system?

Answers are on page 269.

# Lesson 3   Financial Institutions

**What is the difference between a *commercial bank* and a *savings institution?***

Banks provide a safe place to keep valuable and important legal papers. Many offer **checking accounts**, also called **demand deposits**. Many provide **loans** and bank **credit cards**. Some banks offer their customers **debit cards**. A debit card allows people to pay at stores without borrowing. The user electronically subtracts the amount paid from his or her account. Debit cards are also used at automated teller machines. Many banks also provide **trust fund** services. They act as managers, or **trustees**, of money and property.

Commercial banks maintain checking accounts and interest-paying **savings accounts**. They make loans to individuals and businesses.

The primary economic function of commercial banks is to hold demand deposits and to honor checks drawn upon them—in short, to provide us with the most important component of the economy, our money supply.

Savings institutions, sometimes called **thrifts**, are more limited than commercial banks. There are two main types of thrifts—**savings and loan associations** (S&L's) and **mutual savings banks.** Savings and loans were set up mainly to grant loans secured by home **mortgages**. They offer savings accounts that pay **interest**. Mutual savings banks are owned and run for a profit by those who deposit money in them. They offer savings and checking accounts.

**Credit unions** are owned by their depositors. Members often work for the same company. Credit unions are not run for profit. They offer higher interest rates on savings accounts and charge less for loans. They offer **draft accounts**, which are similar to checking accounts.

## Lesson 3 Exercise

1.  Are the following statements TRUE or FALSE?
    (a) Credit unions are run for profit.
    (b) Thrifts make most big loans to business.
    (c) Another name for a checking account is a demand deposit.
    (d) Mutual savings banks and credit unions are owned by their depositors.

2.  Identify whether, according to this lesson, the following services are provided by commercial banks, mutual savings banks, savings and loan associations, or credit unions. Some services may be offered by more than one type of bank.
    (a) checking accounts
    (b) loans to businesses
    (c) mortgage loans to help people buy houses
    (d) high-interest savings accounts

3.  Mrs. Lopez is trying to decide between acquiring a credit card and acquiring a debit card. What could you tell her to help her decide?

**4.** What are some advantages of belonging to a credit union?

Answers are on page 269.

## Lesson 4    Government's Role in the Economy

**What does it mean to say that the Federal Reserve Act provided for a more elastic currency?**

The **Federal Reserve Act** of 1913 divided the United States into twelve areas. Each area has a Federal Reserve Bank and branch banks. The banks are run by the **Federal Reserve Board**. Board members, called governors, are appointed to 14-year terms by the president. The Senate must approve the appointments.

All **national banks** must join the **Federal Reserve System**. **State banks** do not have to join, but many do. Nearly half of all banks belong to the system.

In addition to creating the Federal Reserve System, the Federal Reserve Act provided for a more **elastic currency** by controlling the national supply of money. The Federal Reserve Board decides the amount of the cash reserves all banks must keep on hand. Requiring banks to keep more money on hand reduces the money available for loans; lowering the **reserve limit** makes more money available. The board also fixes the **discount** rates on loans made by Federal Reserve Banks to private banks. Finally, the board directly affects the national money supply by buying or selling **U.S. bond issues**.

In 1933, Congress passed a Banking Act that created the **Federal Deposit Insurance Corporation** (FDIC). The FDIC and the **Federal Savings and Loan Insurance Corporation** (FSLIC) today insure deposits up to $100,000.

The government controls banking and the economy in other ways as well. Today, all bank notes are issued by Federal Reserve Banks rather than individual banks. The Federal Reserve Board, the **Treasury Department**, and the FDIC work together to prevent bank failures.

## Lesson 4 Exercise

1. What are three powers the Federal Reserve Board has that help to control the national supply of money?

2. Which one of the following statements is implied in this lesson?
   (1) The Federal Reserve Act increased the government's control over banking, credit, and money.
   (2) Congress has greater power than the president in appointing Federal Reserve Board members.
   (3) There are more bank failures today than there were before 1933.

Item 3 is based on the following graphs.

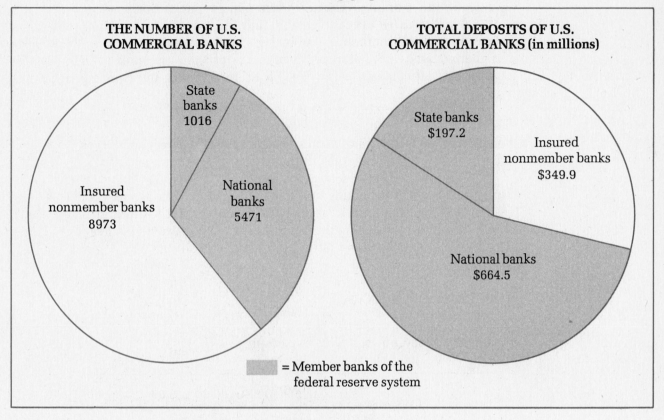

THE NUMBER OF U.S.
COMMERCIAL BANKS

State banks 1016

Insured nonmember banks 8973

National banks 5471

TOTAL DEPOSITS OF U.S.
COMMERCIAL BANKS (in millions)

State banks $197.2

Insured nonmember banks $349.9

National banks $664.5

= Member banks of the federal reserve system

**3.**  Answer the following questions.

   **(a)** Are more commercial banks members or nonmembers of the Federal Reserve System?

   **(b)** Is there more money in member or nonmember banks?

   **(c)** In which kind of bank is more than half of the total deposits?

Answers are on page 269.

# Lesson 5  Taxes

**How do tax revenues benefit citizens?**

Government in this country employs millions of people, and is a supplier and a consumer as well. To pay for a vast array of expenditures, the government accumulates **revenue** (income), mainly through a variety of taxes.

In addition to **personal income taxes**, other sources of revenue include the **Social Security tax** (a proportional tax taken out of payroll), **corporate income taxes**, **excise taxes** (taxes on nonessential items), **tariffs** on imports, **state income taxes**, **school** and **property taxes**, highway **tolls**, **fines**, **licensing fees**, and **sales taxes**.

The government has considerable power in industries, such as banking, that affect the economy directly. The redistribution of the country's wealth, accomplished through taxes, is a more obvious way that government partic- ipates in the economy. There are two main types of taxes.

A **progressive tax** is one by which the amount to be paid increases as income or profit increases. The income tax is a progressive tax. People with higher incomes pay a higher percentage of their incomes than do people with lower incomes. People are placed in different **tax brackets** according to incomes.

A **regressive** tax is one that places the heaviest burden upon individuals and groups with the lowest incomes. A sales tax is a regressive tax because everyone pays the same amount. Therefore, poorer people pay a higher percentage of their incomes than wealthy people do.

The government uses some tax money to pay for **social welfare** pro- grams. These are programs that improve the "quality of life." Social welfare spending includes public assistance (welfare), Medicaid, grants for educa- tion, funding for housing projects, grants to consumer agencies, and money to maintain and improve public park lands.

## Lesson 5 Exercise

*Item 1* is based on the following graph.

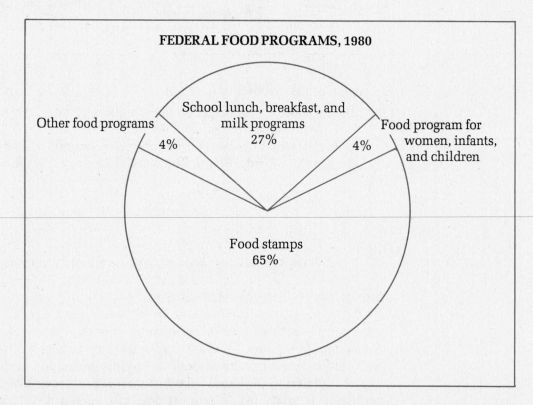

**FEDERAL FOOD PROGRAMS, 1980**

Other food programs 4%

School lunch, breakfast, and milk programs 27%

Food program for women, infants, and children 4%

Food stamps 65%

1.  Answer the following questions about the food program costs reported in the graph.

    (a) Which food program used more than half of federal food program funds?

    (b) What percentage of federal food program costs involved schools?

**2.** What is the difference between a progressive tax and a regressive tax? Give an example of each.

**3.** According to this lesson, each of the following is a way in which the government affects the economy EXCEPT

    **(1)** collecting taxes
    **(2)** taking over failing businesses
    **(3)** regulating banking practices

Answers are on page 270.

## Lesson 6    Measuring Our Economy

**Why is inflation most damaging to people with fixed incomes?**

A country's economy is not static. As conditions change, the economy fluctuates. Generally, the economy moves in cycles from prosperity to **recession**. In a recession, production decreases and unemployment increases. Sometimes the government tries to stimulate the economy during a recession. The government may create public works projects and grant low-cost loans to businesses to encourage production.

    **Inflation** is another condition that affects the economy. Inflation occurs when wages and prices rise. People are able to buy fewer goods with the same amount of money. In other words, inflation causes the real value of the dollar to go down. The government sometimes sets controls on wages and prices to curb inflation.

    Studying business cycles and conditions is one way to measure our economy. Another way is to look at certain economic statistics.

    The **Gross National Product** (GNP) is the value of everything that is produced and sold in one year. It is measured in terms of **fixed** or **constant** dollars because the value of the dollar can change from year to year.

    The **Consumer Price Index** (CPI) is another method of measuring the economy. The CPI is the average price of essential goods and services, such as food, housing, and transportation.

    To measure the health of the economy, it is also necessary to consider such factors as growth in wages, growth of new industries, and housing starts.

## Lesson 6 Exercise

**1.** How does the creation of public works projects help combat recession?

**2.** All of the following items would be included in the CPI EXCEPT

    **(1)** average apartment rents
    **(2)** new car prices
    **(3)** cost of meat
    **(4)** cost of gold
    **(5)** cost of milk

3. Provide a brief definition of the Gross National Product.

4. Prices for goods are higher during times of inflation. What are some other negative effects of inflation?

5. Of what use are statistics in studying the economy?

Answers are on page 270.

## Lesson 7   Labor and the Economy

What role do *human resources* play in the economy?

Human resources in the economy include **management** and **labor**. The people who supervise and make the major decisions about how a business is run are part of management. The people who do the actual work it takes to produce a good or provide a service are part of labor.

Labor can be classified in different ways. **Blue-collar** workers are **manual laborers**, such as carpenters, plumbers, drivers, and factory workers. **White-collar** workers are people who work at "desk jobs" in offices. They include accountants, insurance agents, and editors.

In earlier years, workers worked long hours for low wages and no **benefits**. Workers first began to form **labor unions** during the late 1800s. Unions help to promote and protect the interests of workers. Unions began to become a powerful force during the early 1900s.

Labor unions **negotiate** contracts for workers. The process by which contracts are negotiated is called **collective bargaining**. When a contract cannot be set, a union may call for a **strike**. Strikes hurt management because they shut down production. Strikes hurt labor because workers do not collect regular wages, although some unions maintain **strike funds** to supply some money to striking workers.

In order to settle a strike, the two sides may call in a **mediator**. The mediator is an impartial third party who makes suggestions about how to settle the strike. Sometimes, management and labor agree before meeting the mediator to accept whichever **compromises** the mediator believes are fair. This is called **binding arbitration**.

## Lesson 7 Exercise

1. Which of the following is NOT directly determined by collective bargaining?
   (1) wages of union members
   (2) working conditions for union members
   (3) annual raises for management employees

Item 2 is based on the following chart.

| The Number of Days U.S. Workers Spent on Strike | |
| --- | --- |
| Year | Person-Days Idle (in millions of days) |
| 1930 | 3,320 |
| 1940 | 6,700 |
| 1950 | 38,800 |
| 1960 | 19,100 |
| 1970 | 66,414 |
| 1980 | 30,984 |

From Jack Abramowitz *et al.*, *Economics and the Free-Enterprise System* (New York: Globe Book Company, 1983), page 292.

2.  Which on of the following conclusions CANNOT be supported by the chart?

    **(1)** U.S. workers spent more time on strike in 1970 than in 1960.
    **(2)** There were more strikes in 1940 than in 1930.
    **(3)** People spent less time on strike in 1980 than in 1970.

3.  What are some reasons for strikes?

Answers are on page 270.

# Lesson 8    International Trade

**How does an embargo affect the economy of a country?**

Every morning millions of Americans begin the day with a cup of coffee. Yet not one single coffee bean is grown in the United States. The coffee Americans drink is **exported** from Brazil, Colombia, and several other Latin American countries. Exported and **imported** goods play a major role in international economics.

In order to supply all goods demanded by its citizens, a country imports various items. In return, a country exports its excess resources and products. The combination of imports and exports make up a country's **balance of trade**. A country that exports more than it imports has a favorable balance of trade. A country that imports more than it exports has an unfavorable balance of trade.

Sometimes countries that normally trade with each other enter into a conflict. As a result, they may decide to prohibit trade. This is called an **embargo.** After the Soviet Union invaded Afghanistan in 1979, the United States placed an embargo on all grain shipments to the Soviet Union.

There are two main theories about the regulation of international trade. One view is that there should be **free markets**, that is, trade with no tariffs or other restrictions. The other view is that tariffs should be used to create protected markets. A **protected market** is a region or country in which certain industries are protected from foreign competition.

# Lesson 8 Exercise

Item 1 is based on the following chart.

| Major Imports and Exports of the United States (in billions of dollars) | | |
|---|---|---|
| Item | Imports | Exports |
| Food and live animals | $15.8 | $27.7 |
| Beverages and tobacco | $2.8 | $2.7 |
| Crude materials (hides, rubber, wood, ores, etc.) | $10.5 | $23.8 |
| Mineral fuels (coal, oil, natural gas) | $79.1 | $8.0 |
| Chemicals (medicines, fertilizers, etc.) | $8.6 | $20.7 |
| Machinery and transport equipment (cars, tractors, airplanes) | $60.5 | $84.6 |
| Other manufacturered goods (tires, clothing, scientific equipment, etc.) | $55.9 | $42.7 |

From Jack Abramowitz et al., *Economics and the Free-Enterprise System* (New York: Globe Book Company, 1983), page 237.

1. Answer the following questions.

   **(a)** In terms of dollars, what is the largest U.S. import?

   **(b)** Does the United States import more machinery than it exports?

   **(c)** For which items is the dollar amount of imports almost the same as the dollar amount of exports?

2. Which of the following affect a country's balance of trade?

   **(a)** tariffs

   **(b)** imports

   **(c)** exports

3. If a country exports twice as many foodstuffs as it imports, what is the benefit to that country?

4. Which person listed below would be more likely to favor a protected market? Which would be more likely to favor a free market?

   **(a)** a consumer

   **(b)** an automobile manufacturer

5. List some negative effects of tariffs.

Answers are on page 270.

# Chapter 4 Quiz

1. Briefly describe the difference between an economic good and a service.

2. Match the economic system with the proper description.

   Capitalism        Communism        Socialism

   (a) All wealth and products are shared equally by all citizens.
   (b) Business success is determined by a free marketplace.
   (c) Some businesses are owned by individuals while major industries are controlled by the government.

3. Briefly explain how advertising can affect both supply and demand.

4. Complete the following sentences.
   (a) Checking accounts are also called _____.
   (b) Savings institutions are also called _____.
   (c) Credit unions offer _____, which are similar to checking accounts.

5. Is each of the following statements TRUE or FALSE?
   (a) Federal Reserve Board members are appointed by the president.
   (b) Cash reserves for all banks are set by the Federal Reserve Board.
   (c) The FDIC sets the discount rate for loans to private banks.

6. What do you think Benjamin Franklin meant when he said, " . . . in this world, nothing is certain but death and taxes"?

*Item 7* is based on the following graph.

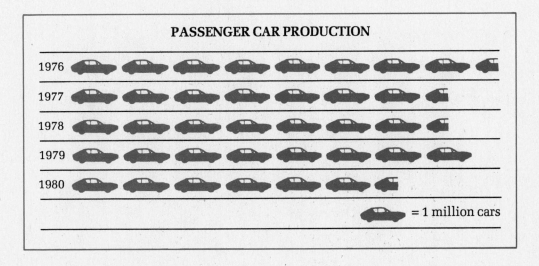

**PASSENGER CAR PRODUCTION**

1976
1977
1978
1979
1980

= 1 million cars

From Linda L. Thompson, *Consumer Mathematics* (Encino, Calif.: Glencoe, 1978), page 237. Used with permission.

7. Answer the following questions.

    **(a)** During which year were the most cars produced?
    **(b)** What does each symbol represent?
    **(c)** How many cars were produced in 1980?
    **(d)** How many more cars were produced in 1976 than in 1980?

---

8. In theory, it is not supposed to be possible for recession and inflation to exist at the same time. Briefly explain why this is so.

9. Briefly explain how the increase in industrialization in the early 1900s contributed to the increase in the power of labor unions.

10. All of the following statements about embargo are true EXCEPT:

    **(1)** Politics is frequently a cause of embargo.
    **(2)** An embargo has a profound effect on the economies of both the import and export countries.
    **(3)** An embargo does not affect the balance of trade.

Answers are on page 270.

# Chapter 5 Political Science

## Objective

In this chapter you will read and answer questions about

- Types of governments
- The Declaration of Independence
- The Articles of Confederation
- American colonial government
- The Constitutional Convention
- The Constitution
- The Bill of Rights
- The Federal Government
- State and local government
- The political process
- Government and social welfare
- International politics

## Lesson 1 Types of Government and How They Function

**What is a principal characteristic of each of the major types of government?**

Laws provide security, order, and, one hopes, justice. **Government** refers to the way laws are made and executed in large social units. **Political science** is the study of how different types of governments function.

One of the oldest types of government is the **monarchy**, in which one person inherits the power to rule. In an **absolute monarchy** the monarch has total, unrestricted power over the country. In a **constitutional monarchy** the monarch's power is limited by a system of laws. Some countries have a **symbolic monarchy** in which the ruler has little real power.

A **dictatorship** is a form of government in which one person has total rule. The dictator usually comes to power in a time of emergency and controls all aspects of life. **Fascism**, a form of dictatorship or **totalitarian government**, is characterized by a highly emotional glorification of the state, economic and social regimentation, and suppression of opposition.

In an **oligarchy** the people are ruled by a governing class, usually made up of a small group of powerful families. In a **democracy** all of the citizens have some say in how the country is to be run.

In the United States, the purest form of democracy to be found is the New England town meeting, in which all the citizens gather to make decisions. This is called a **direct democracy**. Most governmental decisions, however, are made by elected representatives, such as members of the Senate, the House of Representatives, state legislatures, or local lawmaking bodies. The United States is a **representative democracy**.

## Lesson 1 Exercise

1. General Smith takes control after the army overthrows the government. He now controls the military, the schools, the newspapers, television, and radio. What form of government is this?

2. Name two forms of democracy found in the United States. Give an example of each.

3. In England during the feudal period, a king or queen ruled the country, and a powerful nobility governed the lives of the peasants, who lived and worked on the nobles' property. These nobles also advised the king or queen on affairs of state. Which two types of government existed during this time?

4. Tell whether the following statement is TRUE or FALSE, and then explain your answer. Fascism stresses the importance of the individual.

Answers are on page 271.

## Lesson 2    The Declaration of Independence and the Articles of Confederation

In which ways were the Declaration of Independence and the Articles of Confederation the basis of U.S. political philosophy and government?

**The Declaration of Independence**, in which the thirteen colonies expressed their determination to be free of British rule, announced the American philosophy of **individualism**, the right to personal freedom and independence. Included in these individual rights were " . . . life, liberty, and the pursuit of happiness." The document also stated that all men were created equal. The colonies' insistence on self-determination was expressed in these sentiments: " . . . governments . . . [derive] their just powers from the consent of the governed. That whenever . . . government becomes destructive to these ends, it is the right of the people to alter or to abolish it. . . . "

While the leaders of the **American Revolution** were resolving to break away from England, they were also developing a plan for the new government. This plan, **The Articles of Confederation**, was approved seven months before the end of the **Revolutionary War**.

Having lived under the domination of powerful rulers, the people who drafted the articles were unwilling to grant control to a central ruling power. Under the articles, more power was invested in the individual states. The central government could not raise an army, levy taxes, or regulate trade among the states or with foreign countries. It could not make laws without the unanimous consent of all thirteen states.

The weakness of this government was that there was no provision for resolving conflicts between the states, maintaining order when citizens took up arms, raising money by taxes, or issuing a common currency. The articles provided for neither a president nor a national court system.

## Lesson 2 Exercise

1.  Which words in the Declaration of Independence summarize the philosophy of individualism?

2.  The idea that the power of government rests on the will of the people is the cornerstone of democracy. Which statement from the Declaration of Independence quoted in the lesson most clearly indicates how powerful the will of the people is? Explain.

3.  The Confederation of States has been described as "a league of friendship entered into by sovereign states." What does this definition mean?

4.  According to the description of the Articles of Confederation in this passage, does it follow that a stronger form of government was needed?

5.  Why did many colonial people not want a strong central government?

Answers are on page 271.

## Lesson 3   The Constitution

**How does the U.S. Constitution provide for the distribution of political power?**

In 1787, the Founding Fathers held a **Constitutional Convention**. Their purpose was to draft a constitution that would give the central government more power, but not at the expense of individual freedom.

Finally ratified in 1790 by the last of the thirteen states, the U.S. **Constitution** is the supreme law of the land. No laws may conflict with it. It embodies the principle of **limited government**: the government has only those powers that are stated in the Constitution. This limitation of powers is established in three ways: (1) a **separation of powers**, which defines each of three branches of government with separate powers and controls; (2) a system of **checks and balances**, which allows each branch to oversee the other branches as shown in Table 1; (3) a **federal system**, which divides the governing power between the federal government and the states.

The three branches of the federal government are the **executive branch**, or the president of the United States; the **legislative branch**, or the **Senate** and the **House of Representatives**; and the **judicial branch**, or the **Supreme Court** of the United States.

| TABLE 1  The System of Checks and Balances | | |
|---|---|---|
| President | Congress | Supreme Court |
| **Powers** | **Powers** | **Powers** |
| 1. Enforces laws.<br>2. Can veto bills.<br>3. Can appoint judges and other officials. | 1. Make the laws.<br>2. By a two-thirds vote of members Congress can pass a law over President's veto.<br>3. Can impeach President.<br>4. Must approve President's appointment of judges and other officials. | 1. Interprets the laws.<br>2. Can declare laws unconstitutional. |
| **Controls** | **Controls** | **Controls** |
| 1. Can be removed by Congress.<br>2. Congress can override veto.<br>3. Appointments must first be approved by Congress. | 1. President can veto a bill passed by Congress.<br>2. Laws passed by Congress can be declared unconstitutional by Supreme Court. | 1. Judges appointed for life by the President.<br>2. Appointments must first be approved by Congress.<br>3. Judges can be removed by Congress for improper behavior. |

The legislative branch, or **Congress**, is composed of two senators from each state and a number of representatives from each state determined by population. Members of the judicial branch are judges appointed for life terms by the president.

## Lesson 3 Exercise

1.  On November 8, 1985, President Reagan vetoed a bill that had been passed by Congress to reauthorize biomedical research at the National Institute of Health. His veto was overridden by the House on November 12 and by the Senate on November 20. Which aspect of "limitation of powers" does this illustrate?

2.  Why did the members of the Constitutional Convention provide for the "separation of powers"?

3.  Based on information in this lesson (including Table 1), does it follow that the Constitution would allow the president to assume total power if he or she felt it were necessary?

4.  The number of senators and the number of representatives elected by a state is usually not the same. Why was the Congress organized this way?

5.  A question arises over whether a state's abortion law is contrary to the Constitution. Which branch of the government will answer this question?

Answers are on page 271.

# Lesson 4    Amendments to the Constitution

**In what ways is the Constitution a result of compromises?**

The writing of the Constitution involved a series of compromises, particularly between the **Federalists**, who wanted a strong central government, and the **anti-Federalists**, who wanted more power for the states and a guarantee of individual liberties. In order to gain support, the Federalists agreed to pass a **Bill of Rights** in the first congress.

The Bill of Rights is the first ten amendments to the Constitution. They are the citizen's guarantee of civil rights and liberties. They provide for freedom of speech, press, and religion; the right to life, liberty, and private property; and the right to a speedy trial by an impartial jury. The impact of the Bill of Rights was to restrain the influence of government over the rights of individuals.

To date, there are 26 ratified amendments to the Constitution, including the Bill of Rights. An example of the importance of the amendment process is the Fourteenth Amendment. Described sometimes as an extension of the Fifth Amendment, which provides for due process under the law, the Fourteenth Amendment requires that no state shall "deny to any person within its jurisdiction the equal protection of the laws." In 1954, the Supreme Court ruled that, based on the Fourteenth Amendment, racial segregation in public schools was unconstitutional.

For an amendment to become law it must be passed by Congress and be ratified by the legislatures of three-fourths of the states.

# Lesson 4 Exercise

1.  In which ways are the first ten amendments to the Constitution a guarantee of Americans' civil rights?

2.  Why is the Fourteenth Amendment referred to as the "equal protection" amendment?

3.  What are the civil rights of a Greek national residing in and working in Ohio? Explain.

4.  The system of laws set up under the Constitution guarantees individual rights. Why is it true to say that in totalitarian state such rights are not guaranteed?

5. Amendments must be approved by a two-thirds vote of Congress. Which futher requirement must be fulfilled before an amendment is incorporated into the Constitution?

Answers are on page 271.

## Lesson 5    The Federal System—National, State and Local Government

**Why does the federal system provide for a division of power among many governments?**

One major result of the Constitutional Convention compromises was the creation of a system in which power is shared between the federal government and state governments. The Constitution gave certain powers to the federal government and denied certain powers to the states.

| TABLE 2    The Federal System's Division of Powers | |
|---|---|
| Residual Powers | Laws regulating all matters not controlled by the federal government, such as police, marriage, and education |
| Federal Powers | Foreign relations, coining money, postal services, declaration of war, international trade, interstate trade, the armed forces |
| Concurrent Powers | Taxation, court systems, social welfare |

Table 2 shows which powers remained with the states—**residual powers**—which ones were given to the federal government, and which ones are shared by state and federal governments—**concurrent powers**.

Sometimes a disagreement arises over whether a particular matter is a federal or a state concern. Usually these matters are resolved by the courts. State powers often are actually exercised by the local governments of towns, cities, and counties. Education, for example, is a state function. The state gives the power to run schools to the local community. Therefore, the local school board, rather than the state itself, makes decisions concerning schools.

By dividing power among a federal government, fifty state governments, and thousands of local governments, political power is placed in many hands. This is supposed to prevent any small group of people from having too much power.

## Lesson 5 Exercise

1. New York and New Jersey have a dispute over the size of trucks traveling between the two states. Should a federal or a state court be asked to solve this problem?

2. Some of the services that government provides are fire protection, highway maintenance, garbage collection, mail delivery, snow removal, and training the handicapped. By which level of government—federal, state, or local—is each of these services provided?

3. What is the prime advantage of strong local government?

4. The Unites States Congress passes a law making twenty-one the legal marriage age. Why should such a law be contrary to the Constitution?

Answers are on page 271.

## Lesson 6 The United States Political Process

**How can an individual citizen participate in the political process?**

Any citizen at least eighteen years old may vote in elections. He or she may also vote directly to enact or repeal a law.

Members of the House of Representatives are elected every two years. Each representative is elected from a **congressional district** of about 500,000 people. Senators are elected for six-year terms. About one-third of the Senate is up for election every two years. Two senators are elected from each state.

The president is elected every four years. The people, however, do not vote directly for the president. They vote for members of the **electoral college**, who then vote for the president. Each state has one **elector** for each of its senators and representatives. By custom, all of each state's electors vote for the same presidential candidate—the one who receives the most popular votes in their state. In order to be elected president, a candidate must receive a **majority** vote from the electoral college.

Before presidential elections, **primaries** are held. These are preliminary elections in which voters choose delegates from each major political party who pledge to vote for a certain candidate at the party's national convention.

In addition to choosing federal officeholders, voters elect state and local officials. These include governors, mayors, members of state and county legislatures, and representatives of city and town councils.

Candidates for public office are **nominated** by **political parties**, which are made up of people who share similar political beliefs. The Democratic party and the Republican party are the largest political parties in the United States today.

Individuals may also participate in politics in other ways. They may do volunteer work for their political party and may work with interest groups that try to advance special causes. Through **lobbies** these interest groups attempt to enlist the aid of legislators to introduce or vote for measures favorable to them.

## Lesson 6 Exercise

1. Tai Lee, a 25-year-old resident alien, is interested in the presidential election. May she vote for the candidate of her choice?

2. Explain the purpose of a presidential primary.

3. What role in the political process do the following groups have: the American Legion, the NAACP, a city chamber of commerce?

4. Is it possible for a presidential candidate to receive more than half of the country's popular votes, but less than half of the electors' votes? Explain your answer.

Answers are on page 272.

## Lesson 7   Government and Social Welfare

**What are some of the ways that government works to improve the quality of life?**

The first role of government is to maintain peace, order, and security. This includes peace at home and security against attacks from other nations. These were problems for the American government in the early years after the Revolutionary War.

When stability and peace are established, the government often inaugurates programs to improve the quality of life in the areas of employment, education, health, and food and housing for the poor and disadvantaged. Many of these programs started when Franklin D. Roosevelt instituted the **New Deal** during the Great Depression. In general, social welfare programs have grown since the New Deal; there are occasionally cutbacks, however, in some programs.

In the 1960s, Medicare, Medicaid, food stamps, and other programs were established to help people maintain at least a minimum standard of living. They were instituted under President Lyndon Johnson's **Great Society** program. Social welfare programs are concurrent responsibilities of the federal and state governments. In some instances, funding is provided to states by federal tax dollars: states actually run the programs.

Government also intervenes to promote justice and to protect civil rights. Many of the actions that have helped to combat racial segregation in schools, for example, were taken by the federal government.

## Lesson 7 Exercise

1. Name two government programs designed to improve the quality of life.

2.  Federally funded CETA programs were designed to train workers for jobs. Was CETA a social welfare program? Explain your answer.

3.  A portion of the taxes collected by the Internal Revenue Service supports some school lunch programs. How does that demonstrate that social welfare programs are concurrent responsibilities in the federal system?

Answers are on page 272.

# Lesson 8    International Politics

How do nations interact with each other to maintain peace and security?

One way a government protects its people from threats from other countries is to maintain armed forces. Another security measure is to work toward world peace. One way this is done is through the **United Nations** (U.N.). The United Nations was organized in 1945. The United States and about 150 nations are now members. The purpose of the United Nations is to provide a forum for nations to discuss their differences. This forum is supposed to prevent nations from settling their differences through war. The United Nations also has special agencies to work on various problems. A few of these agencies are the **United Nation's International Children's Emergency Fund (UNICEF)**, the **International Labor Organization (ILO)**, and the **World Health Organization (WHO)**.

Nations also maintain contact with other nations through diplomatic relations. **Embassies** are set up through which diplomats try to work out problems and maintain cordial relations between their respective countries.

A third kind of international arrangement involves groups of countries bound together by **treaties**, or formal agreements. These can be military arrangements like the **North Atlantic Treaty Organization (NATO)** formed by the United States and its European allies. There are also economic associations such as the **Common Market**, a union of western European nations. There are also regional groups like the **Organization of American States (OAS)**.

## Lesson 8 Exercise

1.  Which of the following is a military alliance?
    (1) UNICEF        (4) ILO
    (2) NATO          (5) WHO
    (3) OAS

2.  Is the following TRUE or FALSE? A controversy involving the price of French wine sold in Italy could be settled by the Common Market.

3.  Briefly state reasons that nations join international organizations.

4.  Based on the lesson, what are some of the goals of the United Nations?

Answers are on page 272.

# Chapter 5 Quiz

1.  What are some of the fundamental beliefs of the United States political system that were set forth in the Declaration of Independence?

2.  Which two branches of government did the Constitution provide for that the Articles of Confederation did not?

Item 3 is based on the following cartoon.

Jim Morin, *The Miami Herald*, King Features Syndicate. Used with permission.

3.  Justice William Rehnquist and Judge Antonin Scalia were appointed to the Supreme Court by President Reagan. What does the cartoon imply about how the Senate exercised its power under the system of checks and balances?

4.  In October 1986, Congress passed and the President signed a law establishing longer prison terms for those convicted of smuggling drugs into the country. Which branch of the government must see that this law is applied?

5.  If the population of one state is about 17 million and the population of another state is one million, how many representatives does each state elect to the House?

6.  Which branch of the federal government has no members who are elected by the people?

*Item 7 is based on the following table.*

### Party Representation in Congress

| | Senate | | | House of Representatives | | |
|---|---|---|---|---|---|---|
| Years | Total | Demo-crats | Repub-licans | Total | Demo-crats | Repub-licans |
| 1967–69 | 100 | 64 | 36 | 435 | 248 | 187 |
| 1969–71 | 100 | 58 | 42 | 435 | 243 | 192 |
| 1971–73 | 100 | 54 | 44 | 435 | 255 | 180 |
| 1973–75 | 100 | 56 | 42 | 435 | 242 | 192 |
| 1975–77 | 100 | 61 | 37 | 435 | 291 | 144 |
| 1977–79 | 100 | 61 | 38 | 435 | 292 | 143 |
| 1979–81 | 100 | 58 | 41 | 435 | 277 | 158 |
| 1981–83 | 100 | 46 | 53 | 435 | 242 | 190 |
| 1983–85 | 100 | 46 | 54 | 435 | 269 | 166 |
| 1985–87 | 100 | 47 | 53 | 435 | 253 | 182 |

*Sources: Clerk of the House of Representatives; Secretary of the Senate.*

From: *World Almanac 1986* (New York: Newspaper Enterprise Association), page 231. Used with permission.

7.  According to the table, the Democratic Party controlled both houses of Congress until which year?

---

8.  What are three peaceful ways that nations interact with each other?

*Item 9 is based on the map on the next page.*

9.  If the electors in the five states that have the most votes all voted for the same presidential candidate, what would be the minimum number of electoral votes that candidate would need in order to win the election?

*Item 10 is based on the table above and the map on the next page.*

10. Compare the information in the table and the map. What conclusion can be drawn about how residents of the nation's capital are represented at the federal level of government?

Answers are on page 272.

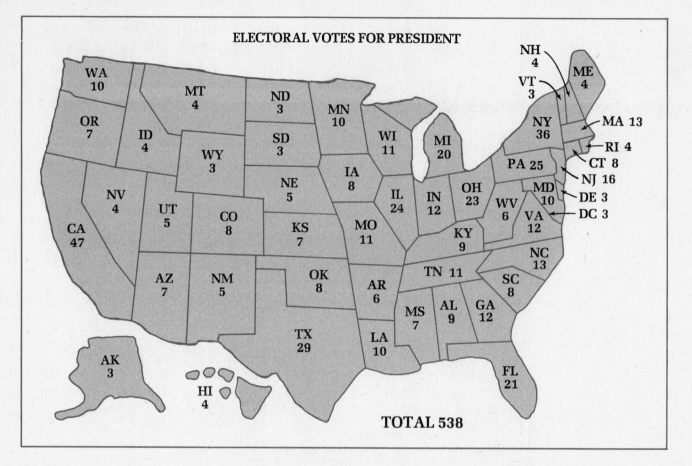

ELECTORAL VOTES FOR PRESIDENT

TOTAL 538

*Chapter*

# 6 | Behavioral Science

## Objective

In this chapter, you will read and answer questions about

- What behavioral scientists study
- Methods used to gather information
- Subfields in psychology
- Perspectives in psychology
- The study of society in sociology
- Group dynamics
- The study of cultures in anthropology
- Attitudes toward cultures

## Lesson 1    Introduction to Behavioral Science

**How do behavioral scientists gather data?**

The behavioral sciences focus on the behavior of animals and humans. There are three main branches of behavioral science. **Psychology** is the behavioral science that studies the behavior and thoughts of individuals. **Sociology** is concerned with the behavior of people in groups and with group dynamics. **Anthropology** studies and compares behaviors in different cultures.

**Behavior** is anything an animal or a person does that can be observed. Crying is a behavior because it can be seen and heard. Sadness is not a behavior because it cannot be observed. Behavior can provide important clues to what is going on in the mind.

Different methods are used in the behavioral sciences to gather information. In a **survey,** a group of people are questioned about their opinions and their behavior. A **case study** involves a detailed examination of an individual or of one particular group. A **field study** is the observation of people in their everyday environment. The method of **participant observation** is used when the scientist joins in the activities of the group, rather than just observing, in order to obtain more detailed information. When the **experimental method** is used, the behavioral scientist must try to control the environment of the people or the animals being studied. The scientist alters one **variable** in the environment and then watches for a difference in behavior.

## Lesson 1 Exercise

1. As part of a field study, a sociologist sat quietly in a classroom, watched the behavior of children, and took down the notes that appear below. Which one of the following notes is an observation of behavior?

    **(1)** The child covered her eyes and turned away from the teacher.
    **(2)** Charles looked like a happy boy.
    **(3)** Diane was distressed when she left the room.
    **(4)** It seemed as if the child was exhausted.
    **(5)** Two of the children seemed to be brother and sister.

2. The questions below address aspects of people's behavior. Choose the branch of behavioral science that might best deal with the question.

    **(a)** How does parenting in South Africa compare with parenting in the United States?
    **(b)** Which group of children is more likely to have a record of juvenile delinquency, those who go to public schools or those who go to private schools?
    **(c)** Which group shows behavior that is associated more closely with prejudice, people who belong to a church or those who do not?
    **(d)** Why do people continue to smoke even though they know that it is a hazard to their health?

3. What word should go in each of the blanks?

    **(a)** The three main branches of behavioral science are _____, _____, and _____.
    **(b)** An anthropologist would be likely to compare behaviors in different _____.
    **(c)** *Behavior* is anything an animal or a person does that can be _____.

*Item 4* is based on the following graph.

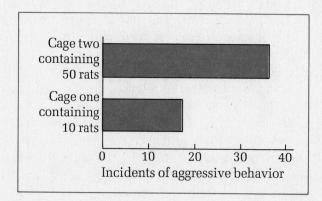

4. A psychologist studied the effects of overcrowding on animal behavior by taking two identical cages and treating the rats in them exactly the

same, except for one thing. The results of the study appear in the graph. Complete the sentences below.

**(a)** This method of data collection is called the _____.

**(b)** The two cages were identical, and the rats were treated exactly the same because the behavioral scientist tried to _____ the environment.

**(c)** The scientist altered one variable, which was _____.

Answers are on page 272.

# Lesson 2   Psychology: Subfields and Perspectives

**How does a perspective shape the way in which the psychologist helps people?**

There are many different branches of psychology. **Clinical** psychologists use psychotherapy to diagnose and treat psychological disorders. **Educational** and **school** psychologists are concerned with how people adjust to school and how learning takes place. **Experimental** psychologists try to discover and understand the causes of behavior, sometimes by studying the behavior of animals in an experiment. **Developmental** psychology includes both **child** and **adolescent** psychology and focuses on the process of maturation.

A **perspective**, or **approach**, describes a particular way of looking at behavior. Psychologists often use principles and ideas from different approaches. The **cognitive** approach studies the ways in which people think and perceive. The **humanistic** approach emphasizes the belief that people can be whatever they want to be, despite what may have happened in their lives.

The **psychoanalytical** approach focuses on the revelation of desires and conflicts that are stored in the **unconscious** mind. The **repression** of painful memories from childhood is thought to cause behavioral disturbances in the adult. **Defense mechanisms** are patterns of behavior that provide relief from the unpleasant feeling of anxiety. A person may use them constantly to avoid dealing with feelings. For example, **sublimation** occurs when a person lessens anxiety by replacing an unattainable desire with something useful and constructive.

## Lesson 2 Exercise

**1.** What psychological approach does the statement below indicate?

"There may have been a traumatic event in the patient's past that has been repressed and is now in the unconscious mind."

**2.** The psychoanalytic approach recognizes fantasizing as a defense mechanism. How does fantasizing work as a defense mechanism?

*Item 3* is based on the following graph.

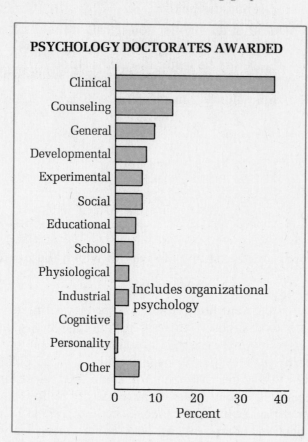

**PSYCHOLOGY DOCTORATES AWARDED**

Clinical
Counseling
General
Developmental
Experimental
Social
Educational
School
Physiological
Industrial — Includes organizational psychology
Cognitive
Personality
Other

0    10    20    30    40
Percent

3. **(a)** More psychologists are involved in _____ psychology than in educational psychology, and this type of psychologist focuses on the process of maturation.

   **(b)** The largest subfield is _____ psychology, and the psychologist who works in this subfield is primarily involved with the use of _____ to help people.

   **(c)** Fewer psychologists are involved in _____ psychology than in clinical psychology, and this type of psychologist might be found studying the behavior of rats in a cage.

Answers are on pages 272–273.

# Lesson 3    The Biological Perspective and Behaviorism

**How do heredity and environment work together to shape personality?**

Newborn infants show differences in personality from the outset. Some newborns are hardly bothered by loud noises, while others cry at the drop of a pin. These differences to a great extent are determined by **heredity.** Differences between individuals can be inherited and then shaped by the

**environment.** The biological perspective relates behavior to heredity or to physical factors. As maturation occurs, heredity provides the potential for development. For instance, wide variations can be seen in the height of individuals at a particular age; the potential for height is determined by heredity. But the influence of environment, such as through diet, can keep a person from attaining full height.

The family environment is considered to be important in the shaping of behavior, especially in childhood. The approach of **behaviorism** provides definitions for the conditioning of behavior. Parents often use **operant conditioning** to train behavior: they use punishment to discourage behavior or **positive reinforcement** to encourage it. When a child learns to stay in the backyard to avoid a spanking, the child has learned through **negative reinforcement.** When the learning of the alphabet by the child is rewarded, the child receives positive reinforcement. In **classical conditioning,** an individual learns that the appearance of one thing tends to be accompanied by another. For example, a baby is fed with a bottle and feels good when hunger goes away. The baby begins to associate the sight of the bottle with being fed and, eventually, just having a bottle will make the baby feel good.

## Lesson 3 Exercise

1. A certain psychologist thinks that heredity has no influence on the development of personality. There is evidence to contradict that idea. Give an example of such evidence.

*Items 2 to 4 are based on the following graph and passage.*

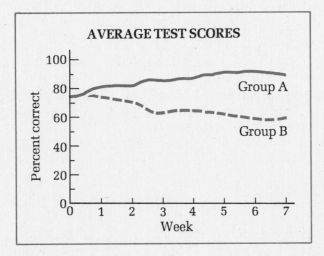

An educational psychologist wanted to run an experiment to see how the ideas of behaviorism would affect the behavior of schoolchildren. A class was to be divided into two groups, based on test scores. Group A would receive praise, encouragement, and rewards when they did well on a test. Group B would receive scoldings and punishment when they did poorly on a test. Based on similar studies of animals, the psychologist predicted that the results of the study would look similar to those in the graph.

2. Which type of conditioning would the psychologist use in this experiment?

3. Which type of reinforcement would the psychologist use to condition the behavior of the children in group A?

4. What would the psychologist most likely recommend teachers do to encourage students' improved performance?

Answers are on page 273.

## Lesson 4  The Study of Society in Sociology

Why are social institutions important to society?

A **society** is a group of people who share a way of life and who live in the same general area. We can refer to all the people who live in the United States as the American society. The sociologist often studies different groups of people within society, such as **peer groups** or people who live in the suburbs. Societies are stratified, or divided into classes. **Social class** can be determined by such things as family income, area of residence, education, and occupation. An individual can move from one class to another; this is called **social mobility.**

The sociologist studies the **social institutions** in a society. Social institutions satisfy different needs that individuals may not be able to satisfy on their own. The school system is a social institution that provides education. Churches and synagogues are also social institutions. The family is a social institution that provides for the care of children. The family also provides a great deal of the **socialization** that teaches children the behaviors that are acceptable to society.

Members of society are concerned with how other members conform to the basic beliefs and rules of society. The behaviors that are acceptable to a society are called **norms.** A person whose behavior goes against the norm may be punished by being ostracized or excluded. Behavior that goes against the norm is said to be **deviant.**

## Lesson 4 Exercise

1. Is government a society, a social class, or a social institution?

2. What word or phrase completes each of the following sentences?
   **(a)** The behaviors that are accepted by a society are called _____.

   **(b)** Moving from one class to another is called _____.
   **(c)** Behavior that goes against the norm of society is called _____ behavior.

3. Which of the following is a deviation from the norms of American society?

**(1)** A man uses a knife to cut food at the dinner table.
**(2)** A boy claps his hands to show appreciation.
**(3)** A woman goes to the supermarket in a bikini.
**(4)** A male infant is dressed in blue.
**(5)** A woman makes up her face with different colors to look attractive.

Answers are on page 273.

## Lesson 5    The Study of Group Behavior

**How do people know how to act when they assume a role?**

Sociologists consider the family to be an important institution. The **nuclear family** consists of a couple and their children. The **extended family** includes relatives outside the nuclear family. The family is called a **primary group** because there is personal and continued contact between the members of the group. In a primary group, the members are concerned with how the other members conform to the basic beliefs and rules of the group. Another example of the primary group is the peer group. Adolescence is considered to be a time of conflict because the young adult looks to two different primary groups, the family and the peer group, for approval. In contrast, a **secondary group** is characterized by limited contact and short-lived relationships among members. Examples of secondary groups include a church organization or a professional association of doctors.

Norms provide guidelines for the different **roles** people play in life. As we take on different roles—husband, wife, parent, friend, employee—we behave in different ways according to other people's expectations.

## Lesson 5 Exercise

Items 1 to 3 are based on the following graph and passage.

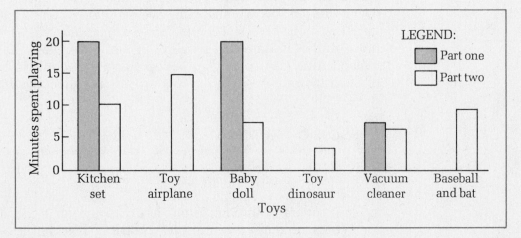

In Part One of an experiment, a sociologist noted the type of toys that a group of four-year-old girls played with. In Part Two, the sociologist observed the same girls playing with toys, but only let one girl at a time into the room. The sociologist's observations are recorded on the graph.

1.  Comparing the two parts of the experiment, what were the differences in the girls' toy choices?

2.  What does the girls' behavior in Part One of the experiment show about the girls' socialization?

3.  What does the experiment suggest about the influence of a peer group's expectations on an individual's behavior?

Answers are on page 273.

## Lesson 6   Introduction to Anthropology

**How do cultural traits help define a society?**

Anthropology studies the development of societies' cultures. A **culture** is a system of values, beliefs, and traditions that are shared by a society and passed down to its children. Culture provides a shared language and a common way of life. A **cultural trait** is any behavior that is common in a particular culture. The **dominant culture** of a society holds it together. **Subcultures** share some of the traits of the dominant culture, but have others that produce little conflict with the dominant culture. The members of a **counterculture** behave in ways that clash with the larger society. The "hippie movement" of the 1960s could be considered to have been a counterculture.

Sometimes, a culture influences other cultures. Before the twentieth century, several European countries, including England, France, and Spain, maintained colonies around the world. The Europeans brought their cultures to their colonies. Cultural traits from one place spread to another by a process called **cultural diffusion**. In some countries, such as Japan, the dominant culture is very strong. In others such as the United States, there is **cultural pluralism** because people from many different cultures participate in the dominant culture, even though they keep characteristics of their own culture. Many women who have emigrated from India continue to wear their traditional dress. They may also raise their children according to the rules of their culture and speak their native language. Eventually, the customs of American society are accepted by the immigrants and mixed with those of their native culture. This process is called **acculturation.**

## Lesson 6 Exercise

*Item 1 is based on the map on the next page.*

1.  The letters *A* through *E* on the map represent five different cultures. Which of those five cultures probably has the greatest influence on others of the five by cultural diffusion?

2.  Do cultures remain the same or do they change? Support your answer.

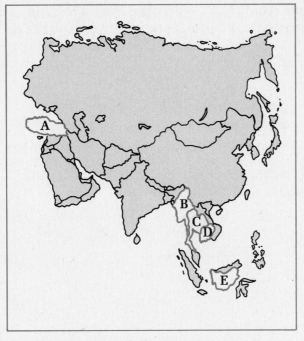

3. Complete the following.
    **(a)** The _____ _____ of a society in-
    cludes values, beliefs, and traditions that hold it together.
    **(b)** A _____ differs in many ways from a
    _____, but because the second contains the first,
    there would be little conflict between the two.

4. Why might a dominant culture react strongly against a counterculture?

Answers are on page 273.

## Lesson 7    The Study of Different Cultures

**Why is objectivity important to the study of anthropology?**

Children learn the values and the beliefs of their culture when appropriate behaviors are reinforced and inappropriate behaviors are punished. They learn the **taboos,** or rules that forbid certain behaviors. They also learn **rituals,** which are ceremonies that symbolize the values and the beliefs of their culture. **Rites of passage** are rituals that symbolize movement from one stage of life to another, such as a marriage rite.

A society is made up of many smaller groups, each with its own organization, leadership, and rules for behavior. These basic groups can vary. In most cultures, the basic group is the family. Another type of basic group is called the **clan,** a large group of people who believe that they all descended from one ancestor. Another basic group is the **tribe,** which is made up of people who cooperate and work together to provide basic needs. Certain members of a tribe may hunt; others farm; still others cook.

Different cultures can have very different values and beliefs. An anthropologist must recognize the fact that values and beliefs that may seem strange are not wrong but are simply different from one's own. This is called **cultural relativity,** and it enables the anthropologist to observe cultures more objectively in order to understand behavior. It is important that anthropologists avoid **ethnocentrism,** or the belief that their own culture is superior to all others.

## Lesson 7 Exercise

1. An anthropologist writes the following passage in a book about a particular culture:

   "This culture has a strange and rather cruel rite of passage that requires an adolescent boy to go alone into the jungle for a week."

   This sentence demonstrates a lack of _____ _____.

2. How are cultural relativity and ethnocentrism related?

3. Give some examples of rites of passage that are common in contemporary U.S. culture.

Answers are on page 273.

# Chapter 6 Quiz

1. All people do not consider the same things to be rewarding. In the behavioral approach to psychology, why is it important to know this if you want to reinforce a behavior?

2. Fill in the blanks.
   **(a)** According to the psychoanalytic approach, childhood memories that are repressed are stored in a person's _____.
   **(b)** The idea that people can be whatever they want to be, despite what may have happened in their lives, is part of the _____ approach to psychology.
   **(c)** The _____ approach studies the perceptions and the thoughts of people.

3. Behavioral Books is planning to publish a three-part book about suicide. Part 1 will include a case study of Martin Harris, who committed suicide when he was 17. Part 2 will deal with suicide in the United States—how many people try it, who they are, and the methods they use. Part 3 will be concerned with how suicide in this country differs from suicide in other parts of the world. What kind of behavioral scientist would be the best choice to write each of the three parts in this book?

4.  Today, many families in the United States consist of a divorced woman and her children. How does this differ from the traditional nuclear family?

5.  Complete the following.

    (a) The _____ perspective relates behavior to heredity or physical factors.

    (b) _____ discourages a certain behavior; _____ encourages it.

    (c) Differences between individuals can be inherited and then shaped by the _____.

*Item 6* is based on the following graph.

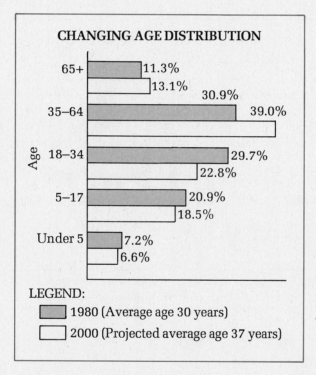

6.  According to the graph, the largest group of people in the United States at the beginning of the next century will be

    (1) infants
    (2) children
    (3) adolescents
    (4) middle-aged adults
    (5) senior citizens

7.  Which type of group is more likely to have a greater influence on a person's values, a primary group or a secondary group? Explain briefly.

8. Given sociology's definition of *roles* in society, what does *role conflict* mean?

9. Fill in the blanks.

   (a) Immigrants to the United States eventually begin to speak some English. This is an example of _____.

   (b) Many immigrants brought methods of food preparation from their countries that are now widely used in the United States. This is an example of _____ _____.

   (c) If immigrants use their culture as a standard by which to judge another society, they may be guilty of _____.

*Item 10 is based on the following graph.*

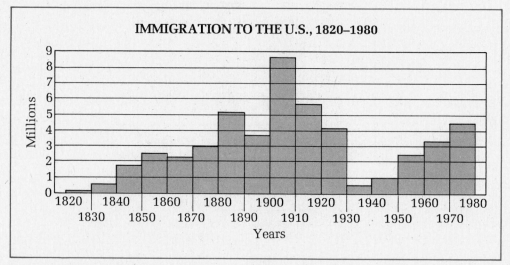

**IMMIGRATION TO THE U.S., 1820–1980**

*Source:* Robert L. Hardgrave, Jr., *American Government: The Republic in Action* (New York: Harcourt Brace Jovanovich, 1986), page 209. Used with permission.

10. Choose the statement that best describes the effect of immigration on the United States.

    (1) The cultural plurality of American society is slowly decreasing.
    (2) The immigration rate between 1930 and 1940 helped decrease the number of subcultures in our society.
    (3) Immigration into the United States, especially between the years 1900 and 1910, has greatly contributed to the establishment of a pluralistic society.
    (4) More countercultures came to the United States between the years 1950 and 1970 than in any other period of time.
    (5) The group of immigrants who arrived in the United States from 1900 to 1910 established the largest dominant culture.

Answers are on page 273.

## Chapter 7

# Interrelationships Among the Branches of Social Studies

## Objective

In this chapter, you will read and answer questions about passages in social studies. The passages illustrate the fact that most events can be viewed from the vantage point of more than one of the branches of social studies. Passages demonstrate that

- The economy of the United States influences domestic employment and foreign economies
- Political events influence social roles
- Economic decisions influence political legislation
- Geography influences international politics
- Politics influences human welfare

## Lesson 1  The Stock Market Crash: National and International Effects

**How did the practice of buying stocks on margin contribute to the stock market crash?**

*The stock market crash directly affected companies whose stocks were traded in the market, it affected stockholders, and it affected the stock market itself. The health of the economy of the United States (like that of any country) depends on the maintenance of a delicate balance among many factors. When an imbalance occurs, its effects are felt throughout both the country and the world.*

*As you read the following passage, notice the direct effects of the crash; consider the implications of its broader indirect effects.*

\*　　\*　　\*

On October 30, 1929, the show-business newspaper *Variety* carried the headline "Wall Street Lays an Egg." In show business, when something "lays an egg," it flops or fails. By October 30, 1929, it was clear that investment in the stock market had let to financial ruin for millions of people.

The 1920s had been a decade of growth and prosperity that saw United States production increase by 50%. There was plenty of work. Families bought radios, vacuum cleaners, automobiles, washing machines, and other products of the boom economy. New companies were formed.

Americans invested in the stock market even though they knew little about the companies whose stock they were buying. The investors' goal was to gain by selling the stock at a profit.

People often bought stock on credit, or **on margin**. Credit buying allowed people to pay out only a small part of the value of the stock up front. When the value of the stock increased, they sold it and paid off the rest of the purchase price with part of the profit. Large amounts of money were made this way, but in October 1929, stock prices fell.

| TABLE 1   Unemployment During the Great Depression | |
| --- | --- |
| Year | Percent Unemployment |
| 1929 | 4 |
| 1930 | 10 |
| 1931 | 15 |
| 1932 | 24 |
| 1933* | 25 |
| 1939 | 17 |

\* After 1933, unemployment slowly declined.

The stock market began to collapse, or *crash*, on October 23, 1929. Brokers began to make *margin calls*, that is, to demand the money that was still owed by those who had bought on margin. The supply of consumer goods exceeded the public's ability to buy, so companies failed. As prices fell and stocks were lost, a panic began. Everyone wanted to sell, but there were no buyers.

The collapse of the stock market was the beginning of the worldwide economic depression of the 1930s. As shown in Table 1, unemployment was rampant.

## Lesson 1 Exercise

*Item 1 is based on Table 1.*

1.  New Deal agencies such as the Civilian Conservation Corps (1933–1942) and the Public Works Administration (1933–1939) sponsored conservation projects both to conserve natural resources and to help combat unemployment. Does Table 1 show how effectively these two agencies combated unemployment? Explain your answer.

2.  Identify effects of the stock market crash that helped cause worldwide depression and explain how they did so.

3.  Most companies strive for a supply/demand ratio of 1:1 per product: for each item manufactured, there is a consumer. At the time of the stock market crash, which of the following supply/demand ratios were recorded by many companies?
    (1) less than 1:1
    (2) more than 1:1
    (3) 1:1
    (4) 1:less than 1
    (5) 1:more than 1

Answers are on page 274.

## Lesson 2   The World Wars and Women's Liberation

**How did United States involvement in two world wars contribute to the feminist movement?**

*Every major event in the world society has some degree of impact on most spheres of life everywhere. History records two world wars: they have had a profound influence on the economic and the social landscapes of the United States (not to mention of the whole world). These wars caused changes in the makeup of the United States work force, which, in turn, affected the status of both women and men in society. Those changes that began early in this century continue to interest historians, economists, and behavioral scientists, among others.*

*As you read the following passage, notice how change breeds change and how change pervades many facets of society.*

\*     \*     \*

Women in the United States have always worked hard, but before the twentieth century, most women worked as homemakers. Beginning in the early 1900s, the number of women who worked outside the home began to increase slowly but steadily. A major increase came during World War I when many men left jobs in factories and offices to become servicemen. At the same time, more jobs were created to support the war effort.

During World War II, hundreds of thousands of women worked in defense plants to produce guns, airplanes, warships, and ammunition.

Women also joined the armed forces. More than 216,000 women served in the army or the navy during World War II. After the war, many women left their defense-plant jobs, but others remained in the work force. World War II changed United States society. Women were becoming more independent and more involved in work outside the home.

The women's liberation movement began in the 1950s and the early 1960s with the publication of two books—*The Second Sex* by Simone de Beauvoir and *The Feminine Mystique* by Betty Friedan. The movement fostered awareness of the facts that all jobs ought to be open to women and that women and men should be paid the same rate for the same work.

The women's movement has made great advances: more and more women are entering professions that were traditionally open only to men. However, sex discrimination in the work place is not yet a thing of the past.

## Lesson 2 Exercise

1. How did twentieth-century political events encourage changes in women's roles in society?

2. What does the title, *The Second Sex,* suggest Simone de Beauvoir says about the status of men and women in society?

3. Based on ideas in the passage, explain how war can have a positive effect on a nation's economy.

Answers are on page 274.

## Lesson 3     United States Economic and Political History and School Desegregation

**What brought about school desegregation in all parts of the United States?**

*The need for cheap labor encouraged the early colonists to bring indentured servants and slaves to North America. Slavery in the United States, therefore, had its origin in colonial economics. The country's politics, history, and society are full of the effects of seventeenth-century economics.*

*As you read the following passage, notice how the different branches and levels of government interacted as they addressed one aspect of one of those effects.*

*     *     *

In 1619, a Dutch ship carried 20 black people to Jamestown. Soon after that, slavery had the status of an institution in colonial society. By the time of the Declaration of Independence, there were about a half-million slaves in the 13 colonies, and since then racial discrimination in a variety of forms has been part of United States culture.

In the 1896 *Plessy v. Ferguson* decision, the Supreme Court ruled that laws that required segregated public facilities, which includes schools, did not violate the Constitution. However, in 1954 the court ruled in *Brown v. Board of Education of Topeka* that school segregation violates the Fourteenth Amendment. The decision held that "separate educational facilities are inherently unequal."

The Supreme Court's decision was unpopular with many people and led to a move to impeach Chief Justice Earl Warren. Some Southern governors vowed never to allow racially integrated schools. President Eisenhower sent troops to Little Rock, Arkansas, in 1957 to defend the constitutional rights of students there by ensuring that the schools would integrate. Under federal protection, nine black students began to attend a previously all-white school.

## Lesson 3 Exercise

1.  What evidence is there in this passage that some states have had laws requiring racial discrimination?

2.  Why did the Supreme Court's decision about a case in Kansas have an effect on schools in the south?

*Item 3 is based on the following time line.*

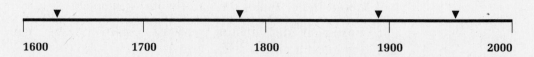

| 1600 | 1700 | 1800 | 1900 | 2000 |

3.  The time line graphically demonstrates how far apart in time specific events mentioned in the passage were. A United States historian might

conclude that since *Brown v. Board of Education of Topeka*, laws that combat racial discrimination in the United States have encouraged rapid social change. Which observations could lead the historian to call the rate of recent social change *rapid*?

4. Each of the three branches of government has a different role in relation to the laws of the United States. Explain the role of each of the branches in regard to the Fourteenth Amendment and its requirement of school desegregation in Little Rock.

Answers are on page 274.

## Lesson 4    Soviet Geography and the Cold War

**What role did geography have in the development of the cold war?**

*Geography and politics have always been closely intertwined. Before the age of air and space travel, geographic features played a critical role in any nation's security from attack. Even now, geography and national security are related, if not as intimately as in earlier times.*

*The following passage illustrates the influence of geography on modern-day international relations.*

\*          \*          \*

The Soviet Union covers the largest land area of any nation in the world today. It is more than twice the size of the next-largest country, Canada. The geography of the Soviet Union has benefited the country in many ways; it has also caused many problems.

The Soviet Union has few natural defenses against its enemies because, like most of the country, its border areas are flat. It has been invaded many times by foreign armies. The French, under Napoleon, invaded in 1812, and the Germans invaded during World Wars I and II. The Soviet Union sustained heavy damage during these invasions. Twenty million Soviet people were killed in World War II alone.

The Soviet Union's lack of natural defenses has influenced its foreign policy since World War II. At the end of the war, there were Soviet troops in the countries between Germany and the Soviet Union. Those troops stayed where they were in order to provide a **buffer zone** between the Soviet Union and the rest of Europe. The Soviets believed this zone would protect them from future invasions. Soviet control of the affected countries (Bulgaria, Czechoslovakia, East Germany, Hungary, Poland, and Rumania) has caused a great deal of conflict.

Soviet presence in Eastern Europe and United States opposition to that presence was the foundation for the **cold war**. Western European nations, Canada, and the United States formed the North Atlantic Treaty Organization (NATO) in 1949 to guard against further incursions. Since then there has been strain within and between both of the sides in the cold war. The cold war goes through periods of **escalation** when verbal or other confrontations are prevalent, and periods of **détente** when a spirit of constructive accord marks East-West relations.

## Lesson 4 Exercise

1. According to the passage, how does the Soviet Union justify its presence in Afghanistan?

2. What is the difference between *cold war* and *war*?

3. Does the cartoon in Figure 1 represent a period of détente in the cold war? Explain your answer by summarizing the point that the cartoon makes.

" 'Coo' Yourself!"

Herb Block, *The Washington Post.* Copyright 1952. Used with permission.

4. The Soviet Union was building missile bases in Cuba until President Kennedy and Premier Khrushchev reached agreements in 1962 that resulted in the removal of weapons. What role did geography play in the Cuban missile crisis?

Answers are on page 274.

## Lesson 5    Famine in Africa: The Geography and the Politics

**On what basis can starvation in Africa be called a political issue?**

*At first glance, it might seem that the causes and spread of famine are always strictly an aspect of geography. However, recent events in Africa demonstrate that politics can also be a factor in a famine's origin and duration.*

*In the following passage, notice how geography and both local and international politics conspire to bring about and prolong a famine. Consider famine's long-term, devastating effects on society—communities as well as individuals.*

*       *       *

In the mid-1980s the world's attention began to focus on the famine in Africa. Nature was part of the cause of the African famine. For a number of years, the sub-Saharan area suffered extended periods of drought. Crops died and valuable topsoil was blown off the land. Where farms had once produced grain, there were deserts.

Political problems also contributed to the famine. Civil wars in Ethiopia, for example, created great numbers of **refugees**, thousands of people who fled their homelands for safer areas. Farms were abandoned, or they were destroyed by fighting troops. Areas that had been unaffected became overpopulated and, therefore, increasingly less able to feed growing numbers of people. As the famine spread, more and more refugees wandered from place to place in search of food.

Efforts at famine relief were complicated by politics. Millions of dollars worth of food that was sent to Ethiopia never reached many areas because of the continuing civil war. The **terrain** was also a hindrance: access to remote areas was often difficult, and relief supplies could not be delivered to the neediest people.

The consequences of famine are far-reaching. Land that has been destroyed by drought does not easily become fertile again. Malnutrition has serious, long-term effects on people: when it impairs physical or mental development, permanent damage can result. A whole generation of both young adults and children is likely to suffer mental disability and physical disease for the remainder of their lives.

## Lesson 5 Exercise

1.  Name three ways in which the civil war's effect on farms and farmers in Ethiopia hastened the depletion of resources that could have helped fight famine.

2.  How do the effects of famine on an organized society demonstrate that there is a hierarchy of human needs?

3. What roles might the United Nations play to arrest the progress of famine in a country that is at war with another?

Answers are on pages 274–275.

# Chapter 7 Quiz

*Items 1 and 2 are based on the following dialogue.*

The following is part of a conversation between members of an energy commission.

**Speaker 1:** Gasoline wholesale prices are down, the reserve stock is up, and demand is low. High inventories indicate that we may soon see further reduction in prices.

**Speaker 2:** Prices have hit bottom and could go up at any time. Crude imports are going up. Increased dependence means that higher prices are possible.

1. Which of the speakers is more likely to favor increased construction of nuclear power stations? Explain your choice.

2. Explain, in terms of supply and demand, why Speaker 2 predicts that "increased dependence means that higher prices are possible."

---

3. After the stock market crash in 1929, laws were enacted to require companies to disclose information about their financial standing before they would be allowed to sell stock. How might such laws help prevent another stock market crash?

4. The equal-rights amendment says that it is illegal to discriminate against a person because of sex. Many believe that even though laws against it exist, sex discrimination cannot be eradicated without a constitutional amendment to prohibit it. Why might a constitutional amendment be more effective in curbing sex discrimination than other laws might be?

5. Which one of the following headlines might have appeared concerning an event in 1957?

   (1) Supreme Court Upholds School Segregation
   (2) Supreme Court Sends Troops to Little Rock
   (3) President Enforces Court's Decision
   (4) Congress Votes for Integration
   (5) Topeka Loses; Brown Wins

6. Which factors of its geography have encouraged United States economic development?

*Items 7 to 10 are based on the following map.*

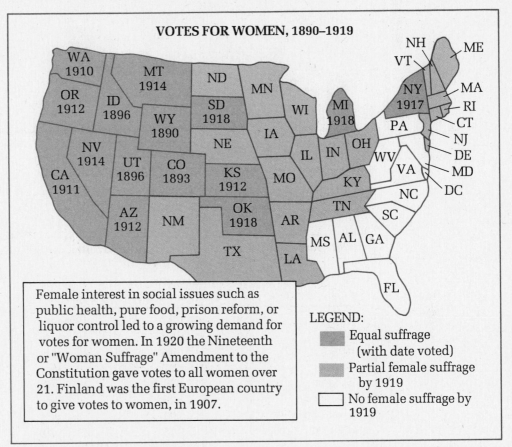

From Martin Gilbert, *The American History Atlas* (New York: Macmillan Publishing Co., Inc., 1969).

7.  World War I helped create a climate that allowed passage of the women's suffrage amendment. Which of the following explains how that climate was created?

    **(1)** Most of those who voted on the amendment were women.
    **(2)** The war was looming on the horizon: it was practical to grant women the vote so that they could be drafted.
    **(3)** It's generally easier to pass amendments during wars.
    **(4)** Women's contributions to the war effort heightened respect for their impact on the nation's welfare.
    **(5)** The spirit of national unity, common during wars, made the time just right for the passage of the amendment.

8.  According to the map, did any of the 13 original states have equal suffrage by 1919? If so, which?

9.  What role did the states have in the process of adding the Nineteenth Amendment to the Constitution?

10. Two states are not represented on the map. Given the purpose of the map, why would it have been inappropriate to have shown them?

Answers are on page 275.

# Unit II Test

Item 1 is based on the following chart.

| Comparison of the Quality of Life in Different Countries | | | |
|---|---|---|---|
| | Per Capita Income per Person per Year | Life Expectancy | Infant Mortality |
| Bolivia | $ 933 | 49 years | 77 per 1,000 |
| China | $ 250 | 68 years | not available |
| East Germany | $ 5,945 | 72 years | 13 per 1,000 |
| Japan | $ 8,627 | 76 years | 16 per 1,000 |
| Sweden | $12,831 | 76 years | 8 per 1,000 |
| Taiwan | $ 1,826 | 72 years | 14 per 1,000 |
| United States | $11,596 | 73 years | 14 per 1,000 |
| Vietnam | $ 113 | 53 years | not available |
| Zaire | $ 224 | 46 years | 104 per 1,000 |

Source: Jack Abramowitz et al. *Economics and the American Free-Enterprise System* (New York: Globe Book Company, 1983), page 206.

1. Based on information in the chart, the soundest hypothesis is that there is a direct relationship between a country's

   (1) per capita income and life expectancy
   (2) per capita income and infant mortality rate
   (3) per capita income and birth rate
   (4) infant mortality rate and life expectancy
   (5) infant mortality and birth rate

Items 2 to 5 are based on the following passage.

Most of the fighting during the Civil War took place in the South, so life in the South, unlike that in the North, changed radically. Many Southerners fled their homes to get away from the fighting. Southern railroads, ports, and cities were destroyed. Richmond, the capital of the Confederacy, sustained serious damages. Atlanta was burned by Union troops. Food and clothing became extremely scarce.

Even greater changes were felt after the war. Because the South's economy had relied on slavery, the end of slavery in 1863 (by Lincoln's *Eman-*

*cipation Proclamation*) forced the South to find new ways to live and work. Many large plantations were divided and sold as small farms. Some plantation owners held on to their land, seeds, and sometimes tools and workhorses. The sharecroppers planted and harvested the crops, which were later divided, often unequally, between the landowner and the sharecropper.

Adapted from Kenneth Uva and Shelley Uva. *The United States in the Making*, volume 2. (New York: Globe Book Company, 1986), page 95.

2. The point of the passage is that the Civil War's greatest effects were felt
   **(1)** during the war  **(4)** in the South's economy
   **(2)** in cities  **(5)** by plantation owners
   **(3)** in the North

3. Which of the following headlines might have appeared in a Southern newspaper shortly after the Civil War?
   **(1)** Sharecroppers Buy Up Plantations
   **(2)** Sharecroppers Keep Plantations Going
   **(3)** Small Farms Replace Plantations
   **(4)** Plantation System Unchanged
   **(5)** Plantations Gone Forever

4. Why were there shortages of food and clothing in the South during the Civil War?

5. What was the relationship between the *Emancipation Proclamation* and the introduction of sharecropping?

---

6. A "victimless crime" is defined as the willing exchange of illegal goods or services between adults. Illegal gambling and prostitution are victimless crimes by that definition.

   Which one of the following could be considered a victimless crime?
   **(1)** burglary  **(4)** arson
   **(2)** selling illegal drugs  **(5)** embezzlement
   **(3)** auto theft

7. Few economies are purely capitalistic or socialist. In many capitalist countries there is government ownership of certain large industries. Some socialist countries permit some private ownership of property.

   The passage implies that
   **(1)** in a pure capitalist economy, all industry is privately owned
   **(2)** in a pure capitalist economy, there is some private ownership of property
   **(3)** in a pure socialist economy, all property is privately owned
   **(4)** in a pure socialist economy, most industry is privately owned
   **(5)** in pure capitalist and socialist economies, the government owns large industries

*Items 8 to 10 are based on the following chart.*

| The Separation of Power in the Federal Government | | |
|---|---|---|
| Executive Branch | Judicial Branch | Legislative Branch |
| Enforces the law. President is commander in chief of the armed forces. President appoints ambassadors, cabinet members, federal judges. President makes treaties with foreign nations. President has the power to pardon people for crimes. President can veto bills. | Interprets the law and the Constitution. Federal courts handle cases involving federal laws, treaties with foreign nations, the U.S. government, and foreign ambassadors. Supreme Court can declare a law unconstitutional. Supreme Court can declare a presidential act unconstitutional. | Makes laws. Regulates trade between states and with foreign countries and Indian tribes. May raise an army, navy, air force. May impeach and convict any federal official. Senate must approve the president's appointments. Senate must approve treaties. |

Based on Kenneth Uva and Shelley Uva, *The United States in the Making*, vol. 2 (New York: Globe Book Company, 1986), page 17.

8. Which two powers named in the chart most clearly demonstrate that no president is above the law?

9. According to the chart, who has the last word about laws in the United States?

   (1) the president
   (2) federal courts
   (3) the Supreme Court
   (4) Congress
   (5) the Senate

10. How does the distribution of powers with regard to treaties demonstrate the benefits of checks and balances?

*Items 11 and 12 are based on the following chart.*

| U.S. Immigration by Decades | | | | | |
|---|---|---|---|---|---|
| Years | Immigrants | Years | Immigrants | Years | Immigrants |
| 1820–1829 | 128,502 | 1870–1879 | 2,742,287 | 1920–1929 | 4,295,510 |
| 1830–1839 | 538,381 | 1880–1889 | 5,248,568 | 1930–1939 | 699,375 |
| 1840–1849 | 1,427,337 | 1890–1899 | 3,694,294 | 1940–1949 | 856,608 |
| 1850–1859 | 2,814,554 | 1900–1909 | 8,202,388 | 1950–1959 | 2,499,268 |
| 1860–1869 | 2,081,261 | 1910–1919 | 6,347,380 | 1960–1969 | 3,213,749 |

*Source:* Kenneth Uva and Shelley Uva, *The United States in the Making*, vol. 2 (New York: Globe Book Company, 1986), page 35.

11. The best hypothesis that information in the chart supports is that the Civil War caused the trend in United States immigration to

    **(1)** increase
    **(2)** continue
    **(3)** stop
    **(4)** slow
    **(5)** reverse

12. The National Origins Plan went into effect the same year the Depression began. One goal of the plan was exceeded by the effects the Depression had on immigration rates. What goal was that?

*Item 13 is based on the following quote.*

We the people of the United States, in order to form a more perfect Union, establish justice, insure domestic tranquility, provide for the common defense, promote the general welfare, and secure the blessings of liberty to ourselves and our posterity, do ordain and establish this Constitution for the United States of America.

—Preamble to the Constitution

13. The Preamble cites six reasons for the establishment of the Constitution. Which one best emphasizes that the Constitution was designed to establish a nation rather than a confederation of states?

*Items 14 to 16 are based on the following material.*

Each year millions of people in developing countries starve. In developed countries, people suffer the effects of overeating. The following table compares rates of food intake.

| **Average Person's Daily Intake** | | |
|---|---|---|
| | Developed Countries | Developing Countries |
| Calories (C) | 1.5 C | C |
| Protein (P) | 2P | P |
| Food* (F) | 3F | F |
| * Counts grain fed to livestock. | | |

From *GAIA: An Atlas of Planet Management* (New York: Anchor Press/Doubleday, 1984), pages 48–49. Used with permission.

The table shows, for example, that an average person in a developed country gets one and one-half times the calories every day that an average person in a developing country gets.

The diets of more than one-tenth of the world's population (500 million) cannot sustain a person's health or body weight. Most of the people whose diets are so poor live in Asia; about one-third live in Africa and in Latin America.

14. Five questions follow. If there is enough information in the passage to help you answer any question, answer it. If there is not enough information, write "Not enough information."

    (a) What is the approximate population of the world?
    (b) What is the approximate population of the developing countries in the world?
    (c) What is the minimum amount of food a person must eat in order to stay healthy?
    (d) How many more calories does an average person in a developing country get per day than an average person whose diet cannot sustain health?
    (e) Ounce for ounce of grain consumed, is the average diet in a developing country richer in protein than the average diet in a developed country?

15. A person who regularly eats less than the minimum critical diet is most likely to live in which of the following countries?

    (1) Cambodia
    (2) Iceland
    (3) Nicaragua
    (4) Ethiopia
    (5) Bolivia

16. Which one of the following statements is best supported by information given in the passage?

    (1) Starvation rates are increasing every year.
    (2) People in developed countries eat more meat than people in developing countries.
    (3) People have healthier diets in North America than in Europe.
    (4) Hunger is greatest where populations are largest.
    (5) Cattle in the developed world eat more than people in the developing world.

Items 17 to 19 are based on the maps on the next page.

17. Most of one area of today's United States was under continuous British control from 1689 to 1763. Which area is that?

    (1) the Northwest
    (2) the West Coast
    (3) the Midwest
    (4) the South
    (5) the East Coast

18. Under the *Treaty of Paris*, France lost all its colonial power in North America. The map for which year shows North America after that treaty?

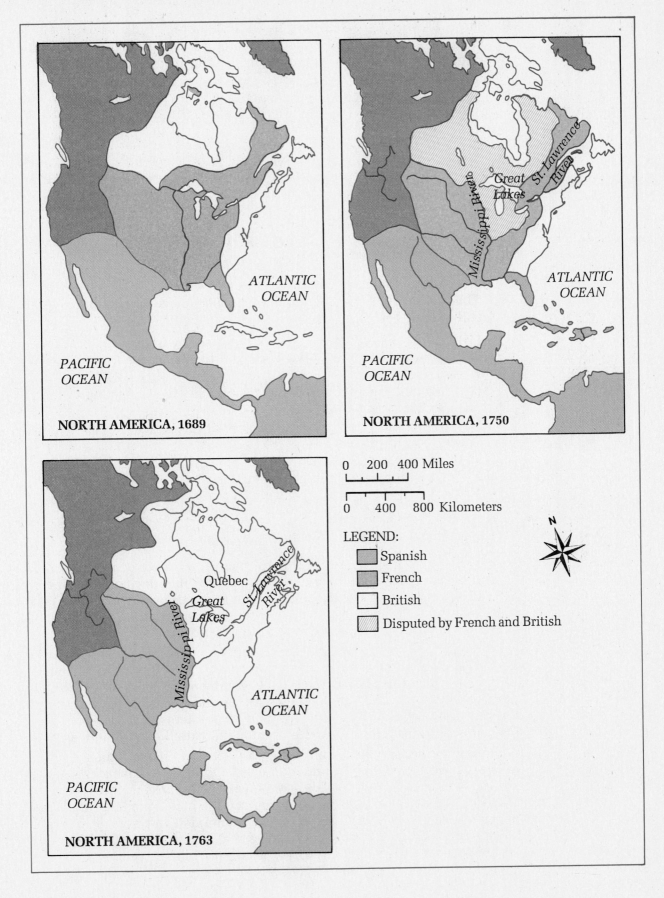

**NORTH AMERICA, 1689**

**NORTH AMERICA, 1750**

Great Lakes

St. Lawrence River

Mississippi River

ATLANTIC OCEAN

PACIFIC OCEAN

**NORTH AMERICA, 1763**

Quebec

Great Lakes

St. Lawrence River

Mississippi River

ATLANTIC OCEAN

PACIFIC OCEAN

0   200   400 Miles

0   400   800 Kilometers

LEGEND:

Spanish

French

British

Disputed by French and British

**19.** In 1732 King George II gave James Oglethorpe a charter to establish Georgia as the last of the thirteen colonies. One reason it was established was to serve as the king's only military outpost against the

  **(1)** French
  **(2)** Spanish
  **(3)** British
  **(4)** Indians
  **(5)** colonists

Item 20 is based on the following quote.

Congress shall make no law respecting an establishment of religion, or prohibiting the free exercise thereof. . . .

—First Amendment to the Constitution

**20.** The portion of the First Amendment quoted above was included in the Bill of Rights to

  **(1)** encourage people to be religious in their own ways
  **(2)** allow people to take tax deductions for donations to religious organizations
  **(3)** prevent the government from making any laws affecting religious organizations
  **(4)** prevent the government from supporting or restricting religious expression
  **(5)** increase the amount of freedom people have by allowing them to choose from many different religions

Items 21 to 25 are based on the following passage.

Before the stock market crash of 1929, many American economists held conservative, laissez-faire theories. They believed that during times of economic depression, businesses should be left on their own to find ways back to prosperity. A proposed "way back" was to lower prices to increase consumer demand for goods.

When the stock market crashed, spurring worldwide depression, the laissez-faire approach did not create prosperity. John Maynard Keynes, a British economist, proposed ways for governments to provide the buying power that would spark economic growth: establish work programs for the unemployed, welfare aid for the needy, and low-interest loans for homebuyers and businesses. The United States adopted many Keynesian ideas.

Some conservative economists oppose the Keynesian approach. They argue that government programs cause inflation and hold back business growth. A program of supply-side economics they propose requires reducing the influence of government and cutting taxes. They argue that large-scale tax cuts encourage savings and investment, stimulate business growth, and balance the federal budget. They believe that improvement in the overall economy eventually helps the poor, to whom public welfare assistance should be more sparing than Keynesians advocate.

21. With the benefit of the unemployed in mind, a liberal economist would most likely agree with

    **(1)** tax increases to support public assistance
    **(2)** tax reductions to stimulate business growth
    **(3)** tax increases to slow big business growth
    **(4)** tax reductions to encourage private saving
    **(5)** tax increases to balance the federal budget

22. A supply-side economist would be likely to support all of the following items EXCEPT

    **(1)** a cut in federal income taxes
    **(2)** an amendment to the Constitution calling for a balanced federal budget
    **(3)** an increase in savings and investment by private citizens
    **(4)** an increase in loans to businesses
    **(5)** a cut in social welfare programs

23. Would a supply-side economist favor airline deregulation? Explain.

24. Supply-side economic theories became popular during the 1980s. Which one of the following is the most likely explanation for that?

    **(1)** Keynesian economics had gone out of date.
    **(2)** Government influence on the economy had been decreasing.
    **(3)** Inflation had been a major economic factor in the 1970s.
    **(4)** Most people dislike paying taxes.
    **(5)** Keynesian economics had led to a business boom.

25. Supply-side economists believe their theories benefit the poor. Which of the following goals of supply-side theory best argues for that belief?

    **(1)** encourage saving
    **(2)** encourage investment
    **(3)** stimulate business growth
    **(4)** balance the federal budget
    **(5)** reduce public welfare assistance

*Item 26* is based on the following passage.

United States Senators are elected for six-year terms. About a third of the Senate is up for election every two years. In the 1986 election, 22 of the 34 seats up for vote had been held by Republicans. Before the election, Republicans had held 53 Senate seats.

26. In 1986, to maintain or gain the majority of seats in the Senate, which party needed to win more state elections?

Items 27 and 28 refer to the following maps.

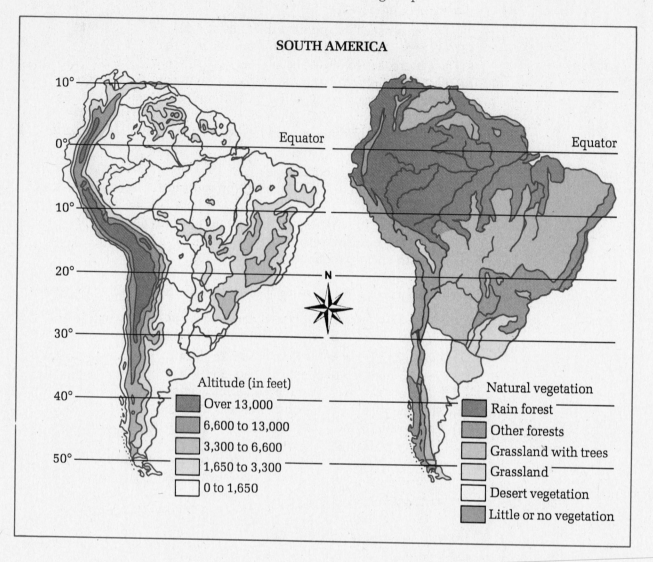

**SOUTH AMERICA**

27. Typically, equatorial areas are covered with dense jungle. What accounts for the large areas of sparse foliage in the tropical and subtropical regions of South America?

28. Most of the continental United States lies between 30°N and 50°N. What conclusions can be drawn about the dominant climate and the seasons of the portion of South America south of 30°S?

Items 29 to 32 refer to the following information.

Every culture is made up of layers of organized standards or patterns for behavior. The smallest elements of behavior are parts of larger patterns for behavior. Five terms sociologists use to classify cultural behavior patterns are listed and defined on the following page.

**(1) trait:** The smallest material or nonmaterial element in a culture. Material elements include electric appliances and fast food in United States culture. Nonmaterial elements include symbols, such as a green traffic light that means "go," and ideas, such as the idea that social mobility is desirable.

**(2) complex:** A combination of several traits that comprise a cluster of standards for correct behavior. The many material and nonmaterial elements that make up a cultural pattern of behavior after a person's death form a complex.

**(3) institution:** Several complexes that combine together to meet a particular cultural need. The family, for example, is an institution made up of such complexes as those for parenting and for maintaining appropriate relationships with members of the extended family.

**(4) role:** The pattern of behavior expected or required of a person who occupies a particular position in an institution or in society. In families, for example, parental roles are different from children's roles.

**(5) subculture:** Within a large, complex society, there is a smaller, self-contained set of behavior patterns. Immigrant, occupational, and religious groups are subcultures that have distinctive behaviors that are more or less compatible with behaviors appropriate in the broader culture.

In each of the following items, there is a description of a behavior or situation that can be classified by one of the sociological terms defined. Choose the term that best labels each description. The terms may be used more than once, but no one item has more than one correct answer.

29. In the United States the influence of religion is apparent in many sectors of the culture. "Blue laws," court oaths, the Pledge of Allegiance, the legality of weddings performed by clergy, and some national holidays are all products of religious influence. Religion is an example of a(n)

    **(1)** trait
    **(2)** complex
    **(3)** institution
    **(4)** role
    **(5)** subculture

30. In Borneo, in an Iban wedding ceremony, the man and woman are recognized as married after a chicken is waved over their heads. In that society, waving the chicken is an example of a(n)

    **(1)** trait
    **(2)** complex
    **(3)** institution
    **(4)** role
    **(5)** subculture

31. A shop steward wants to improve his chances for promotion to supervisor. With his wife's support he takes courses to prepare himself for the GED. In different situations, this man (a) represents a group of workers, (b) studies under a teacher's guidance, and (c) participates in the life of a family. Each of his activities is an example of a(n)

    **(1)** trait
    **(2)** complex
    **(3)** institution
    **(4)** role
    **(5)** subculture

32. In the United States, when a couple who are not engaged elope, their behavior is different from the behavior that is normal in their society. The norm they depart is an example of a(n)

    **(1)** trait
    **(2)** complex
    **(3)** institution
    **(4)** role
    **(5)** subculture

Answers are on pages 275–277.

# Performance Analysis Chart

**Directions:** Circle the number of each item that you got correct on the Unit II Test. Count how many items you got correct in each row; count how many items you got correct in each column. Write the amount correct per row and column as the numerator in the fraction in the appropriate "Total Correct" box. (The denominators represent the total number of items in the row or column.) Write the grand total correct over the denominator, **32,** at the lower right corner of the chart. (For example, if you got 28 items correct, write 28 so that the fraction reads *28*/**32**.) Item numbers in color represent items based on graphic material.

| Item Type | History (page 85) | Geography (page 103) | Economics (page 112) | Political Science (page 125) | Behavioral Science (page 137) | TOTAL CORRECT |
|---|---|---|---|---|---|---|
| Comprehension (page 34) | 2, 3 | 17 | 7 | | | /4 |
| Application (page 43) | | 15, 27, 28 | 22, 23 | | 6, 29, 30, 31, 32 | /10 |
| Analysis (page 51) | 4, 5, 12, 18, 19 | | 21 | 9, 26 | 1 | /9 |
| Evaluation (page 61) | 11 | 14, 16 | 24, 25 | 8, 10, 13, 20 | | /9 |
| TOTAL CORRECT | /8 | /6 | /6 | /6 | /6 | /32 |

The page numbers in parentheses indicate where in this book you can find the beginning of specific instruction about the various fields of social studies and about the types of questions you encountered in the Unit II Test.

# Practice

# Introduction

When a theater group is about to open a new play, they have something known as a "dress rehearsal." During the dress rehearsal, the actors and stagehands run through the play as if it were a real performance, even though there is no audience. The dress rehearsal allows the group to judge how ready they are to open the play to the public. It allows them to realize the parts of the play that succeed, and discover areas that may need further work. The activities in this GED Practice section will be your dress rehearsal. The scores do not really count, but you can benefit a great deal from them. And come GED "show time," you will be able to obtain your best possible score.

This section is filled with GED-like test questions, or *items*. It provides valuable practice on the kinds of items found on the Social Studies Test. Arranged in two groups, the practice makes it easy to apply your knowledge to items based on content areas in social studies, as well as to a collection of items structured like the actual test.

On the pages that follow, you will find:

- **Practice Items** This practice contains 64 simulated GED test items, grouped according to the branches of social studies covered on the test. For example, you will find history items grouped together, geography items grouped together, and so on.

- **Practice Test** This is a 64-item test structured like an actual Social Studies Test. The passages are *not* grouped together according to content. Rather, the content varies from item to item.

As on the actual Social Studies Test, all the questions are multiple choice. By completing the Practice Items and the Practice Test, you will discover your strong points and weak points in social studies. And if you discover any weak points, *don't worry*—you will be shown how to strengthen them. The answer key not only provides the correct answer to each practice question, but it also explains *why* each answer is correct. The Performance Analysis Chart following each practice will direct you to parts of the book where you can review the skills or subjects that give you trouble.

You can use the Practice Items and the Practice Test in a number of different ways. The introductions that precede the practices will provide you with choices for using them to best advantage. You may also wish to talk with your teacher to get suggestions about how best to make use of the Practice Items and Practice Test.

# Practice Items

These Practice Items are similar to the real Social Studies Test in many ways, but there is one major difference. The items that follow are grouped according to the branches of social studies: history, geography, economics, political science, and behavioral science. As you work on the Practice Items, you will focus on one branch at a time. (The actual Social Studies Test presents passages from the various branches in mixed order.)

The whole group of 64 Practice Items is the same length as an actual test; the items are as challenging as the actual test items. Your results will help you determine which skills you have mastered and which you should study further.

## Using the Practice Items to Best Advantage

You can use the Practice Items in the following ways:

- After you finish a chapter in Unit II, you can test your ability by completing the section of the Practice Items that corresponds to the same branch of social studies. You can save the Practice Items until you've completed all the chapters in Unit II. You can do the Practice Items one group at a time and then review the chapters for the areas in which you have difficulty.

- You can use the Practice Items as a practice test. To do this, complete the Practice Items in one sitting. Since the actual test allows you 85 minutes, you may want to time yourself. If 85 minutes elapse and you have not finished, circle the last question you answered, and then continue. This way, you can learn what score you'd earn within the time limit, as well as your total score counting the untimed portion of the practice. This will give you a rough idea of how you would perform on the actual Social Studies Test.

Keep an accurate record of your performance. Write your answers neatly on a sheet of paper, or use an answer sheet provided by your teacher.

### Using the Answer Key

The answer key can be a very helpful study tool. Compare your answers to the correct answers in the answer key beginning on page 278, and check each item you answered correctly. Whether you answer an item correctly or not, you should read the explanations of correct answers in the answer key. Doing this will reinforce your knowledge of social studies and develop your testtaking skills.

### How to Use Your Score

Regardless of how you use these Practice Items, you will gain valuable experience with GED-type questions. After scoring your work with the answer key, fill in the Performance Analysis Chart on page 202. The chart will help you determine which skills and areas you are strongest in, and direct you to parts of the book where you can review areas in which you need additional work.

# Practice Items

**Directions:** *Choose the one best answer to each question.*

### History Items

Item 1 refers to the following map.

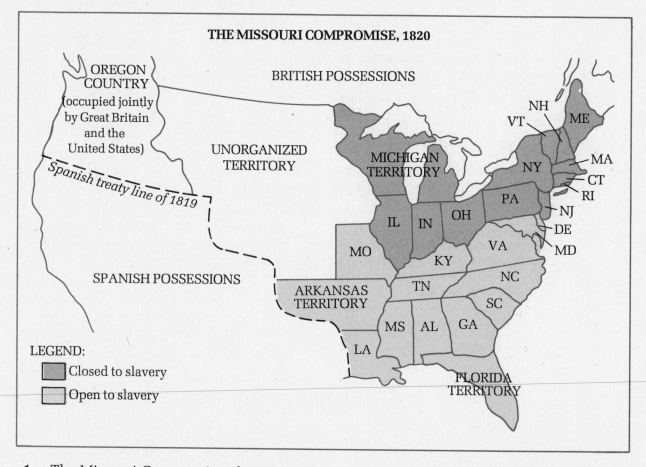

**THE MISSOURI COMPROMISE, 1820**

LEGEND:
- Closed to slavery
- Open to slavery

1. The Missouri Compromise of 1820 created two new states, Maine and Missouri. Maine became a free state, while Missouri became a slave state. Based on the information provided in the map, which of the following is the best explanation for the adoption of the Missouri Compromise?

   (1) It was the most convenient way to open the unorganized territories to new settlement.

   (2) It maintained the balance between slave states and free states, allowing neither to control Congress.

   (3) It divided the country between North and South, permitting separate federal legislation for each.

   (4) It protected citizens in the new state against hostile Indian tribes in the unorganized territories.

   (5) It pacified southerners who worried that the South would lose control of the Mississippi River.

*Items 2 to 4 refer to the following passage.*

During the 1950s and 1960s, numerous protests, legal decisions, political actions, mass marches, and government interventions brought an end to legal segregation in the United States. On December 1, 1955, Rosa Parks, a black woman, refused to give her seat to a white man on a bus in Montgomery, Alabama, and was arrested. In response to this event, blacks in Montgomery refused to use any buses. This boycott of the bus service led to an important decision by a federal court. The court ruled that a law that allowed buses to separate, or segregate, blacks and whites was not legal under the Constitution.

In 1957, President Eisenhower sent troops to Little Rock, Arkansas, to protect black students who were entering a high school that had been open only to white students. A previous decision by the U.S. Supreme Court had declared that segregated public schools were unconstitutional. In 1960, college students in Greensboro, North Carolina, began to protest segregation. In 1962, James Meredith became the first black to attend the University of Mississippi.

The civil rights movement received tremendous support on August 28, 1963, when 200,000 people came to Washington, D.C., to demand equal rights for blacks. On that day, Dr. Martin Luther King, Jr. delivered his famous "I have a dream" speech. The following year, the strongest civil rights bill in the history of the United States, the Civil Rights Bill of 1964, was signed into law.

**2.** According to the passage, which event touched off the movement to end racial segregation in the United States?

 **(1)** James Meredith's entry into the University of Mississippi
 **(2)** the Supreme Court's ruling to make segregated public schools illegal
 **(3)** President Eisenhower's decision to send troops to Little Rock, Arkansas
 **(4)** Rosa Parks's refusal to give up her seat on a bus in Montgomery, Alabama
 **(5)** Dr. Martin Luther King, Jr.'s "I have a dream" speech in Washington, D.C.

**3.** Which of the following best explains why the civil rights movement was successful in achieving the laws that were set forth by the Civil Rights Bill of 1964?

 **(1)** Dr. Martin Luther King, Jr.'s nonviolent actions convinced the southern whites to support civil rights.
 **(2)** College-student protests gathered the backing of students everywhere to support civil rights.
 **(3)** The United States Constitution guarantees equal rights for all.
 **(4)** The national attention that was received by the march on Washington, D.C., raised American consciousness.
 **(5)** The Supreme Court ruled in 1954 that segregation in public schools denied equality to blacks.

**4.** Court decisions on the civil rights cases that are mentioned in the passage were most likely based on which of the following amendments?

 **(1)** the First Amendment, which guarantees freedom of speech, press, and religion
 **(2)** the Tenth Amendment, which guarantees to the states all rights that are not prohibited by the federal government
 **(3)** the Eleventh Amendment, which declares that no state shall be sued in a federal court by another state
 **(4)** the Thirteenth Amendment, which abolished slavery in the United States
 **(5)** the Fourteenth Amendment, which prevents states from denying equal protection of the laws to any person

**5.** In 1986, two authoritarian national leaders left office under duress. One was Jean-Claude Duvalier, the "President for Life" of Haiti. The other was Ferdinand Marcos, president of the Philippines for twenty years. In both countries, there was widespread poverty and government corruption. Both leaders had been accused of stealing millions from their countries.

Which of the following statements would make the best newspaper headline for this passage?

(1) Duvalier flees Haiti
(2) Marcos accused of theft of millions
(3) Great poverty in Haiti and the Philippines
(4) Marcos and Duvalier leave office
(5) Corruption common in Haiti and the Philippines

Brooks in The Birmingham News

"First things first!"

*Items 6 and 7 refer to the following illustration and text.*

The *Great Society* refers to a set of social programs that were designed by President Johnson and that were intended to end poverty and racism, to eradicate disease, to rebuild cities, to banish ignorance, and generally to live in harmony and abundance.

**6.** Based on the illustration, which of the following statements best describes the economic impact of the Vietnam War on the Great Society in the 1960s?

(1) American taxpayers were reluctant to spend more money on the war in Vietnam.

(2) President Johnson's Great Society had proved to be too expensive to support.

(3) The gas shortage was made worse by the need to supply the U.S. troops in Vietnam.

(4) Great Society programs were deprived of funds by the expense of the Vietnam War.

(5) The war caused a recession, which made it impossible to provide funds for domestic programs.

**7.** Which of the following statements is NOT supported by the illustration?

(1) President Johnson was compelled to spend money on the Vietnam War that would have been spent on the Great Society.

(2) President Johnson's roles included head of the armed forces and domestic-programs legislator.

(3) Foreign-policy programs had a higher priority in the Johnson administration than domestic programs did.

(4) Funds for the war and for domestic programs were drawn from the same budget.

(5) More money was spent to achieve military aims than to improve social conditions.

*Item 8 refers to the following map.*

**8.** Based on the map, which of the following was the most likely benefit of the Panama Canal when it was built in 1914?

(1) It became cheaper to ship fruit and other produce from the west coast to the east coast.

(2) It opened new territories for American exploration and colonization.

(3) It increased U.S. trade with the countries of South America.

(4) It removed any obstacles to U.S. conquest of the Pacific Islands.

(5) It reduced the navy's difficulties in protecting U.S. coastal waters.

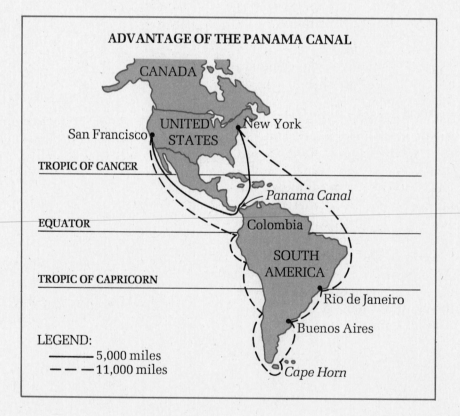

ADVANTAGE OF THE PANAMA CANAL

*Items 9 to 11 refer to the following passage.*

Before 1776, the Americans had been slow to settle the interior, which they called the "back-country." After 1800, the "back-country" became
"frontier" in American speech, and the line of
settlement advanced westward with astonishing
speed. By its conventional definition, the "frontier" is commonly understood to be the outer edge
of the area with a population density of at least
two persons per square mile. Before 1783 that line
was still largely east of the Appalachian Mountains except for a small settlement on the dark
and bloody ground of Kentucky. Thirty years later,
the great center of the continent was occupied. By
1820 the frontier had crossed the Mississippi.
And by 1840, it had reached the 100th meridian.
The plains beyond were subdued after 1865 with
the aid of a new technology—the steel plough, the
six-shooter, and the barbed-wire fence. After the
census of 1890, the superintendent of the census
observed that for the first time in American history, a single frontier line was no longer visible
on his map. The frontier, in that sense, had come
to an end.

From Geoffrey Barraclough, ed., *The Times Atlas of World
History*, New York: Hammond, 1984, with permission.

**9.** Which of the following statements
about the United States before 1800 is
implied by the passage?

(1) The population was moving steadily westward.
(2) The population density was less
than two persons per square mile.
(3) Most Americans lived on or near
the eastern seaboard.
(4) The steel plough was used only in
the East.
(5) Most Americans lived in the "back-
country."

**10.** Based on information that is provided
in the passage, which of the following
was the "frontier"?

(1) New York in 1776
(2) California in 1783
(3) Kentucky in 1800
(4) Kansas in 1820
(5) Oregon in 1890

**11.** Which of the following statements is
supported by information that is provided in the passage?

(1) The myth of the frontier has become
very important in American society
and consciousness.
(2) Unlike many colonial nations, the
United States was fortunate to have
an internal empire to conquer.
(3) After 1890, the frontier line extended in the Pacific to Hawaii and
in the north to Alaska.
(4) The frontier advanced by pushing
back the Native American tribes
that it encountered.
(5) Improved agricultural tools were a
cause of the frontier's rapid advancement.

**12.** As the United States expanded westward in the early nineteenth century,
Americans felt that their country was
destined to reach its natural boundary—the Pacific Ocean. This belief
came to be called *manifest destiny*.
Based on this information, which of the
following is an action that was motivated by manifest destiny?

(1) the division of Oregon with Britain
in 1846
(2) the declaration of war against Mexico in 1846
(3) the purchase of California from
Mexico in 1848
(4) the California gold rush in 1849
(5) the annexation of Hawaii in 1898

*Items 13 to 16 refer to the following passage.*

On June 17, 1972, five men were arrested at the offices of the Democratic Party's National Headquarters in Washington, D.C. The offices were located in a hotel called the Watergate. The men, who were trying to steal private papers, all had connections to the White House.

President Richard Nixon denied knowledge of the Watergate crime, but newspaper reporters began to uncover proof that some of the White House staff members were involved in the attempted burglary. Other administration officials also denied participation, but further investigations implicated them in the use of secret funds and wiretapping as well.

In July of 1973, it was discovered that President Nixon held secret tape recordings of conversations in the White House that concerned the Watergate scandal. President Nixon refused to turn over the tapes to the courts as he felt it was his right to withhold them. The Supreme Court ruled against the president.

The Judiciary Committee of the House of Representatives began impeachment hearings, and in July 1974 the committee recommended impeachment. On August 5, 1974, President Nixon released the tapes that proved his involvement with Watergate and then resigned on August 9, 1974.

**13.** Many of those connected to the Watergate scandal were charged and tried by jury. With which of the following crimes are they LEAST likely to have been charged?

(1) burglary
(2) treason
(3) fraud
(4) obstructing justice
(5) lying to a grand jury

**14.** Based on information that is provided in the passage, which of the following relationships is most similar to that of President Nixon to the Watergate scandal?

(1) President Hoover and the stock-market crash
(2) President Roosevelt and the New Deal

(3) President Kennedy and the Bay-of-Pigs invasion
(4) President Carter and the Iranian Hostage Crisis
(5) President Reagan and the Iran-Contra Affair

**15.** Which of the following statements is best supported by the Supreme Court decision regarding the tape recordings?

(1) The Supreme Court believed that President Nixon was guilty of a crime.
(2) President Nixon was required by law to prove his innocence before the Supreme Court.
(3) The Supreme Court may suspend the president's constitutional rights.
(4) The president of the United States has the right to take the Fifth Amendment.
(5) The office of the president is not above the law.

**16.** Which of the following best explains why the Judiciary Committee recommended the president's impeachment?

(1) It is illegal for the president to record conversations in the White House.
(2) The president was a proven accomplice in the attempted burglary.
(3) It is illegal to harbor or to protect known criminals.
(4) The president knowingly interfered with the course of justice.
(5) The president had incriminated himself by illegal wiretapping.

*Item 17 refers to the following graph.*

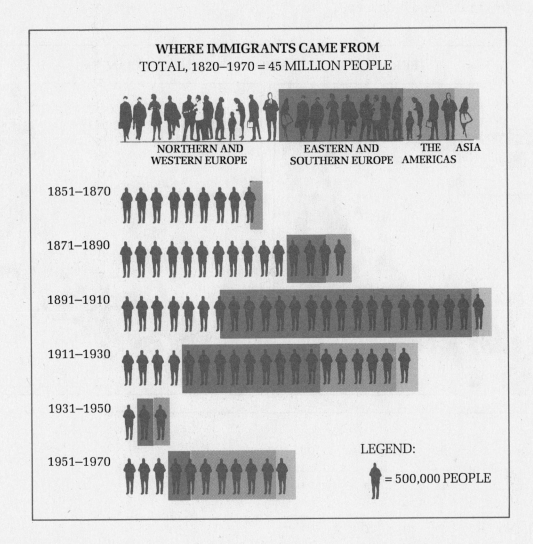

**WHERE IMMIGRANTS CAME FROM**
TOTAL, 1820–1970 = 45 MILLION PEOPLE

NORTHERN AND WESTERN EUROPE    EASTERN AND SOUTHERN EUROPE    THE AMERICAS    ASIA

1851–1870

1871–1890

1891–1910

1911–1930

1931–1950

1951–1970

LEGEND:

= 500,000 PEOPLE

**17.** Based on information that is provided in the graph, which of the following immigrants to the United States would you be least likely to find?

**(1)** a German in 1860
**(2)** an Italian in 1900
**(3)** a Mexican in 1925
**(4)** a Russian in 1954
**(5)** a Canadian in 1965

## Geography Items

*Item 18* refers to the following maps.

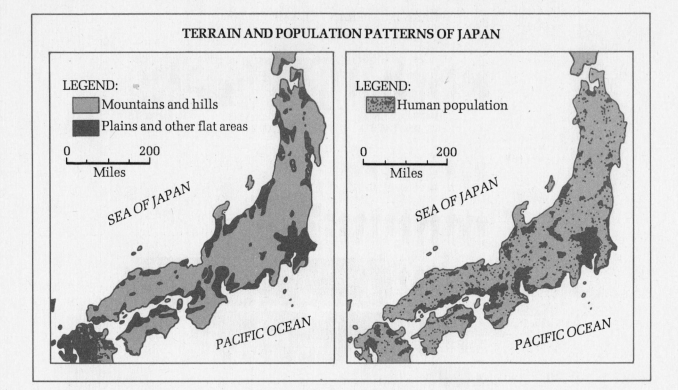

**TERRAIN AND POPULATION PATTERNS OF JAPAN**

LEGEND:
Mountains and hills
Plains and other flat areas
0    200
Miles
SEA OF JAPAN
PACIFIC OCEAN

LEGEND:
Human population
0    200
Miles
SEA OF JAPAN
PACIFIC OCEAN

**18.** Based on the information that is provided in the maps, which of the following is an explanation for the population distribution in Japan?

**(1)** No large urban population is more than 100 miles from another.

**(2)** The south is more densely populated than the north.

**(3)** The population is most dense on the Pacific coast.

**(4)** The population is concentrated where the farming is easiest.

**(5)** The mountains separate one part of the country from the other.

*Items 19 and 20* refer to the following passage.

Humankind has had a great impact on the landscape. Through urbanization, forest clearance, irrigation, agricultural terracing, mining and land reclamation, we have altered our environment in many astounding ways, not all of them for the good. While once-arid deserts have been made to bloom with fruits and vegetables, much natural beauty and wildlife has been lost to industrial expansion and pollution. As the world's population continues to grow—and its needs to increase—the necessity for careful environmental control becomes more and more apparent. Fortunately, modern science enables us to monitor almost every aspect of environmental change and either to avoid potential problems or to plan for their solution.

**19.** Which of the following statements is the most accurate summary of humankind's relationship to the environment?

   **(1)** The landscape is easily altered to suit our purposes.
   **(2)** We must be cautious in the ways in which we change the environment.
   **(3)** Humanity must forge ahead in its conquest of nature.
   **(4)** Industry has destroyed the environment and must be stopped.
   **(5)** Natural resources have recently become dangerously scarce.

**20.** An action that is based upon which of the following statements would be opposite in effect to that prescribed by the passage?

   **(1)** In order to continue growing and prospering, humanity must make use of the resources that are available to it.
   **(2)** The beauty of nature is a gift that we have inherited from our forebears, and we must try to use it wisely.
   **(3)** Industry is the most important of humankind's activities, and nothing should be done to hinder its efficiency.
   **(4)** The world's population can be decreased by cutting back on our use of natural resources.
   **(5)** The deserts are growing larger by the year, and we must take action to halt the process.

Items 21 to 23 refer to the following model.

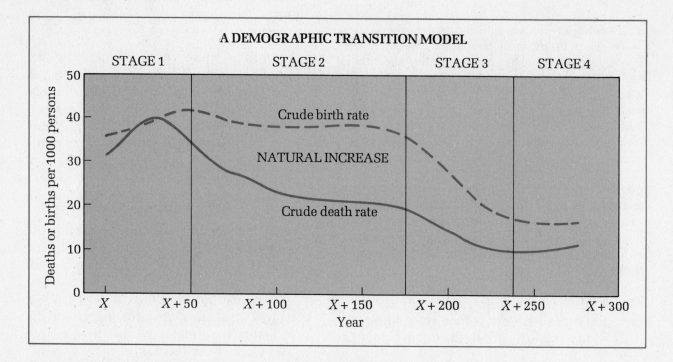

The model above illustrates the evolution of a typical society from an agrarian economy to an urban-industrial one. This transition, where *Year X* marks the beginnings of change, can be documented in terms of mortality and fertility rates, and their relationship to each other.

**21.** Which of the following stages will be marked by a high rate of population growth?

    **(1)** Stage 1
    **(2)** Stage 2
    **(3)** Stage 3
    **(4)** Stages 3 and 4
    **(5)** Stages 1 and 4

**22.** A country that is in Stage 4 is most likely to be one in which

    **(1)** health services are strong and family planning is encouraged

    **(2)** large families are regarded as status symbols

    **(3)** health services have been disrupted by civil wars

    **(4)** religious laws discourage the use of family planning

    **(5)** medical facilities and family planning are only for the rich

**23.** A possible conclusion to be drawn from the data that is provided in the model is that

    **(1)** if the birth rate exceeds the death rate, population growth will increase

    **(2)** the population will grow when the death rate is below 30 per 1,000

    **(3)** a change in the death rate is affected by a change in the birth rate

    **(4)** the birth rate must exceed the death rate for the population to grow

    **(5)** it will require more than 250 years for any signs of change to become apparent

---

**24.** Climate, or the weather in a given place during a period of time, is ultimately determined by a number of factors. Two of the most important factors are a region's proximity to, or distance from, the equator and its proximity to the ocean.

On the basis of this information, which of the following American cities should have similar climates?

    **(1)** New Orleans and Salt Lake City

    **(2)** Seattle and San Francisco

    **(3)** Kansas City and Boston

    **(4)** Chicago and Detroit

    **(5)** Washington, D.C., and Miami

*Items 25 and 26 refer to the following map.*

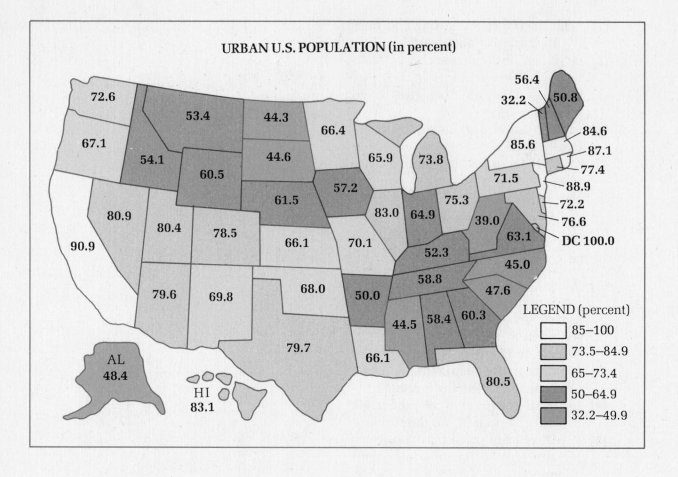

**URBAN U.S. POPULATION (in percent)**

LEGEND (percent)
- 85–100
- 73.5–84.9
- 65–73.4
- 50–64.9
- 32.2–49.9

**25.** Based on this map, which of the following states are the most urbanized?

  **(1)** the New England states
  **(2)** the Southwestern states
  **(3)** the noncontinental states
  **(4)** the Southeastern states
  **(5)** the North Central states

**26.** For which of the following applications would the data that is given in the map be adequate?

  **(1)** to calculate the total percent of urban population for the United States
  **(2)** to estimate the number of people per state who reside in urban areas
  **(3)** to rank all the states in order of urbanization
  **(4)** to determine whether urbanization patterns across the states relate to the presence of industry
  **(5)** to predict changes in U.S. urban population percents

## Economics Items

Item 27 refers to the following graph.

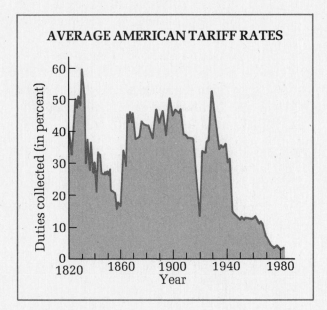

**AVERAGE AMERICAN TARIFF RATES**

Items 28 and 29 refer to the following passage.

A *balance of trade* exists when the percent of goods that are exported to other nations is approximately equal to the percent of goods that are imported from other countries. A trade deficit occurs when the percent of imports is greater than the percent of exports. At present, the United States has a trade deficit.

Many factors affect the balance of trade. For example, a strong currency has more buying power; therefore, a country that has a strong currency tends to import more from countries that have weak currencies. When a country is at war, domestic industries are employed in defense production, and more manufactured goods and raw materials may be needed from other countries. In times of economic depression, fewer goods are imported. Inflation may also affect the balance of trade because it raises production costs and weakens the currency.

27. Based on information provided in the graph, which of the following statements about tariff rates is true?

    (1) Tariff rates steadily declined during the Civil War.
    (2) The Great Depression was marked by low tariffs.
    (3) Tariff rates plummeted during World War I.
    (4) The Nixon administration imposed heavy tariffs.
    (5) Tariff rates have remained steady since World War II.

28. Based on the passage, which of the following strategies would be most helpful toward the elimination of the U.S. trade deficit?

    (1) increasing the production of domestic goods
    (2) raising tariffs on imported goods
    (3) lowering the value of the dollar
    (4) increasing the defense budget
    (5) reducing inflation

29. A manufacturer in the United States wishes to increase its sales in France. Based on information that is provided in the passage, which of the following situations would be most favorable to the manufacturer's achievement of its goals?

    (1) The United States experiences a depression.
    (2) U.S. import tariffs are raised.
    (3) The French economy is currently inflated.
    (4) The franc is strong compared to the dollar.
    (5) The U.S. economy is currently inflated.

**30.** A *mixed economy* is one in which private ownership and government ownership of industries exist side by side. The United States, for instance, has a capitalist economy in which private enterprise is the guiding principle; yet, the government owns and runs many industries, such as the postal service. Likewise, in many socialist countries, a good deal of property is privately owned.

Based on the passage, which of the following best describes a country that has a mixed economy?

(1) The government does not regulate business.
(2) All property is owned by the government.
(3) The government runs only the postal service.
(4) The government owns large industries, but private citizens own small businesses.
(5) Business and property are owned by both the government and private citizens.

*Item 31 refers to the graph below.*

**31.** In a time of economic inflation, the federal government decides to lower prices in an area of the economy that most affects the budget of the average wage earner. Which of the following government agencies would most likely be chosen to lower prices in the area of the economy under its control?

(1) the Department of Energy
(2) the Department of Agriculture
(3) the Department of Transportation
(4) the Department of Health, Education, and Welfare
(5) the National Parks Service

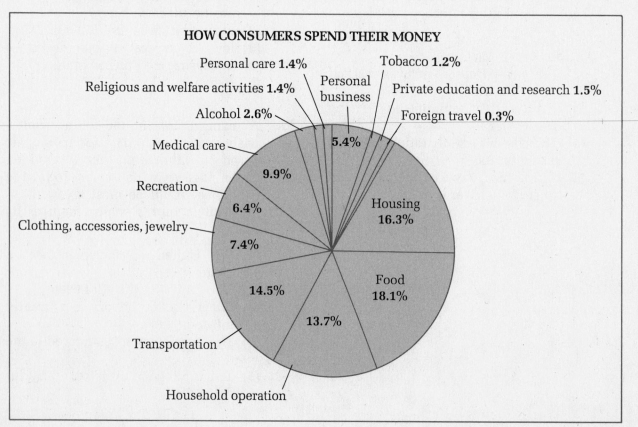

**HOW CONSUMERS SPEND THEIR MONEY**

Personal care **1.4%**
Tobacco **1.2%**
Religious and welfare activities **1.4%**
Personal business
Private education and research **1.5%**
Alcohol **2.6%**
Foreign travel **0.3%**
Medical care
**5.4%**
**9.9%**
Recreation
Housing **16.3%**
**6.4%**
Clothing, accessories, jewelry
**7.4%**
Food **18.1%**
**14.5%**
**13.7%**
Transportation
Household operation

*Items 32 and 33 refer to the following graph.*

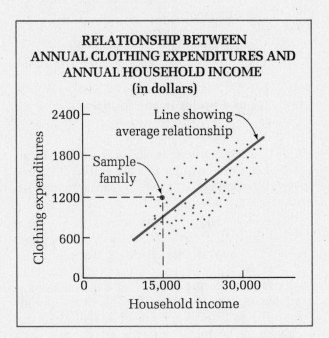

**RELATIONSHIP BETWEEN
ANNUAL CLOTHING EXPENDITURES AND
ANNUAL HOUSEHOLD INCOME
(in dollars)**

Clothing expenditures

Line showing average relationship

Sample family

Household income

**32.** Based on information that is provided in the graph, which of the following statements about the sample family is true?

(1) The family's annual household income is less than the average.

(2) They spend more on clothing than an average family of the same income.

(3) The family's annual household income is more than the average.

(4) Their clothing expenses are half those of a family whose income is $30,000.

(5) The family is average in terms of annual clothing expenditures.

**33.** Which of the following statements is supported by information that is provided in the graph?

(1) A family's annual clothing expenditure can be predicted based on its annual income.

(2) A household that has two wage earners will spend twice as much on clothing as a household that has one wage earner.

(3) Annual clothing expenditure is determined not only by a household's income, but also by the number of people that it comprises.

(4) The average expenditure of clothing increases at a constant rate that is proportional to income level.

(5) An average household does not spend more than it can afford on clothing.

Items 34 and 35 refer to the following passage.

The federal government has several means of intervening in the economy to assist vital or troubled industries, as well as, in many cases, unemployed workers or economically depressed regions. A *tax incentive* aids an industry by lowering, eliminating, or deferring certain taxes. A *subsidy* is a direct payment or credit given to a company or an industry. A new method has been proposed, in which the government could insure loans from private institutions, which may otherwise be reluctant to invest in risky projects.

**34.** Which of the following situations is an example of government subsidy?

  **(1)** A hotel that is built in a depressed rural area in 1987 pays 10 percent of its property tax in 1987, 40 percent in 1990, and 100 percent in 2000.

  **(2)** A steel mill in Pennsylvania does not pay sales tax on newly purchased processing equipment.

  **(3)** An auto plant in Michigan obtains a federal grant to train displaced steelworkers for positions on its assembly line.

  **(4)** A company that makes business machines gives word-processing training to welfare recipients, who are paid a salary by the federal government.

  **(5)** A nonprofit environmental organization is not required to contribute to the unemployment fund.

**35.** Based on information that is provided in the passage, which of the following would be an advantage of federal loan insurance over tax incentives and subsidies?

  **(1)** It encourages the development of innovative technologies.

  **(2)** It increases federal control over civilian industries.

  **(3)** It is comparatively inexpensive for the government.

  **(4)** It makes the government liable for private debts

  **(5)** It rewards the most profitable industries.

Items 36 to 40 refer to the following passage.

In the United States, there are several legal forms that a business organization may take. The three basic forms are proprietorships, partnerships, and corporations.

A *proprietorship* is a firm that is owned by a single individual and is usually a small business, such as a shop, a restaurant, a garage, etc. The advantages of a proprietorship are that its owner has complete control over it and that it is easy and inexpensive to establish. Disadvantages include the fact that the owner has unlimited liability for the business—if it fails, all of the owner's personal assets may be taken by creditors to cover its debts.

A *partnership* is a business in which two or more people agree to own and run the organization. Each partner contributes money and labor in return for a proportion of the profits or losses. One advantage of partnerships over proprietorships is that they can generally put together more financial resources and specialized skills. However, each partner remains personally liable for the bills of the firm—even if a partner owns only 30 percent of the firm, he or she must pay all of its debts if the other partners cannot do so.

A *corporation* is a form of organization that is considered by law to be separate and distinct from its owners. An owner in a corporation contributes money in return for stock, or shares. The greater the amount of money a person spends, the greater number of shares the person receives. Each share represents one vote in the corporation's management. It also entitles the stockholder to a proportion of the company's profits or losses. Unlike a proprietorship or a partnership, a corporation is run by directors who are hired by the stockholders. The advantages of a corporation are that it is able to raise large sums of money, and an owner's liability is limited to the amount of stock he or she holds; if the firm goes bankrupt, stockholders may lose only the value of their own stock.

**36.** Based on information that is provided in the passage, which of the following statements about business ownership is true?

(1) Only owners of proprietorships and partnerships are liable.
(2) A partnership is the best way to raise money for a business.
(3) All owners are liable to a certain extent for their firms.
(4) A stockholder is a partner in the corporation.
(5) A business partner fully controls the company's finances.

**37.** Which of the following describes a situation that would occur in a partnership?

(1) Six people own equal parts of a pizza parlor, in which they each spend one night a week behind the counter.
(2) An executive owns a large department store and shares the responsibility of management with two other executives.
(3) A business falls into debt, and its owner must sell the family car to pay back the creditors.
(4) A farmer owns all of the equipment on the farm but rents the land from another farmer.
(5) An oil company is run by twelve people, who are paid large salaries but do not share in its profits.

**38.** Which of the following statements best explains why someone would choose to invest in a corporation over other forms of business?

(1) A corporation is the most profitable form of business.
(2) If one goes bankrupt, liability for debts may be shifted to other owners.
(3) A person would be most likely to benefit from the skills of one's associates.

(4) A person's personal assets will be best protected.
(5) Less money is tied up in a corporation.

**39.** A shopkeeper declares that proprietorship is the best form of ownership. Based on the passage, which of the following arguments best supports this opinion?

(1) Unlimited liability can have little or no effect on one's life.
(2) Compromise amongst several owners may lead to weaker policies.
(3) No money can be made by investing in someone else's business.
(4) The greatest personal risks bring the greatest personal rewards.
(5) Owning your own business is the only satisfying way of life.

**40.** The passage provides evidence to support which of the following statements?

(1) The form that a business takes is determined by the number of people who own it.
(2) The amount of profit that a person makes is determined by the form of business that has been chosen.
(3) The type of personality that a person has determines the kind of business that he or she chooses.
(4) The amount of liability that a person has in a partnership is determined by the amount of money that she or he invested.
(5) The amount of influence that a person has in a corporation is determined by the number of stocks that she or he owns.

## Political Science Items

*Items 41 to 45 refer to the following information.*

The American judicial system is composed of many different types of courts to be found at three levels: federal, state, and local. Listed below are five different categories of courts and brief descriptions of the types of cases that are to be found in their jurisdiction.

**(1) Federal Supreme Court:** considers cases that are appealed from lower federal courts or from the highest state courts; also considers cases that involve ambassadors, foreign ministers, and consuls. Supreme Court decisions are final.

**(2) Court of Appeals:** considers appeals from individuals and from groups who seek to reverse the ruling of lower courts. Both the federal and the state court systems have courts of appeals.

**(3) Federal District Court:** tries cases that involve federal law and also those cases that involve persons or situations in more than one state.

**(4) State Superior Courts:** are distributed throughout the counties of a state; hear cases that involve state law, where all parties are residents of that state and the situation occurred in that state only.

**(5) County or Municipal Courts:** hear only those cases that involve persons and situations that are within the actual physical boundaries of their jurisdiction.

Each of the following cases would be decided by one of the courts that are described above. Choose the category of courts that is most likely to try the case. The categories may be used more than once in the set of items, but no one question has more than one best answer.

**41.** The laws of a certain state declare that all school taxes must be based on local property taxes. The school board from a district where the property taxes are low contests this law on the grounds that its school will have less financial support. The school board takes the case to the

(1) Federal Supreme Court
(2) Court of Appeals
(3) Federal District Court
(4) State Superior Court
(5) County or Municipal Court

**42.** A New York City restaurant owner is arrested and taken to court for serving beer to a minor, who is a resident of Albany. The court rules that the restaurant's liquor license be taken away. The restaurant owner contests the ruling on grounds that the minor had presented a forged identification. The restaurant owner takes the case to the

(1) Federal Supreme Court
(2) Court of Appeals
(3) Federal District Court
(4) State Superior Court
(5) County or Municipal Court

**43.** In accordance with integration laws, white students from one high school are bused to another high school, which is in the same school district but in a black neighborhood some distance from their homes. The parents protest against the busing and take their case to the

(1) Federal Supreme Court
(2) Court of Appeals
(3) Federal District Court
(4) State Superior Court
(5) County or Municipal Court

**44.** A newspaper reporter writes an article that is sharply critical of a local politician. The politician sues the reporter for slander. The judge in the case rules that the reporter must pay damages, but the reporter contests the ruling on the grounds that her professional rights are being violated. After a series of legal battles, the case is finally settled in the highest court to which the reporter can legally appeal. This is the

(1) Federal Supreme Court
(2) Court of Appeals
(3) Federal District Court
(4) State Superior Court
(5) County or Municipal Court

**45.** A driver who lives in Muncie, Indiana, has an automobile collision on the Indiana state highway. The driver of the other car, a Chicago resident, is clearly at fault and is sued by the first driver in the

(1) Federal Supreme Court
(2) Court of Appeals
(3) Federal District Court
(4) State Superior Court
(5) County or Municipal Court

**46.** The Second Amendment to the U.S. Constitution gives all citizens the right to bear arms, claiming that a well-regulated militia is "necessary to the security of a free State." If a U.S. senator wished to have this amendment repealed, which of the following statements would be the best argument in support of the senator's position?

(1) A civilian militia is no longer necessary to our security.
(2) A truly free state does not need a militia.
(3) A well-regulated militia does not require weapons.
(4) The security of our country is no longer an issue.
(5) The Second Amendment is unconstitutional.

Items 47 to 49 refer to the following time line.

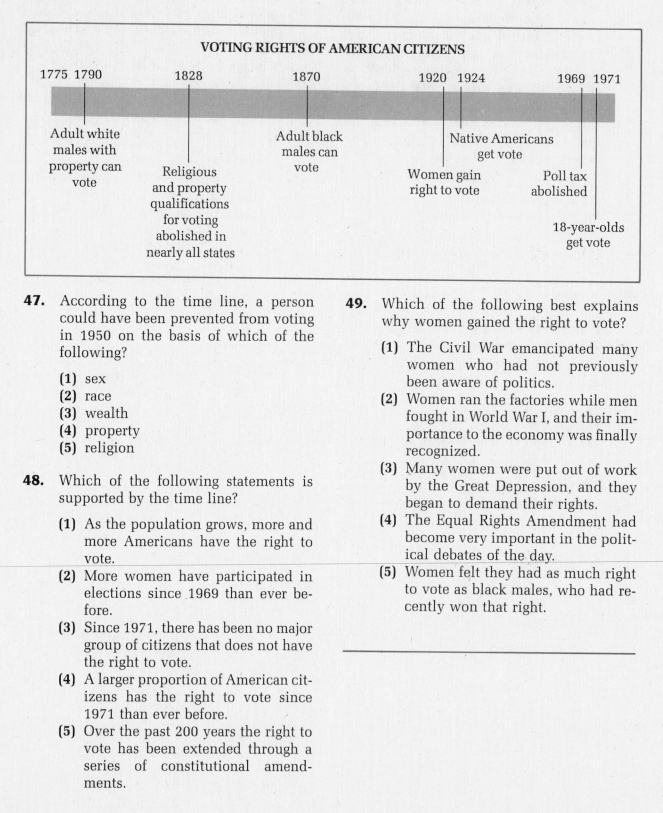

**VOTING RIGHTS OF AMERICAN CITIZENS**

1775 1790 — Adult white males with property can vote

1828 — Religious and property qualifications for voting abolished in nearly all states

1870 — Adult black males can vote

1920 — Women gain right to vote

1924 — Native Americans get vote

1969 — Poll tax abolished

1971 — 18-year-olds get vote

**47.** According to the time line, a person could have been prevented from voting in 1950 on the basis of which of the following?

(1) sex
(2) race
(3) wealth
(4) property
(5) religion

**48.** Which of the following statements is supported by the time line?

(1) As the population grows, more and more Americans have the right to vote.
(2) More women have participated in elections since 1969 than ever before.
(3) Since 1971, there has been no major group of citizens that does not have the right to vote.
(4) A larger proportion of American citizens has the right to vote since 1971 than ever before.
(5) Over the past 200 years the right to vote has been extended through a series of constitutional amendments.

**49.** Which of the following best explains why women gained the right to vote?

(1) The Civil War emancipated many women who had not previously been aware of politics.
(2) Women ran the factories while men fought in World War I, and their importance to the economy was finally recognized.
(3) Many women were put out of work by the Great Depression, and they began to demand their rights.
(4) The Equal Rights Amendment had become very important in the political debates of the day.
(5) Women felt they had as much right to vote as black males, who had recently won that right.

**50.** The United Nations is the largest international organization in the world, established as a forum in which all member nations may air their grievances and where disputes may be settled peacefully. However, many other international organizations exist in order to deal with more specific, regional problems. Some, like the North Atlantic Treaty Organization, are military organizations that were established to protect member nations from common enemies. Others, like the European Economic Community or the Association of Southeast Asian Nations, promote economic and cultural cooperation.

Which of the following statements is a conclusion that can be drawn from the passage?

(1) The United Nations is an arbiter in international affairs.
(2) International organizations serve a variety of functions.
(3) Military alliances serve to protect their members.
(4) International organizations contend with regional difficulties.
(5) The Association of Southeast Asian Nations is an economic community.

*Item 51 refers to the following illustration.*

Historical Pictures Services—Chicago

**51.** From 1919 to 1933, an amendment to the Constitution made it illegal to produce, sell, or transport alcoholic beverages in the United States. According to the illustration, the greatest danger from this law was that

(1) too many arrests would have to be made to enforce the law
(2) public disrespect for this law would encourage disregard for all laws
(3) the law would only result in more liquor being sold
(4) Congress would not be able to enforce it
(5) law-abiding citizens would vote against the amendment

52. Since the days of the Great Depression, the Democratic Party's strength has come from four major sources. The Deep South had been a traditional Democratic stronghold since the end of the Civil War. Big cities also were a traditional source of Democratic strength. The image of the Democratic Party as the party for the working class during the Depression gave the party great support among industrial workers and blacks.

Based on information provided in the passage, which of the following measures would be most likely to lose the Democratic Party a large portion of its support?

(1) decreasing the federal defense budget
(2) subsidizing farm crops and equipment
(3) increasing funds for national education programs
(4) decreasing federal funds for work programs
(5) passing strong affirmative-action legislation

## Behavioral Science Items

53. Reinforcement is one way to influence and to shape behavior. Reinforcement may be either positive or negative. That is, desired behaviors may be rewarded and therefore encouraged, while behaviors that are considered undesirable may be punished and therefore discouraged. Which of the following is NOT an example of reinforcement?

(1) The children in a family all finish their dinner and are given dessert.
(2) A debtor stops making payments on his credit card, and his account is cancelled.
(3) Several students in a class begin to make noise, and the teacher lectures in a louder voice.

(4) A dog snarls at a guest, and its owner yells at it.
(5) A baby smiles and her parents clap and smile back.

*Items 54 to 58 refer to the following information.*

Sociologists have classified social interaction into five broad types, which appear to be universal. These types are as follows:

(1) **cooperation:** people or groups work together to promote common interests or goals
(2) **conflict:** two or more people or groups struggle against each other in order to obtain something that both want
(3) **coercion:** one person or group forces its will on another
(4) **exchange:** one person assists another in order to receive something in return
(5) **competition:** two or more people or groups strive for the same goal under a set of mutually acceptable rules

Each of the following statements describes a social interaction. For each item, choose the one of the above types that most closely fits the interaction being described. The types may be used more than once in the set of items, but no one question has more than one best answer.

54. A group that colonizes an area makes the residents there clear land, build roads, and perform similar labor. The type of social interaction that is described is

(1) cooperation
(2) conflict
(3) coercion
(4) exchange
(5) competition

**55.** A number of baseball clubs in a league play one another. Each is hoping to win the championship. The type of interaction described is

(1) cooperation
(2) conflict
(3) coercion
(4) exchange
(5) competition

**56.** Two individuals are involved in a court case because each claims to be the rightful owner of a certain piece of land. The type of social interaction that is described is

(1) cooperation
(2) conflict
(3) coercion
(4) exchange
(5) competition

**57.** A person lends his lawn mower to a neighbor on condition that the neighbor also mow the owner's lawn. The type of social interaction described is

(1) cooperation
(2) conflict
(3) coercion
(4) exchange
(5) competition

**58.** A new supermarket opens across the road from an already established supermarket. It has a huge opening-day sale and advertises its everyday low prices. The type of social interaction described is

(1) cooperation
(2) conflict
(3) coercion
(4) exchange
(5) competition

Questions *59 to 61* refer to the following graph.

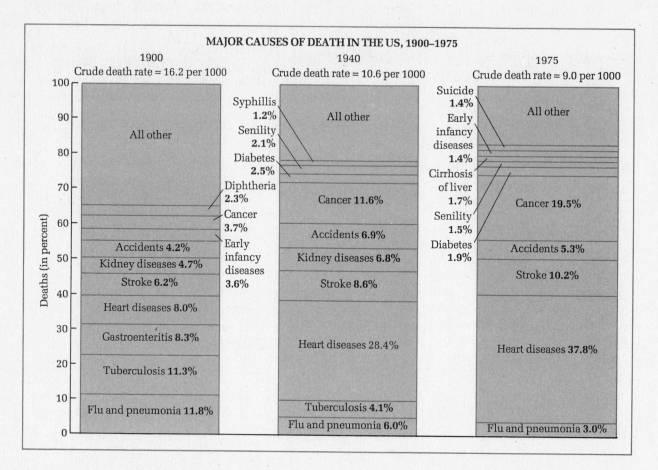

**MAJOR CAUSES OF DEATH IN THE US, 1900–1975**

59. In addition to the information provided in this graph, which of the following factors must be supplied in order to determine the number of deaths caused by heart disease in any given year?

   (1) the percent of the population that has died
   (2) the crude birth rate
   (3) the population of the United States
   (4) the life-span expectancy
   (5) the number of people who have heart disease

60. The graph can be used to predict whether upward or downward trends are likely for the year 2000 for the various causes of death listed. For which of the following causes of death would such a prediction be *most difficult* to make?

   (1) gastroenteritis, because it appeared only once on the graph
   (2) heart disease, because the percent of deaths has been changing so dramatically
   (3) tuberculosis, because it didn't appear on the graph in 1975
   (4) accidents, because the percent of deaths was highest in 1940
   (5) diabetes, because it didn't appear on the chart in 1900

61. Which of the following statements is supported by the graph?

   (1) Infectious diseases have increased as a major cause of death.
   (2) Treatments for cancer have become more effective.
   (3) The percent of stress-related deaths has increased.
   (4) The expected age of death has risen.
   (5) Childhood diseases are increasing in frequency.

*Items 62 to 64* refer to the following article.

Psychologists Michele Paludi and Lisa Strayer asked 300 men and women to evaluate an article supposedly written by a man (John T. McKay), a woman (Joan T. McKay), an author with a sexually ambiguous name (Chris T. McKay) or an anonymous author.

The article was on a subject judged to be either masculine (politics), feminine (the psychology of women) or neutral (education).

As the researchers expected, people rated the articles as better written, more insightful, more persuasive and higher in overall quality when they were told they had been written by a man.

"This pro-male bias was present even for articles in feminine and sex-neutral fields," Paludi and Strayer say.

. . . When the article was on a sexually neutral topic and either anonymously written or by Chris T. McKay, most thought that the author was a man. And they rated the article better than did those who thought the articles had been written by a woman.

Why the pro-male bias?

The researchers cite studies showing that "in North American culture the role of the male is more highly valued by both men and women than the role of the female. As a result, men's behavior is valued more even when their behavior is compared to the identical behavior exhibited by women."

**62.** Psychologists Paludi and Strayer found that when readers rated an article that was on a topic like education and supposedly anonymous, they generally

    **(1)** thought the article was written by a man

    **(2)** rated the article as better written than articles on the psychology of women

    **(3)** gave the article an unfavorable rating

    **(4)** thought the article exhibited a pro-male bias

    **(5)** felt unable to rate the article fairly

**63.** According to the article, which of the following statements is the most likely explanation for the findings that were obtained in the study?

    **(1)** Articles that supposedly were written by men are rated more highly than articles that supposedly were written by women.

    **(2)** In American society certain fields have traditionally been—and still are—associated with men and certain fields with women.

    **(3)** In American society men and, therefore, things that are done by men are more highly valued than women and things that are done by women.

    **(4)** The women's movement of the last few decades has produced significant changes in attitudes toward and beliefs about women.

    **(5)** Readers were fooled by the sexually ambiguous name Chris T. McKay.

**64.** Which of the following conclusions is best supported by evidence that is presented in the study by Paludi and Strayer?

    **(1)** Male authors generally have an easier time getting their writings published than do female authors.

    **(2)** The sex of the author can influence readers' opinions of an article.

    **(3)** Even when writing on similar topics, men and women tend to have significantly different writing styles.

    **(4)** In American culture, the role of the male has traditionally been more highly valued than the role of the female.

    **(5)** The position of women in our society has changed less than people think.

Answers are on pages 278–281.

# PRACTICE ITEMS
# Performance Analysis Chart

**Directions:** Circle the number of each item that you got correct on the Practice Items. Count how many items you got correct in each row; count how many items you got correct in each column. Write the amount correct per row and column as the numerator in the fraction in the appropriate "Total Correct" box. (The denominators represent the total number of items in the row or column.) Write the grand total correct over the denominator, **64,** at the lower right corner of the chart. (For example, if you got 55 items correct, write 55 so that the fraction reads 55/**64.**) Item numbers in color represent items based on graphic material.

| Item Type | History (page 85) | Geography (page 103) | Economics (page 112) | Political Science (page 125) | Behavioral Science (page 137) | TOTAL CORRECT |
|---|---|---|---|---|---|---|
| Comprehension (page 34) | 2, 5, 6, 9 | 19, 25 | 27, 30, 32, 36 | 47, 51 | 62 | /13 |
| Application (page 43) | 10, 12, 14, 17 | 22, 24 | 31, 34, 37 | 41, 42, 43, 44, 45 | 53, 54, 55, 56, 57, 58 | /20 |
| Analysis (page 51) | 1, 3, 8, 13, 16 | 18, 21, 23 | 28, 29, 35, 38 | 49, 50, 52 | 59, 63 | /17 |
| Evaluation (page 61) | 4, 7, 11, 15 | 20, 26 | 33, 39, 40 | 46, 48 | 60, 61, 64 | /14 |
| TOTAL CORRECT | /17 | /9 | /14 | /12 | /12 | /64 |

The page numbers in parentheses indicate where in this book you can find the beginning of specific instruction about the various fields of social studies and about the types of questions you encountered in the Practice Items.

# Practice Test

Like the actual Social Studies Test, the items in the following Practice Test appear in mixed order. On the actual test, after completing items from one branch of social studies, you will be required to switch gears and answer questions from a different branch of social studies. This Practice Test is structured in the same way. It will provide you with two kinds of practice necessary for the GED: practice on the items themselves, and practice on switching from one branch of social studies to another.

This Practice Test is the same length (64 items) as the actual test, and it is equally challenging. By taking the Practice Test, you can gain valuable test-taking experience and you will know what to expect when you sit down to take the actual Social Studies Test.

## Using the Practice Test to Best Advantage

You can use the Practice Test in the following ways:

- To get hands-on, test-taking experience, you may wish to take the Practice Test under conditions similar to those of the actual test. To do this, complete the Practice Test in one sitting and try to answer all the questions within the 85-minute time limit. If time runs out before you finish, circle the last question you have answered. Then continue with the test. This way, you can learn your score within the time limit as well as your total score on the test.

- If you want, you can take the Practice Test in sections. For example, you can plan to answer ten items a day or complete a third of the test at a time. While this does not simulate the actual testing situation, your results will still give you a pretty good idea of how well you would do on the real test.

When you take the Practice Test, write your answers neatly on a sheet of paper, or use an answer sheet provided by your teacher. If you don't know how to answer a question, skip it and come back to it later after you have answered the other questions. Remember that this is not the actual test, just some helpful practice. If your relax, you may discover that you actually perform better!

### Using the Answer Key

Compare your answers to the correct answers in the answer key beginning on page 282, and check each item you answered correctly. Whether you answer an item correctly or not, you should read the information that explains each correct answer. This will help you reinforce your knowledge of social studies and enhance your testing skills.

### How to Use Your Score

However you decide to take the Practice Test, your final score will point out your strengths and weaknesses in the subject of social studies. The Performance Analysis Chart at the end of the test will help you identify those strengths and weaknesses.

# PRACTICE TEST
# Social Studies

**Directions:** *Choose the one best answer to each question.*

Items 1 and 2 are based on the following chart.

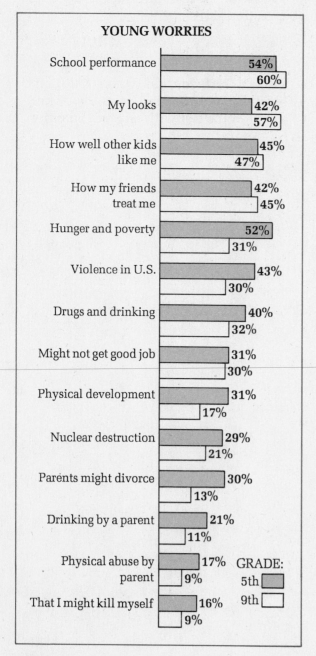

YOUNG WORRIES

| Worry | 5th | 9th |
|---|---|---|
| School performance | 54% | 60% |
| My looks | 42% | 57% |
| How well other kids like me | 45% | 47% |
| How my friends treat me | 42% | 45% |
| Hunger and poverty | 52% | 31% |
| Violence in U.S. | 43% | 30% |
| Drugs and drinking | 40% | 32% |
| Might not get good job | 31% | 30% |
| Physical development | 31% | 17% |
| Nuclear destruction | 29% | 21% |
| Parents might divorce | 30% | 13% |
| Drinking by a parent | 21% | 11% |
| Physical abuse by parent | 17% | 9% |
| That I might kill myself | 16% | 9% |

GRADE: 5th ■  9th □

*Young Adolescents and Their Parents,* a study conducted by the Search Institute, of Minneapolis. Eight thousand students were asked which of several concerns worried them "very much" or "quite a bit." The chart contrasts the responses of fifth graders and ninth graders.

1. Which of the following statements is supported by the chart?

   (1) Few of the ninth graders would be upset if they failed a school examination.
   (2) It is likely that most of the fifth graders questioned will worry less as they mature.
   (3) The suicide rate among younger children is likely to be higher than for older children.
   (4) Younger children tend to worry more about societal problems than older children do.
   (5) As a child matures, he or she is less likely to be concerned about personal appearance.

2. Based on the chart, which book title do you think would be the most appealing to both a young teenager and a younger child?

   (1) *How to Cope With a Problem Parent*
   (2) *Learn and Earn: One Hundred Interesting Jobs for Teenagers*
   (3) *Build a Stronger Body in Thirty Days*
   (4) *How to Win Friends and Influence People*
   (5) *Drugs: Where They Come From and How We Use Them*

*Item 3 is based on the following map.*

**THE WESTERN STATES AND THE YEARS THEY BECAME STATES**

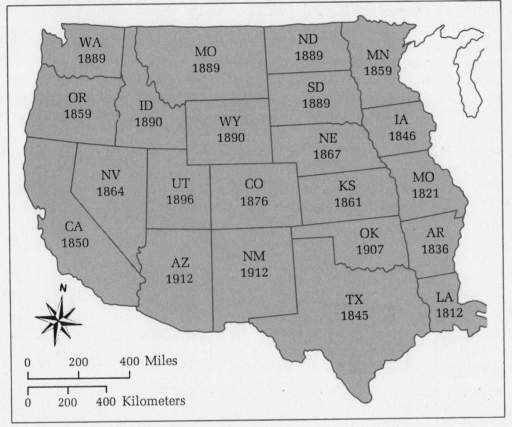

3. Which one of the following statements is supported by information given in the map?

(1) All the Northern states gained independence at approximately the same time.

(2) Statehood status for the territories that bordered Mexico spanned two centuries.

(3) All the states east of the Mississippi gained statehood before the Western states.

(4) Wyoming became a state before Arizona because it was easier to travel to from the East.

(5) Arizona and New Mexico were purchased from Mexico at the same time in the Gadsden Purchase.

**4.** Some insurance companies will lend money to those who hold life insurance policies with them. The policy itself it put up as collateral or security for the loan. The policyholder can borrow only up to the cash value of the policy, which is determined by the amount of money the holder has put into the policy. If the borrower does not repay the loan, the insurance is lost. Because risk to the company is low, the interest rate of the loan against the policy is low as well.

According to the passage, a borrower who defaults on a loan from an insurance policy is required to forfeit which of the following?

A. the life insurance policy
B. the cash amount of the loan
C. the low interest rate of the loan

**(1)** A only
**(2)** B only
**(3)** C only
**(4)** A and B only
**(5)** B and C only

Items 5 to 7 are based on the following chart.

| HOW CONGRESS IS CHOSEN | |
| --- | --- |
| **House** | **Senate** |
| SIZE | |
| 435 members—in proportion to population | 100 members—2 for each state |
| TERM OF OFFICE | |
| 2 years—all members up for election at same time | 6 years—one-third of members up for election every 2 years |
| QUALIFICATIONS | |
| 1. At least 25 years of age<br>2. U.S. citizen for 7 years<br>3. Resident of state from which elected | 1. At least 30 years of age<br>2. U.S. citizen for 9 years<br>3. Resident of state from which elected |

5. Which of the following candidates would be eligible to run for senator from Florida?

(1) a 25-year-old citizen of the United States and a resident of Florida
(2) a 40-year-old Alabama resident who became a U.S. citizen in 1970
(3) a 40-year-old resident of Florida who has been a U.S. citizen for four years
(4) a 35-year-old citizen of the United States who has lived in Florida all her life
(5) a 28-year-old resident of Florida who was born in the United States

6. A Republican president, recently elected, wants to introduce a new bill to Congress. The Senate and the House of Representatives are composed of a Democratic majority that is opposed to the bill. The president might have a better chance of passing the bill through Congress at which of the following times?

(1) February of the president's first year
(2) December of the president's first year
(3) February of the president's second year
(4) December of the president's second year
(5) February of the president's third year

7. A statistician predicts a population growth for the United States of 10% during the next 50 years, with primary growth occurring in states along the Pacific coast. Based on this information, which of the following effects on state representation will most likely occur?

(1) Senate representation in Oregon and Washington will increase.
(2) Congressional representation in Florida and Georgia will increase.
(3) House representation will increase in the West and decrease in the East.
(4) House representation for the United States will increase in two-year increments throughout this period.
(5) Congressional representation will increase by 10% during the next 50 years.

*Items 8 to 12 are based on the following passage.*

Several factors seem to increase the risk of heart attacks. Smoking, obesity, a high-cholesterol diet, and lack of exercise are often contributing factors. Recently, it has been discovered that personality traits also play a part. Two behavior types are associated with high and low risks of heart attacks. They are known as Type A and Type B behavior.

*Type A persons* tend to be hard-working and competitive. They thrive under pressure and constantly drive themselves to succeed. Toward that end, they seek attention and advancement, and they take on many projects with deadlines to meet. Much of the time, they seem alert, efficient people who get things done. When put in a stressful situation that they cannot control, however, they often become hostile and impatient. For example, Type A persons may become angry with slow elevators or slow salespersons or with anything that might interfere with their tight schedule.

*Type B persons* are easy-going and relatively noncompetitive. They usually exhibit a calm and patient demeanor. Everyday problems do not seem to create much stress in their lives. Studies have shown that they are likely to live longer than people with Type A behavior.

**8.** According to the passage, which one of the following statements about heart attacks is true?

(1) The likelihood of a heart attack is influenced by a combination of physical, life-style, and personality factors.

(2) Type B persons are more likely to suffer heart attacks than Type A persons.

(3) There is no way to predict who is more likely to suffer a heart attack.

(4) Smoking is not connected to heart attacks.

(5) Behavior is not connected to heart attacks.

**9.** Which of the following situations would be most stressful to a Type A person?

(1) a high-pressure job

(2) preparing to run the New York marathon

(3) a job promotion that requires meeting deadlines

(4) a traffic jam

(5) a social gathering where most of the people are strangers

**10.** According to the passage, which one of the following types of people would be the LEAST likely to get a heart attack?

(1) a 40-year-old overweight smoker

(2) a 60-year-old Type A nonsmoker

(3) a Type B smoker

(4) a Type B nonsmoker who exercises

(5) an overweight Type B nonexerciser

**11.** Which one of the following statements is best supported by the information given in the passage?

(1) Possible heart-attack victims cannot be identified.

(2) We now know more about the causes of heart attacks than previously.

(3) Smokers are most often Type A persons.

(4) Type B persons are usually nonsmokers.

(5) Exercise best prevents heart attacks.

**12.** All of the information in the passage is provided to support which of the following conclusions?

    **(1)** Type A persons suffer a higher risk of heart attacks because of their stressful life-styles.

    **(2)** A smoker is more likely to suffer a heart attack than a nonsmoker.

    **(3)** Personality traits are now considered to be the primary factor in determining the risk of heart attack.

    **(4)** Type B persons are less bothered by stress than Type A persons.

    **(5)** Life-style, as well as physical characteristics, affect the likelihood of heart attack.

---

**13.** Lines of longitude appear as north-south lines on a map. They show how far east or west of the prime meridian a place is located. Lines of latitude are east-west lines on a map. They show how far north or south of the equator a place is located.

    One way for someone to find out whether San Diego is farther north than New York City would be to

    **(1)** compare the longitude of San Diego with the latitude of New York

    **(2)** compare the longitude of San Diego with the longitude of New York

    **(3)** compare the latitude of San Diego with the longitude of New York

    **(4)** compare the latitude of San Diego with the latitude of New York

    **(5)** compare the distance of San Diego and New York from the prime meridian

*Items 14 and 15 refer to the following passage.*

All persons born or naturalized in the United States, and subject to the jurisdiction thereof, are citizens of the United States and of the State wherein they reside. No State shall make or enforce any law which shall abridge the privileges or immunities of citizens of the United States; nor shall any State deprive any person of life, liberty, or property, without due process of law; nor deny to any person within its jurisdiction the equal protection of the laws.

Fourteenth Amendment to the U.S. Constitution

**14.** Which of the following legal decisions would be most strongly influenced by the Fourteenth Amendment?

    **(1)** A state governor is impeached for accepting bribes.

    **(2)** The Supreme Court orders a state to desegregate its schools.

    **(3)** A state abolishes gambling within its jurisdiction.

    **(4)** An immigrant to the United States is denied citizenship.

    **(5)** A state lowers sales taxes on goods sold within its borders.

**15.** Which of the following most likely was an immediate effect of the ratification of the Fourteenth Amendment?

    **(1)** All immigrants automatically became United States citizens.

    **(2)** Slavery was abolished throughout the United States.

    **(3)** States had to obey federal law regarding citizens' rights.

    **(4)** All state laws became subject to federal authorization.

    **(5)** The residents of some states were granted special privileges.

16. Harvard College is the oldest college in the United States. It was built in Massachusetts 16 years after the Pilgrims first arrived. Most of the people at Harvard studied to become ministers. As ministers, they would become leaders of the New England colonies.

Which one of the following conclusions is best supported by the passage?

(1) Church and state were closely linked in early New England.
(2) There were no ministers in New England before the construction of Harvard College.
(3) The purpose of college education in colonial times was to train people for the ministry.
(4) Most people in the early New England colonies went to college.
(5) Pilgrims were the predominant leaders of the early New England colonies.

*Items 17 to 20 refer to the following information.*

Defense mechanisms are mental processes that people use, often unconsciously, to protect themselves and to resolve conflicts. Psychologists have classified defense mechanisms into a number of types. Listed below are five types of defense mechanisms and brief descriptions of how they are used.

[1] **Rationalization:** An individual gives a false explanation of a threatening situation in order to protect feelings of self-esteem.

[2] **Denial:** An individual acts as though a particular upsetting situation never occurred or does not exist.

[3] **Projection:** An individual attributes to others negative characteristics and impulses that the individual possesses.

[4] **Reaction formation:** An individual displays behavior that is the opposite of all the individual's repressed unconscious attitudes.

[5] **Sublimation:** Impulses that are socially unacceptable (for example, aggressive impulses) are transformed into behavior that is socially acceptable.

Each of the following items describes the use of one of the defense mechanisms listed above. For each item, choose the type of mechanism that is being used. The categories may be used more than once in the set of items, but no one question has more than one best answer.

17. A person applies for a job but is turned down. She decides that she didn't want that job anyway. The type of defense mechanism that she uses is

(1) rationalization
(2) denial
(3) projection
(4) reaction formation
(5) sublimation

18. A person loses weight and shows many signs of serious illness. His friends are very concerned, but he refuses to see a doctor and insists that nothing is wrong. The type of defense mechanism that he is using is

(1) rationalization
(2) denial
(3) projection
(4) reaction formation
(5) sublimation

19. When a widower remarries shortly after his wife's death, his older child is extremely hostile to the new wife. The younger child, in contrast, always seems to be going out of her way to be nice to her. The type of defense mechanism that the younger child is using is

(1) rationalization
(2) denial
(3) projection
(4) reaction formation
(5) sublimation

**20.** A person hates other people but is convinced that it is they who hate him. The type of defense mechanism that he is using is

(1) rationalization
(2) denial
(3) projection
(4) reaction formation
(5) sublimation

*Items 21 to 23 are based on the following graph.*

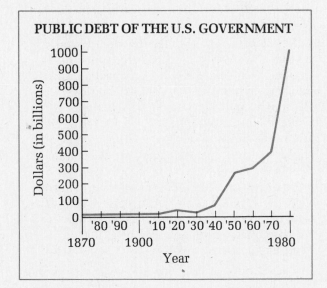

**PUBLIC DEBT OF THE U.S. GOVERNMENT**

Dollars (in billions)

Year

**21.** Based on the graph, during which historical period was the budget most closely balanced?

(1) between the Civil War and World War I
(2) the decade after World War I
(3) the years of the Great Depression
(4) the decade after World War II
(5) the period between the Korean and the Vietnam wars

**22.** Which of the following statements is the best explanation for the decrease in public debt that is shown in the graph?

(1) Industrial expansion after the Civil War created work and prosperity for many, and the government interfered little in the economy.
(2) The Progressive Movement, which lobbied for an increase in federally funded programs, lost its influence after World War I.
(3) Federal income taxes were lowered to boost the business economy in the years preceding the Depression.
(4) The government combatted unemployment that was caused by the Depression by initiating new social-welfare programs.
(5) Individual state taxes were increased, yielding more than $20 billion in extra revenue.

**23.** Which of the following statements about the federal budget is NOT supported by evidence given in the graph?

(1) The expenses of World War I caused the United States to operate for the first time on a deficit budget.
(2) The United States government had to borrow two-thirds of the $330 billion cost of World War II through the sale of war bonds.
(3) President Eisenhower's push to reduce the role of government in business resulted in reducing expenditures and nearly balancing the national budget.
(4) Income taxes were raised by $100 billion during the Kennedy and Johnson administrations to cover increased federal spending.
(5) Defense spending rose sharply in the decade before Reagan was elected president.

**24.** Terrorists are individuals who use threats and violence to frighten populations or governments into meeting political demands. Which of the following historical events is an example of terrorism?

(1) the Boston Tea Party
(2) the Cuban missile crisis
(3) the assassination of President Kennedy
(4) the Iranian hostage crisis
(5) the Chicago gang wars

---

**25.** Although the water cycle keeps the world's water supply fairly constant, *quality* of water is a separate issue. In recent decades, water pollution has become a serious problem. Factories are major contributors to the problem, often spewing wastes directly into rivers and lakes. Chemical fertilizers and pesticides contribute to water pollution when washed from soils in sufficient quantities. Human wastes are also a factor, especially in urban areas.

Which of the following statements is best supported by evidence presented in the passage?

(1) Water pollution occurs through both direct and indirect means.
(2) Water pollution is a recent phenomenon.
(3) Factories are the main source of water pollution.
(4) Technology has provided a way to recycle water but not to purify it.
(5) Commerical sources of water pollution are a bigger part of the problem than noncommercial sources.

*Items 26 to 28 are based on the following passage.*

In its early days, the American labor movement was split into two major camps: reform unionism and trade unionism. The reform unionists rejected and sought alternatives to the factory system. Thus, they downplayed strikes against particular employers and were active in efforts to elect third-party (farm/labor) candidates to political office. The trade unionists, in contrast, accepted the factory system and sought, through strikes, to obtain better working conditions from employers. The most important of the reform-unionist organizations was the Knights of Labor, which grew steadily until the "Haymarket Massacre" of May 1886.

Police broke up a protest by labor unionists, anarchists, and others in Chicago's Haymarket Square. Someone threw a bomb at the police, causing seven deaths and many injuries. Although the identity of the bomber was not discovered, eight anarchists were arrested and tried. The judge ruled that inciting a deed made a person as guilty as the one who perpetrated it. The jury then found the anarchists guilty. Some were executed; the others imprisoned. Several years later, the governor of Illinois, saying the trial had been unfair, pardoned those who were in prison. He was denounced as aiding and abetting anarchy.

Public anger at the anarchists was also turned against the Knights of Labor, although the union had in no way been responsible for the bomb. Membership declined steadily. The recently formed American Federation of Labor soon became the main labor organization. Whereas the Knights were reform unionists, the A.F. of L. favored the trade-unionist approach.

**26.** Which of the following statements is a fact that is given in the passage?

(1) The anarchists were responsible for the murder of a number of policemen in Chicago's Haymarket Square.
(2) The governor of Illinois, in granting a pardon, was aiding and abetting anarchy.

**(3)** Inciting a deed is, for all practical purposes, the same as committing it.

**(4)** Members of the Knights of Labor, although not arrested, were involved in planning the "Haymarket Massacre."

**(5)** The Haymarket incident had begun as a protest by individuals, including anarchists and labor unionists.

**27.** Which of the following is likely to have occurred during the labor movement of the 1890s as a result of developments that are discussed in the passage?

**(1)** The labor movement experienced a severe decline.

**(2)** The anarchists disassociated themselves from the labor movement.

**(3)** An increasing number of candidates who ran on the labor-party ticket were elected to public office.

**(4)** The movement shifted to focus on strikes and on better working conditions.

**(5)** The police were empowered to use more force in the event of demonstrations by labor.

**28.** Which of the following statements is best supported by evidence that is presented in the passage?

**(1)** Early labor leaders disagreed as to methods and goals.

**(2)** In the nineteenth century, public opinion tended to be hostile to labor.

**(3)** Early labor leaders were often associated with anarchists.

**(4)** The A.F. of L. drew most of its early membership from the Knights of Labor.

**(5)** The beginnings of the labor movement were characterized by violent clashes between police and union activists.

**29.** While attending sessions, members of Congress cannot be arrested on civil charges and misdemeanors. Which of the following statements best explains the reason for this privilege?

**(1)** Members of Congress are frequent victims of libel and slander.

**(2)** The House of Representatives and the Senate, like embassies, are outside legal jurisdiction.

**(3)** Arrests would bring members of Congress into disrepute.

**(4)** Arrests on minor charges would interfere unduly with the legislative process.

**(5)** Members of Congress are sometimes required to break the law in their duties.

*Item 30 refers to the following graph.*

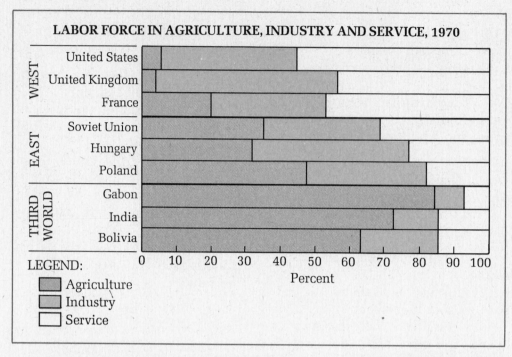

**LABOR FORCE IN AGRICULTURE, INDUSTRY AND SERVICE, 1970**

30. According to the information in the graph, the industrial sector is the largest sector, in terms of percentage of the labor force that is employed, in

(1) all and only the Western countries
(2) all the Western and the Eastern countries, but none of the Third World countries
(3) the United States and the United Kingdom only
(4) the United Kingdom and Hungary only
(5) Poland, Gabon, India, and Bolivia

31. The number of farms in the United States fell from more than 30 million in 1940 to 9 million in 1970, yet the United States continues to be the world's greatest supplier of food. Which of the following statements is an explanation of this phenomenon?

(1) The U.S. population has grown.
(2) Third World need for food has increased.

(3) Third World agriculture has become inefficient.
(4) U.S. agriculture has become very efficient.
(5) U.S. agricultural products are coveted worldwide.

*Items 32 to 35 refer to the following passage.*

By the early nineteenth century, the United States had already fought two major wars on its own soil—the Revolutionary War and the War of 1812. Conflicts such as these had led the young republic—which was still insecure and ill-defined as a nation—to mistrust the intentions of the European powers. As early as 1793, George Washington had proclaimed U.S. neutrality in the war in Europe, and in his Farewell Address of 1796, he recommended that the United States remain free of foreign alliances. Jefferson's policies reinforced this view; his Embargo Act of 1807 prevented United States ships from docking at any foreign port. Isolationism became official policy with Monroe's 1823 year-end congressional message—the Monroe Doctrine. He declared that European nations must halt both their colonization of the Western Hemisphere and their interference in its affairs. The United States would likewise stay out of European affairs and the affairs of their colonies. For nearly 100 years, isolationism was the basis of U.S. foreign policy and largely reflected the country's attitude toward the rest of the world.

By the 1890s, however, the situation had greatly changed. The Industrial Revolution had created the need for new sources of raw materials and for new markets for manufactured goods. Also, the expansion to the West was virtually complete, causing speculators to look outside U.S. borders for economic opportunities. In addition to this, the major European powers had embarked on a policy of imperialism by conquering much of Africa and Southeast Asia. The United States, fueled by these economic and political issues, felt the need to establish its position as a great world power.

In 1893, the United States annexed Hawaii, thereby gaining a valuable and strategic outpost in the Pacific. In 1898, it entered the Spanish-American War. American victory resulted in strengthened economic ties with Cuba, as well as a military base there. It also gave the United States possession of Puerto Rico, Guam, and the Philippines. The U.S. foreign policy of isolationism had given way to that of imperialism.

32. Which of the following actions, if undertaken by the United States, would NOT be in accordance with principles of the Monroe Doctrine?

   (1) defending the Caribbean Islands against Spanish invasion
   (2) preventing British delivery of goods to the confederacy during the Civil War
   (3) sending troops to help liberate Algeria from French control
   (4) denying aid to the Allies in their fight against Napoleon
   (5) sending the navy to the Mediterranean to halt Tunisian piracy of U.S. ships

33. Which of the following statements best explains the shift in U.S. foreign policy during the nineteenth century?

   (1) There became fewer and fewer countries left to conquer.
   (2) As the West was won, the people of the United States became more war-like.
   (3) Latin America became less and less dependent on U.S. protection.
   (4) European nations became increasingly hostile toward the United States.
   (5) United States society experienced rapid economic and political growth.

34. Which of the following conclusions can be drawn from information that is provided in the passage?

   (1) No U.S. ships docked at any foreign port during the nineteenth century.
   (2) Increased European imperialism was a catalyst to U.S. imperialism.
   (3) In the 1890s, the United States adopted a policy of belligerence towards Cuba and Puerto Rico.
   (4) Population growth compelled the United States to seek food supplies abroad.
   (5) The Revolutionary War was the main reason that isolationism flourished.

35. Which of the following best describes an effect that the Embargo Act of 1807 might have had on U.S. trading practices?

   (1) Traders became more reliant on foreign merchant navies.
   (2) Sailors learned to disregard the laws pertaining to U.S. ships.
   (3) Slave trade with Africa ceased.
   (4) Foreign powers increased attacks on U.S. ships.
   (5) Overseas trade was brought to a standstill.

*Items 36 to 38 are based on the following illustration.*

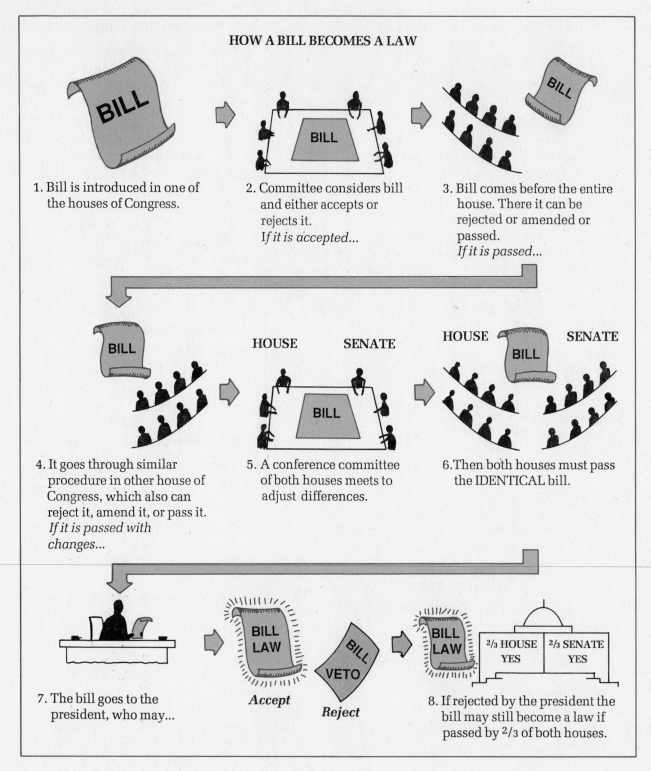

**HOW A BILL BECOMES A LAW**

1. Bill is introduced in one of the houses of Congress.

2. Committee considers bill and either accepts or rejects it.
   *If it is accepted...*

3. Bill comes before the entire house. There it can be rejected or amended or passed.
   *If it is passed...*

4. It goes through similar procedure in other house of Congress, which also can reject it, amend it, or pass it.
   *If it is passed with changes...*

5. A conference committee of both houses meets to adjust differences.

6. Then both houses must pass the IDENTICAL bill.

7. The bill goes to the president, who may...
   *Accept*    *Reject*

8. If rejected by the president the bill may still become a law if passed by 2/3 of both houses.

**36.** One of the values that is inherent in the above procedure for making a bill into a law is that

(1) it serves the primary goal of efficiency and speed in passing important legislation

(2) it is part of the system of checks and balances that keeps any given political party from controlling the country

(3) it ensures that all citizens vote via someone they elected to the Senate, the House of Representatives, or the presidency

(4) it is one of the ways to prevent a single branch of government from becoming too powerful

(5) it allows legislators to reconsider the ramifications of their decisions even after they have accepted a bill

**37.** Based on the illustration, which of the following statements is true of the president's role in passing legislation?

(1) The president's veto cannot keep a bill from becoming law because Congress will override it.

(2) The president can only accept a bill that has been passed by both houses of Congress.

(3) The president's vote is only important when there is disagreement between the two houses of Congress.

(4) The president can accept the version of one house's bill and reject that of the other.

(5) After a veto, the president has the right to reject a bill that has been passed by two-thirds of both houses.

**38.** Which one of the following statements best illustrates the principles of democracy at work in the legislative process?

(1) The bill is introduced in one of the two houses of Congress.

(2) The president, who is elected by majority rule, can veto a bill that has been accepted by Congress.

(3) The people of the United States are given representation via their elected officials.

(4) The Senate, the House of Representatives, and the president all have equal say in the process.

(5) The committee that makes adjustments in a rejected bill is made up of members of both houses.

**39.** The last quarter of the nineteenth century saw fortunes that were made in railroads, oil, steel—any industry that could exploit the revolution in methods of production and distribution. The U.S. economy, which was based on free enterprise, was thriving. But by the 1880s, the people of the United States wanted Congress to pass legislation that would regulate commerce. The Interstate Commerce Act of 1887 restricted railroad commerce, and the Sherman Antitrust Act of 1890 aimed to destroy monopolies.

Which one of the following conclusions can best be supported by the passage?

(1) Many people sought to restrict free enterprise because they were unable to exploit the economic situation.
(2) The economy experienced a period of unchecked growth that ended because of the self-limiting nature of free enterprise.
(3) The people of the United States could not accept limitless freedom and competition as the ultimate way of life in business.
(4) Government regulation is necessary for any system, economic or otherwise, to operate freely and fairly.
(5) Neither piece of legislation was effective, as evidenced by the huge increase in the pace of business consolidation in the 1890s.

**40.** *Society* is often defined as a complex of social relationships between individuals who are bound together by a common language and a common culture. Based on this definition of society, which of the following is NOT a society?

(1) a small tribe of Native Americans
(2) a confederation of English-speaking nations
(3) a nation where two languages are understood
(4) The American colonies before the revolution
(5) the United States after the revolution

*Items 41 and 42 are based on the following table.*

| Asian Immigration to the United States, 1820–1979 | |
|---|---|
| China | 540,000 |
| Japan | 411,000 |
| Turkey | 386,000 |
| Philippines | 431,000 |
| Korea | 276,000* |
| India | 182,000 |
| Indochina (Vietnam, Cambodia, Laos) | 133,000* |

\* Nearly all since 1950

**41.** Which one of the following statements can be supported by the information that is given in the table?

(1) More people can be expected to continue immigrating from Korea and Indochina than from the other countries.

(2) The fewest people have come here from India because most emigrating Indians go to Great Britain rather than the United States.

(3) Proportionate to each country's total population, a higher percent of China's population has immigrated than that of other countries.

(4) More than half of all Korean and Indochinese immigration occurred before 1950.

(5) The physical size and population of each country have little to do with the total number of people who have immigrated to the United States.

**42.** Based on information in the table, which is the most likely cause of immigration of the Koreans and Indochinese?

(1) war
(2) ideology
(3) earthquake
(4) high unemployment
(5) famine and disease

*Items 43 and 44 are based on the following passage.*

The Cabinet is an informal body of executive officers, appointed by the president, that offers advice and opinions on how best to run the government. Although never specifically mentioned in the Constitution, it has by tradition evolved into an important council on which the president depends. It is composed of the principal officers of each executive department (for example, the Attorney General, the Secretary of the Treasury, and so on).

**43.** Which of the following statements best describes the Cabinet's relationship to the federal government?

(1) It ratifies decrees that are made by the president.

(2) It is responsible for controlling the federal budget.

(3) It acts unofficially in the formation of government policy.

(4) It offers advice that the president is compelled to follow.

(5) It is the constitutionally decreed council on federal policy.

**44.** Which of the following actions is one that a member of the Cabinet would NOT be authorized to take?

(1) The Secretary of Labor prepares a report on unemployment.

(2) The Attorney General suggests possible amendments to the Constitution.

(3) The Secretary of Transportation asks Congress to nationalize the railroads.

(4) The Secretary of the Treasury orders the dollar to be devalued.

(5) The Secretary of Defense proposes new aircraft carriers for the navy.

*Items 45 to 49 are based on the following passage.*

Maps are classified according to the type of geographical factor that they depict. Listed below are five different types of maps and brief descriptions of what they contain and how they are used.

[1] **Topographical map:** Shows the natural features of Earth, including continents, oceans, rivers, mountains, plains, forests, deserts, and valleys.

[2] **Contour map:** Shows the elevation or depth of terrain, usually within a very small region; a contour map uses curve, or contour, lines that connect all points of the same elevation in a particular area.

[3] **Political map:** Shows political boundaries of Earth—including borders between countries, states, and regions—and the locations of cities.

[4] **Climatic map:** Shows weather patterns of particular areas; it often includes data on average temperature or rainfall.

[5] **Geological map:** Shows formations and composition of Earth's crust and its interior; it will often include data on the locations of oil, coal, and mineral deposits.

Each of the following items describes a situation that calls for the use of a map. For each item, choose the type of map that would provide the appropriate information to solve the problem that is posed in the situation. Each map type may be used more than once in the set of items, but no one question has more than one best answer.

45. The Food and Agriculture Organization of the United Nations is asked to research the feasibility of rice production in parts of central Africa. To help to determine the areas that present the most favorable conditions for growing rice, the organization could refer to a

   (1) topographical map
   (2) contour map
   (3) political map
   (4) climatic map
   (5) geological map

46. A student is making a model of the United States for a school project and needs to know where to place the Continental Divide. The student could refer to a

   (1) topographical map
   (2) contour map
   (3) political map
   (4) climatic map
   (5) geological map

47. A company is building a factory in an area that is near a lake that experiences some flooding. The company wants to determine the pattern of flooding in the area. The company should refer to a

   (1) topographical map
   (2) contour map
   (3) political map
   (4) climatic map
   (5) geological map

48. A group of bankers is considering industrial investment possibilities in Mexico. A map that they might refer to in their decision-making is a

   (1) topographical map
   (2) contour map
   (3) political map
   (4) climatic map
   (5) geological map

49. A fishing group on Lake Superior is licensed to fish in the United States only. To be certain not to cross into Canadian territory, the group should refer to a

   (1) topographical map
   (2) contour map
   (3) political map
   (4) climatic map
   (5) geological map

**50.** *Status* is a ranked position in a social hierarchy. In our society, status is usually determined by several elements, including occupation, income, education, family background, and in some circumstances, age, sex, and ethnic group. For example, high income carries greater status than low income. *Status inconsistency* occurs when someone ranks high in one element of status and low in another.

Based on the information given in the passage, which of the following is an example of status inconsistency?

(1) a restaurant worker who has a modest income
(2) a retiree who takes a part-time job
(3) a self-made, self-educated millionaire
(4) a lawyer whose parents were both doctors
(5) a woman who is employed as a truck driver

*Items 51 and 52 refer to the following passage.*

The Dawes Act, which was passed in 1887, was a strong attempt to break up the Native American tribal system. Any Native American could become a U.S. citizen by giving up connections to the tribe and, therefore, rights to tribal ownership of the reservation. In this way, between 1887 and 1934, approximately 60% of Native American lands were lost. Yet the Dawes Act failed to destroy the tribes, in part because many Native Americans did not possess the skills or education to become fully assimilated into United States society and chose to remain on the reservations. The Indian Citizenship Act of 1924 sought to remedy this injustice by providing automatic citizenship for all Native Americans.

**51.** Which of the following statements about Native American life prior to the Dawes Act is suggested by information that is provided in the passage?

(1) Native American lands were vast, and their security against encroachment was ensured.
(2) Native Americans actively sought and were granted U.S. citizenship.
(3) The tribal system posed a threat to settlers' designs on Native American lands.
(4) Native Americans were encouraged to seek education and work skills.
(5) The tribal system was already on the verge of collapse.

**52.** Based on the passage, which of the following was a probable result of the Indian Citizenship Act?

(1) All Native Americans were assimilated into U.S. society.
(2) Native American lands lost between 1887 and 1934 were returned.
(3) The tribal system was broken up once and for all.
(4) Tribal power to lobby for change was strengthened.
(5) The Bureau of Indian Affairs was established.

Items 53 to 55 refer to the following table.

```
┌─────────────────────────────────────────────┐
│      DISTRIBUTION OF ADULT AMERICANS          │
│         BY TYPES OF HOUSEHOLD                  │
│                                               │
│  Heading single-parent families        16%    │
│  Other single, separated, divorced, or 21%    │
│     widowed                                    │
│  Living in child-free or post-child-   23%    │
│     rearing marriages                          │
│  Living in extended families            6%    │
│  Living in experimental families or     4%    │
│     cohabiting                                 │
│  Living in dual-breadwinner nuclear    16%    │
│     families                                   │
│  Living in no wage-earner nuclear       1%    │
│     families                                   │
│  Living in single-breadwinner nu-      13%    │
│     clear families                             │
└─────────────────────────────────────────────┘
```

Source: News release, Bureau of Labor Statistics, March 8, 1977; reprinted in Juanita Williams, *Psychology of Women*, New York: Norton, 1983, p. 306.

**53.** According to the statistics provided, which of the following would find themselves in the smallest social minority?

(1) a father who works while the mother manages the household
(2) a mother and a father who both have jobs
(3) a grandmother who lives with her daughter's family
(4) a retired couple who have no children
(5) a father and a mother who are both unemployed

**54.** Which of the following statements about the composition of United States society is suggested by the information provided?

(1) Nuclear family households constitute the major portion of United States society.
(2) Households that involve adults in a nonfamily structure are more common than family-based households.
(3) Marriages that include children are less common households than marriages that do not include children.
(4) Nonmarried households constitute a greater portion of United States society than married households.
(5) No one type of household constitutes a majority in United States society.

**55.** Which of the following changes in percentage is most likely a result of an increase in the divorce rate?

(1) Single-parent families would change to 12%.
(2) Child-free marriages would change to 27%.
(3) Cohabited households would change to 2%.
(4) Dual-breadwinner nuclear families would change to 14%.
(5) Single-breadwinner nuclear families would change to 17%.

*Items 56 and 57* refer to the following temperatures and rainfall graphs.

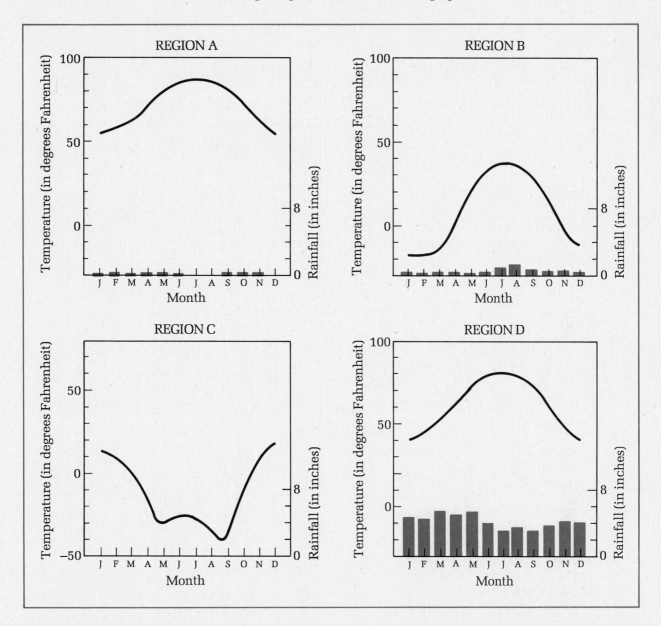

**56.** Which of the following regions would most likely be a desert?

(1) Region A
(2) Region B
(3) Region D
(4) Regions A and C
(5) Regions B and C

**57.** Which of the following best explains the temperature variations of Region C?

(1) There is no rainfall.
(2) It is far to the north.
(3) It is below the equator.
(4) It is far from an ocean.
(5) There is no indigenous vegetation.

**58.** In 1886, the American Federation of Labor (A.F. of L.), a new labor union, was formed. Taking a different approach to labor organization, the A.F. of L. admitted only skilled laborers. The A.F. of L. believed that these workers could strike with greater effect than unskilled workers. The A.F. of L. decided to organize only skilled laborers because these workers would be

(1) more interested in joining a union
(2) more difficult for employers to replace
(3) easier for the union to organize
(4) more likely to agree to a strike
(5) less likely to quit their jobs

*Items 59 to 63 are based on the following passage.*

Although the United States economy is primarily characterized by private enterprise, there are times when the government extends either direct or indirect influence over the production of goods and services. Direct influence occurs when the government enters the economy directly. It may do this by producing goods or providing services (for example, the United States postal service), by controlling the prices of certain items through the placement of price ceilings, or by taking over or directing the production and distribution of certain items. The last usually occurs only during times of war or severe shortage; during World War II, for example, the government established agencies to shift peacetime plants to war production, set priorities for raw materials, ration scarce consumer goods, and even settle labor-management disputes.

The government uses direct methods of economic control usually during times of crisis only. More often it supports the workings of private industry through indirect methods; for example, by trying to give domestic industry an advantage in international competition. One of the most common forms of indirect influence is the tariff, a tax on imported goods. The government would consider passing a low tariff to help domestic manufacturers of an item to compete with significantly lower-priced foreign goods, or a high tariff to prohibit the import of certain goods, thereby stimulating domestic production of these goods.

A more severe measure that the United States government can take to protect domestic industries is to levy an import quota. Import quotas limit the amount of foreign goods that are allowed into the country. Because both high tariffs and import quotas eventually lead to higher prices for domestic goods (since these goods then go virtually unchallenged on the market), the government is unlikely to use these types of economic influences unless domestic industry needs special protection from foreign competition.

**59.** Which of the following best describes the relationship of government to private enterprise in the U.S. economy?

(1) Private enterprise is entirely self-regulating and requires no government interference.
(2) Private investors rely on the government to keep domestic industry competitive in foreign markets.
(3) The government intervenes only in matters of domestic economy, not in matters of global economy.
(4) Private enterprise is generally autonomous, but economic crises often require government stimulus.
(5) Competition is regulated by the government in order to keep the domestic economy free of foreign imports.

**60.** Which one of the following items is an example of direct government influence in the production of goods and services?

(1) a tax on imported electronic parts
(2) a survey on consumer preferences for brand-name appliances
(3) an import quota on foreign cars
(4) a ninety-day wage-and-price freeze
(5) a federal tax exemption to exporters

**61.** Which one of the following government actions might lead to a decrease in domestic car prices?

(1) an import quota on foreign cars
(2) a ceiling that is placed above the current price of cars
(3) a repeal of all tariffs on foreign cars
(4) a law that controls production volume
(5) a federal program to ration steel

**62.** Which one of the following statements best explains how a low tariff on shoes might affect the price of shoes on the United States market?

(1) The price of imported shoes would decrease.
(2) The price of both domestic shoes and imported shoes would remain the same.
(3) The price of domestic shoes only would increase.
(4) The price of imported shoes only would increase.
(5) The price of both domestic shoes and imported shoes would increase.

**63.** In which of the following situations would the government be most likely to impose high tariffs?

(1) Unemployment in the mining industries steadily declines.
(2) A severe worldwide shortage of petroleum occurs.
(3) The price of food rises sharply in Europe.
(4) New computer technology is developed and exported by Japan.
(5) The United States increases its level of exports.

*Item 64 refers to the following passage.*

The Industrial Revolution greatly changed living and working conditions for United States laborers. Compelled to seek work where it was available, in the factories, displaced workers were put in a position that was easily exploited by their employers. Conditions were often crowded and dangerous; housing in the new cities was often inadequate and unhygienic; workers received low wages for long hours. Such conditions eventually led to the formation of labor unions.

**64.** Which of the following statements about working conditions prior to the Industrial Revolution is suggested by the information provided in the passage?

(1) Most workers lived in the cities.
(2) Factories were clean and safe.
(3) People worked in their own homes or shops.
(4) Employers were generous and concerned.
(5) Labor unions safeguarded workers' rights.

Answers are on pages 283–285.

# Performance Analysis Chart

**Directions:** Circle the number of each item that you got correct on the Predictor Test. Count how many items you got correct in each row; count how many items you got correct in each column. Write the amount correct per row and column as the numerator in the fraction in the appropriate "Total Correct" box. (The denominators represent the total number of items in the row or column.) Write the grand total correct over the denominator, **64,** at the lower right corner of the chart. (For example, if you got 54 items correct, write 54 so that the fraction reads 54/**64.**) Item numbers in color represent items based on graphic material.

| Item Type | History (page 85) | Geography (page 103) | Economics (page 112) | Political Science (page 125) | Behavioral Science (page 137) | TOTAL CORRECT |
|---|---|---|---|---|---|---|
| Comprehension (page 34) | 33, 51, 58, 64 | | 4, 21, 30, 59 | 43 | 8, 54 | /11 |
| Application (page 43) | 32 | 13, 45, 46, 47, 48, 49 | 60 | 5, 24, 44 | 2, 9, 10, 17, 18, 19, 20, 36, 50, 53 | /21 |
| Analysis (page 51) | 26, 27, 35, 42, 52 | 56, 57 | 22, 31, 61, 62 | 6, 15, 29, 38 | 12, 55 | /17 |
| Evaluation (page 61) | 3, 16, 28, 34, 41 | 25 | 23, 37, 39, 63 | 7, 14, 40 | 1, 11 | /15 |
| TOTAL CORRECT | /15 | /9 | /12 | /12 | /16 | /64 |

The page numbers in parentheses indicate where in this book you can find the beginning of specific instruction about the various fields of social studies and about the types of questions you encountered in the Practice Test.

# Simulation

# Introduction

By this time, you are probably asking yourself, "Am I ready to take the GED Test?" Your score on the following Simulated Test will help you answer that question.

The test is as much like the real Social Studies Test as possible. The number of questions and their degree of difficulty are the same as on the real test. The time limit and the mixed order of the test items are also the same. By taking the Simulated Test, you will gain valuable experience and a better idea about just how ready you are to take the actual test.

## Using the Simulated Test to Your Best Advantage

You should take the test under the same conditions as the real test.

- When you take the GED, you will have 85 minutes to complete the test. Though this will probably be more than enough time, set aside at least 85 minutes so you can work without interruption.

- Do not talk to anyone or consult any books as you take the test. If you have a question about the test, ask your instructor.

- If you have trouble answering a question, eliminate the choices that you know are wrong. Then mark the best remaining choice. On the real GED, you are not penalized for wrong answers. Guessing a correct answer will better your score, while guessing a wrong answer will not affect your score any more than not answering.

As you take the Simulated Test, write your answers neatly on a sheet of paper, or use an answer sheet provided by your teacher. When time is up, you may wish to circle the item that you answered last, and then continue with the test. When you score your test, you can see to what extent time played a factor in your performance.

## Using the Answer Key

Use the Answers and Explanations (page 286) to check your answers, and mark each item you answered correctly. You should read the information that explains each correct answer. This will reinforce your testing skills and your understanding of the material.

## How to Use Your Score

If you have 52 items or more correct, you scored 80 percent or better. This shows that you are most likely working at a level that would allow you to do well on the actual Social Studies Test. If you have a few less than 52 items correct, then you probably only need to do some light reviewing. If your score was far below the 80 percent mark, then you should spend additional time reviewing the lessons, so that you can strengthen the areas in which you were weak. The Skills Chart at the end of the test will help you identify your strong and weak areas.

# Simulated Test

**TIME:** *85 minutes*
**Directions:** *Choose the one best answer to each question.*

*Item 1* is based on the following illustration.

*Shanks in The Buffalo Evening News*

**"The aspirin's in the upper right drawer."**

1. Which of the following statements is supported by the illustration?

   **(1)** The Johnson administration was responsible for causing national and international troubles.
   **(2)** President Nixon had workable solutions for the world's problems.
   **(3)** The Johnson administration had no immediate solutions for the country's problems.
   **(4)** President Johnson was too old to handle the responsibilities of government.
   **(5)** Johnson and Nixon were willing to cooperate in order to solve the troubles of the world.

2. In the past century, mass-produced goods have almost entirely replaced handmade goods in marketplaces worldwide. The main reason for this is that mass-produced goods, being manufactured on production lines, require less effort and fewer workers, are cheaper to make, and are therefore less expensive to purchase. A great advantage of mass production is that it makes many products affordable for consumers who might otherwise be unable to buy them.

   Which of the following statements about handmade goods is suggested by the passage?

   **(1)** They are of better quality than mass-produced goods.
   **(2)** They are not desired by consumers.
   **(3)** Only the rich can afford them.
   **(4)** They are often not available to consumers.
   **(5)** There are no skilled workers left to make them.

Items 3 to 5 refer to the following graph.

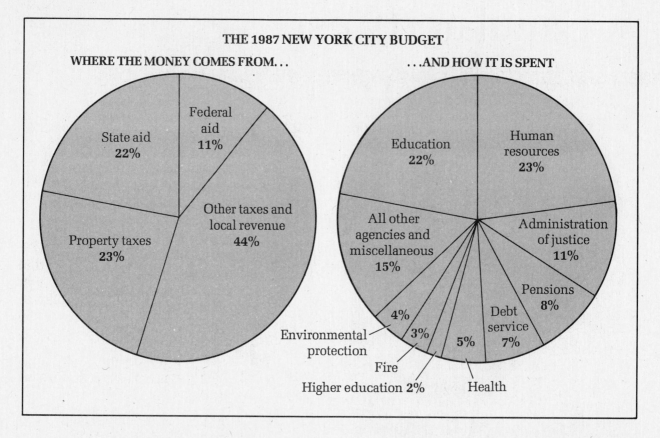

**THE 1987 NEW YORK CITY BUDGET**

WHERE THE MONEY COMES FROM...

State aid
22%

Federal
aid
11%

Property taxes
23%

Other taxes and
local revenue
44%

...AND HOW IT IS SPENT

Education
22%

Human
resources
23%

All other
agencies and
miscellaneous
15%

Administration
of justice
11%

Pensions
8%

Debt
service
7%

4%

3%

5%

Environmental
protection

Fire

Higher education 2%

Health

**3.** Based on information provided in the graph, which of the following form part of the second-largest expense item in New York City's budget?

　(1) courts and jails
　(2) health clinics and hospitals
　(3) sanitation and clean air
　(4) school maintenance and teachers' salaries
　(5) pensions for city workers

**4.** Based on the graph, which of the following groups or agencies probably bears the largest portion of New York City funding?

　(1) the United States Treasury
　(2) New York state consumers
　(3) the New York state Treasury
　(4) New York City corporations
　(5) New York City residents and home owners

**5.** Which of the following statements is supported by information provided in the graph?

   **(1)** Any population increases in New York City will add equally to the city's expenditures and revenues.

   **(2)** New York City relies more heavily on municipal revenues to fund its services than any other city in the country.

   **(3)** New York City's expenses are too high to be covered by its own revenues alone.

   **(4)** New York City's budget is too thinly spread to give adequate funding for all essential services.

   **(5)** New Yorkers would stand to benefit from an increase in state and federal taxes.

*Items 6 and 7* refer to the following passage.

As U.S. society evolves from an industrial into a service economy, the resulting increase in higher-status jobs has greatly affected upward mobility. People whose opportunities were once limited to factory work may now find that more jobs are available in which the pay is higher and the satisfaction greater, and in which better use is made of their abilities.

   Other factors also affect a person's chances for advancement. Studies show that the three major factors are education, race, and sex. Of these, education is by far the most crucial. Three-fourths of all college-educated men move up socially, while only 12 percent of those who are not college educated do so.

**6.** Based on information provided in the passage, which of the following statements about job opportunities is true?

   **(1)** There is more work to be found in factories than ever before.

   **(2)** The service sector has created a wealth of new jobs.

   **(3)** Unemployment has risen since the factories began to close.

   **(4)** Service jobs tend to pay less than industrial jobs.

   **(5)** A person's race or sex has little impact on their job prospects.

**7.** Based on information provided in the passage, which of the following government actions would be most likely to lead to an increase in upward job mobility?

   **(1)** reducing funds for new adult literacy programs

   **(2)** lowering the national minimum wage rate

   **(3)** providing grants to minority scholarship funds

   **(4)** increasing welfare benefits for single mothers

   **(5)** subsidizing companies in the auto and steel industries

*Items 8 to 10* refer to the following passage.

Before the beginning of this century, Sigmund Freud and Josef Breuer had recognized that neurotic symptoms—hysteria, certain types of pain, and abnormal behavior—are in fact symbolically meaningful. They are one way in which the unconscious mind expresses itself. . . . A patient, for instance, who is confronted with an intolerable situation may develop a spasm whenever he tries to swallow: He "can't swallow it." Under similar conditions of psychological stress, another patient has an attack of asthma: He "can't breathe the atmosphere at home." A third suffers from a peculiar paralysis of the legs: He can't walk, i.e., "he can't go on any more." A fourth who vomits when he eats, "cannot digest" some unpleasant fact. I could cite many examples of this kind, but such physical reactions are only one form in which the problems that trouble us unconsciously may express themselves.

From Carl Jung, *Man and His Symbols*, Dell Publishing Co., NY, 1964, p. 9. Used with permission.

8. Based on information provided in the passage, which of the following is NOT a symptom of neurosis?

   (1) A person who is shy inevitably gets migraine headaches in social situations.
   (2) A person who fears challenges becomes dizzy when in tall buildings.
   (3) A person who has had a bad fright cannot talk.
   (4) A person who is overweight goes on a diet.
   (5) A person who finds life has become restrictive feels sick when in small rooms.

9. All of the following can be expressions of unconscious stress. Which differs from the way of expressing stress that is described in the passage?

   (1) limping
   (2) stuttering
   (3) dreaming
   (4) trembling
   (5) nausea

10. Which of the following statements is supported by information provided in the passage?

   (1) Hysteria and neurosis did not exist before the twentieth century.
   (2) Neurosis is a state of mind that can be overcome through psychoanalysis.
   (3) Asthma is generally a neurotic symptom brought about by a person's worries.
   (4) A person's neurosis can sometimes be diagnosed by the nature of its symptoms.
   (5) Physical symptoms of neurosis are usually accompanied by other types of symptoms as well.

*Items 11 and 12* refer to the following passage.

There is no doubt that the world can now produce enough food for everyone. Yet many people in Africa and parts of Asia continue to starve or suffer from malnutrition, while vast surpluses of food are produced in the United States, Australia, Canada, and western Europe. The problem, above all, is one of distribution. One solution might be to ship food from rich countries to the hungry ones. But experience has shown that this can be costly, wasteful, and create a long-term dependency. The hungry nations might be able to make much of their poor soil fertile if they had the tools, irrigation systems, fertilizers, and modern agricultural technology. But they can't afford these things. Neither can they afford to buy food from the rich nations.

**11.** Which of the following actions would lead to the best long-term solution to the problem of world hunger?

   **(1)** provide Third-World countries with low-interest loans to develop and to purchase modern agricultural technology

   **(2)** provide funds for an international relief agency to buy surplus food to be distributed among the hungry nations

   **(3)** encourage Third-World countries to relocate their hungry citizens to the large cities

   **(4)** encourage Third-World countries to repopulate the hungry regions with people from their large cities

   **(5)** provide tax rebates to American and European farmers who would be willing to donate part of their crops to starving countries

**12.** Which of the following statements is supported by information provided in the passage?

   **(1)** The quality of a country's soil will determine whether it is prosperous or hungry.

   **(2)** The rich countries of the world are reluctant to waste their money helping the poorer ones.

   **(3)** There would be no starvation in the world if all the food was distributed evenly among the nations.

   **(4)** The poor nations are unwilling to spend money on agricultural technology and equipment.

   **(5)** The peoples of the West are more wasteful with their food than are the peoples of the hungrier nations.

**13.** In 1981, the U.S. national debt reached $1 trillion, an all-time high. The increasing rate of growth has alarmed many people who believe that the debt will be a burden on future generations. Others point out, however, that in terms of percentage of national output, the debt has declined steadily since 1945. In 1948, for example, the debt represented about 100 percent of national output. By 1981 it had declined to less than 40 percent.

Based on information provided in the passage, which of the following is the best explanation for the decline in the national debt as a percentage of the national output between 1945 and 1981?

   **(1)** The Great Depression caused the government to borrow a lot of money, which it gradually paid off.

   **(2)** Though the national debt continued to rise, the national output rose at an even faster pace.

   **(3)** As the economy improved after World War II, the government was able to borrow more and more money.

   **(4)** The national output is measured in terms of real dollars, whereas the national debt is measured in terms of interest.

   **(5)** The U.S. dollar has grown stronger and stronger since the end of World War II.

*Items 14 to 16* refer to the following passage.

From around 1800 to the 1930s, the fertility rate in the United States was in constant decline. This meant that the average number of children born to each couple continued to decrease through those years. Studies have shown a number of different possible explanations for this trend.

Some sociologists believe that the decline was caused by the desire for a higher standard of living. With less children, couples are able to devote more of their time and resources to leisure activities and material goods. Others believe, however, that the decline was caused by the economic shift from an agricultural society to an industrial one. Whereas large families are helpful to provide labor on a farm, they may often be a burden to industrial workers, who may often live in more cramped conditions than agricultural workers. Still others believe that the decline was caused by the increasing emancipation of women. As education became more available to women, they began to find new opportunities outside the home which made childbearing seem less attractive. Further, as family planning and contraception grew to be more acceptable, more and more couples found themselves rethinking the advantages of large families, and the fertility rate was slowed even more.

**14.** Which of the following would be the most appropriate title for this passage?

(1) U.S. Fertility Rates: Past and Present
(2) Social Changes and Fertility Rates in U.S. History
(3) The Changing Social Order in America
(4) The United States: 1800 to 1940
(5) Fertility Rates and the Role of Women in U.S. Society

**15.** Which of the following statements about life in the United States before 1800 is implied by the passage?

(1) Family planning and contraception were not available to people who wished to limit the size of their families.
(2) Leisure activities and material goods were the privileges of the wealthy only.
(3) The American colonists had one of the highest fertility rates in the world.
(4) Industrial workers tended to have large families and to live in spacious housing.
(5) Women were expected to stay at home and to raise large families.

**16.** Which of the following is a likely explanation for the change in the birth rate that occurred after the period described in the passage?

(1) Because the Great Depression threw many people out of work, more leisure time was available for having large families.
(2) The Great Depression caused more people to see the wisdom of having a large family.
(3) People who had postponed having children during the Great Depression now wanted to have a child.
(4) Many women were forced to go to work while the men were fighting in World War II.
(5) People began to have larger families to replace their loved ones who were killed during the war.

*Item 17* refers to the following graph.

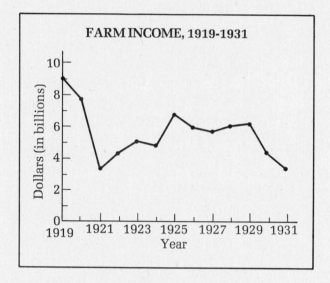

FARM INCOME, 1919-1931

**17.** Which of the following would explain the overall trend in farm income during the 1920s?

(1) After years of economic problems, the Hoover administration brought economic stability to the country.

(2) Many soldiers returning from World War I found that jobs were no longer available on the farms.

(3) The value of crops soared as new markets for U.S. goods were opened up after World War I.

(4) After World War I, the Europeans were able to grow their own crops, and U.S. farmers lost a valuable market.

(5) The Great Depression made most farm crops too expensive for average Americans to afford them.

*Items 18 to 22* refer to the following passage.

Intellectual property laws protect ideas, inventions, and products from being exploited by persons who have no right to profit from their use. These laws cover three main areas.

A *copyright* protects literary, dramatic, musical, artistic, or craft compositions from being copied, published, displayed, or performed by others without permission. Under the Copyright Revision Act of 1979, a work is automatically copyrighted as soon as it is completed. The creator gains additional protection by registering the work with the Federal Copyright Office. Usually a copyright expires 50 years after the death of the creator.

A *patent* is granted only for original inventions, usually of a technical or scientific nature. Determining the originality of an invention is often a lengthy process. A United States patent, once granted, runs for 17 years.

A *trademark* is a word or symbol that a manufacturer places on a product to distinguish it from similar products offered by competitors. In the United States, trademarks are established through use. The first merchant or manufacturer to use a trademark automatically owns it. The owner gains additional protection by registering the trademark. A trademark registration runs for 20 years, under the condition that the trademark is used regularly.

18. Based on information in the passage, which of the following statements is the most accurate?

(1) A patent is automatically granted as soon as an invention is completed.
(2) A plaintiff may sue for copyright infringement even if the copyright is not registered.
(3) Trademarks, copyrights, and patents must be registered with the federal government.
(4) If a trademark is not renewed after 17 years, other companies may use it.
(5) A novel is protected by copyright law only if it is registered with the Federal Copyright Office.

19. Herman Melville, the author of *Moby Dick*, died in 1891. A publisher now wants to print a new edition of *Moby Dick*.

According to the copyright regulations, the publisher

(1) should get permission to publish from Melville's original publisher
(2) should publish the book and send part of the profits to Melville's family
(3) should not publish the book because it is protected by copyright
(4) can go ahead and publish the book because the copyright period has ended
(5) can go ahead and publish the book because there were no copyright regulations when *Moby Dick* was published

**20.** Which of the following explains why manufacturers use trademarks?

   **(1)** They want to distinguish their products in the mind of the consumer.

   **(2)** They want to prevent competitors from selling similar products.

   **(3)** They want to use symbols in their advertisements.

   **(4)** They want to be authorized to charge more for their registered products than their unregistered competitors can charge.

   **(5)** They want to prove the originality of their creations.

**21.** According to the passage, which of the following reasons has NOT been a motivation for the establishment of intellectual property laws?

   **(1)** preventing artists, writers, and inventors from stealing one another's ideas

   **(2)** establishing legal ownership of ideas and creations

   **(3)** maintaining a government record of ideas and creations

   **(4)** recognizing the rights of writers, artists, scientists, and businesspeople to profit from their ideas and creations

   **(5)** preventing unscrupulous businesspeople from profiting from the ideas of others without their consent

**22.** For which of the following conclusions does the passage provide the strongest evidence?

   **(1)** Copyrights, patents, and trademark registrations can be renewed.

   **(2)** Copyrights, patents, and trademark registrations can outlive the people who created the protected material.

   **(3)** Computer software cannot be protected under the current copyright regulations.

   **(4)** Intellectual property laws stifle rather than stimulate technological advancement.

   **(5)** Intellectual property laws are stronger in the United States than in other countries.

*Items 23 and 24* refer to the following passage.

In 1980, 59 percent of all Americans voted in the national elections. Of those aged 65 to 74, 69 percent were voters, while of those aged 18 to 20, only 36 percent were voters.

**23.** Which of the following statements best restates the information provided in the passage regarding the 1980 elections?

   **(1)** The old were more active participants than the young in an election where more than half the population voted.

   **(2)** While barely one-third of those aged 18 to 20 voted, they still represented a larger group than those aged 65 to 74.

   **(3)** The old represented more than half the voting population, while the young represented barely a third.

   **(4)** Less than half of those eligible to vote actually did, and of those, nearly two-thirds were over 65.

   **(5)** While more than half the young and half the old turned out, less than half the population actually voted.

**24.** Which of the following is a conclusion that can be drawn from the information provided in the passage?

   **(1)** The old are a more powerful voting group than the young.

   **(2)** More than half of all Americans are ineligible to vote.

   **(3)** The old are a more reliable voting group than the young.

   **(4)** The voting age should be lowered so that more young can vote.

   **(5)** Elected officials do not represent a true majority.

**25.** In recent years, cities in the developing countries have experienced enormous growth. Steady streams of impoverished rural workers have abandoned the land in the hopes of finding employment in the industrial centers. While many succeed, overburdened city services often cannot keep up with the growth. As a result, these migrants and other urban poor must often make do with extremely inadequate housing and sewage conditions and with minimal health care.

Which of the following would be the best title for this passage?

   **(1)** Development of Third-World Natural Resources

   **(2)** Health Care in Poor Countries

   **(3)** Dilemma of the Poor in Developing Countries

   **(4)** The Agricultural Division of Labor

   **(5)** Real Estate Development in Growing Cities

**26.** The U.S. Constitution grants certain specific rights to the legislative branch of the federal government. These powers include the drafting of all laws, taxation, the regulation of trade between states and with foreign governments, the raising of an army, navy, and air force, the printing of currency, and the prosecution and impeachment of federal officials.

Which of the following actions by the legislative branch is NOT sanctioned by the U.S. Constitution?

   **(1)** passing a protective tariff

   **(2)** calling out the National Guard

   **(3)** removing a president from office

   **(4)** reinstating obligatory national service

   **(5)** authorizing the issue of new Federal Reserve notes

*Items 27 and 28 refer to the following chart.*

| Employment and Unemployment in the United States | | | |
|---|---|---|---|
| Year | Employed | Unemployed | Unemployment Rate in Percent |
| 1970 | 78,678,000 | 4,093,000 | 4.9 |
| 1975 | 85,846,000 | 7,929,000 | 8.5 |
| 1976 | 88,752,000 | 7,406,000 | 7.7 |
| 1977 | 92,017,000 | 6,991,000 | 7.1 |
| 1978 | 96,048,000 | 6,202,000 | 6.1 |
| 1980 | 99,303,000 | 7,637,000 | 7.1 |
| 1981 | 100,000,397 | 8,273,000 | 7.6 |
| 1982 | 99,526,000 | 10,678,000 | 9.7 |
| 1983 | 100,834,000 | 10,717,000 | 9.6 |
| 1984 | 105,005,000 | 8,539,000 | 7.5 |

**27.** According to the chart, which of the following years experienced the largest change in the number of unemployed?

**(1)** 1970 to 1975
**(2)** 1976 to 1977
**(3)** 1978 to 1980
**(4)** 1981 to 1982
**(5)** 1983 to 1984

**28.** According to the chart, the number of unemployed was lower in 1982 than in 1983, yet the unemployment rate was higher. This is best explained by the fact that

**(1)** the overall population increased
**(2)** the economy was weakened in 1983
**(3)** the number of employed increased in 1983
**(4)** the rate had been rising for many years
**(5)** the number of employed was less in 1983 than in 1984

*Items 29 to 31* refer to the following passage.

The invention of the cotton gin by Eli Whitney in 1792 greatly changed the agricultural and economic structure of the South. In the eighteenth century, the main crop had been tobacco. Cotton was not grown because of the great labor and expense required to remove the seed from the lint. But with the cotton gin, this process was greatly simplified, and cotton became a profitable crop. In 1800 the United States produced less than 100,000 bales of cotton. This number had grown to 400,000 in the 1820s, 1,500,000 in the 1840s, and to nearly 4 million by 1860.

One important effect of the "King Cotton" boom was on the slave population of the South. As the demand for cotton grew, the need for cheap labor to pick cotton grew proportionally. In 1800 there had been fewer than 1 million slaves. By 1860 there were more than 4 million slaves, 60 percent of whom were employed in picking cotton. At the same time, the price for one slave more than tripled. Slave traders profited as much from the cotton gin as did the plantation owners, and support for slavery became deeply entrenched in the South.

29. Based on information provided in the passage, which of the following statements about the cotton gin is true?

   (1) It had a deep impact on U.S. society in the eighteenth century.
   (2) Its use put many farm laborers out of work.
   (3) It revitalized the ailing cotton industry.
   (4) It helped to create the slave-trading industry.
   (5) It helped to provide a new source of U.S. wealth.

30. Which of the following was probably an effect of the cotton boom on Southern society?

   (1) It helped to concentrate wealth in the hands of the large plantation owners.
   (2) By raising the price of cotton, it helped the smaller, "one-horse" farms.
   (3) It destroyed the large tobacco farmers, who began to import tobacco from the Caribbean.
   (4) It encouraged "carpetbaggers" from the North to buy cheap Southern land.
   (5) It helped to dramatize the plight of the slaves to Southerners who had been unaware of their suffering.

31. Which of the following statements is the best explanation for the effect of the cotton boom on attitudes toward slavery in the South?

   (1) Whites began to resent slaves because of the added expense of keeping them.
   (2) Keeping slaves was profitable as never before, and those who benefited did not want to lose this bounty.
   (3) Increasing rebelliousness among the slaves caused fear among the slave owners.
   (4) Many abolitionists from the North and the South wanted the slaves to return to picking tobacco.
   (5) The slave population became larger than the free population, and people saw this as an indication that changes were needed.

*Item 32* refers to the following graph.

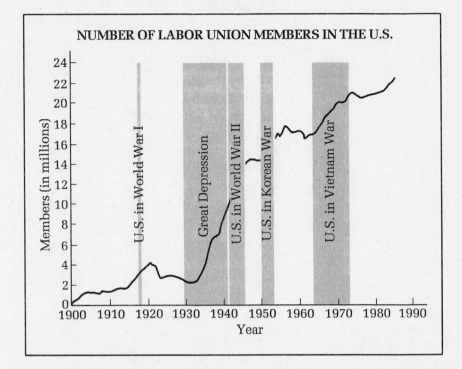

**NUMBER OF LABOR UNION MEMBERS IN THE U.S.**

32. Which of the following statements is supported by information provided in the graph?

   **(1)** Union membership in 1900 was at its lowest in U.S. history.
   **(2)** Union membership rises more slowly in times of prosperity than in times of crisis.
   **(3)** The major U.S. wars of the twentieth century had a devastating effect on union membership.
   **(4)** The rise in union membership is directly proportional to the increase in population.
   **(5)** U.S. labor unions profit most from a strong dollar and a healthy economy.

33. The number of American children who live in poverty rose steadily from 1979 to 1984. Many of these children live in urban areas; a good number of them end up becoming unwed parents and/or dropping out of school. In 1979, 16 percent of Americans under 18 lived in poverty. By 1984, 21 percent of Americans under 18 lived in poverty. These figures represent an increase from 10 million youths to almost 13 million youths in just 5 years.

   Which one of the following statements is suggested by the passage?

   **(1)** Most poor people are children and live in inner cities.
   **(2)** Prior to 1979, childhood poverty was not a major social problem.
   **(3)** Teenage pregnancy is a major cause of teenage poverty.
   **(4)** Public and private poverty policies from 1979 to 1984 failed to reduce poverty among children.
   **(5)** The increase from 1979 to 1984 reflects a general increase of the population caused by "baby-boomers" having babies.

*Items 34 to 38* refer to the following information.

Congress has a number of powers in addition to its main function of passing laws. Listed below are five types of nonlegislative powers entrusted to Congress.

**(1) Constituent powers:** powers related to changing the Constitution

**(2) Electoral powers:** powers related to the selection of the president and vice-president

**(3) Executive powers:** powers used to exert control over the administrative sector of the executive branch

**(4) Investigatory powers:** power to order and to conduct special investigations

**(5) Judicial powers:** power to pass judgments and sanctions on certain individuals

Each of the following statements describes the use of one of the types of nonlegislative powers of Congress listed above. The types may occur more than once in the set of items, but no one question has more than one best answer.

34. In 1868, the House of Representatives impeached President Andrew Johnson, charging that he had violated the Tenure of Office Act. The Senate then acquitted Johnson, by a mere one-vote margin. In this example, Congress used its

   (1) constituent powers
   (2) electoral powers
   (3) executive powers
   (4) investigatory powers
   (5) judicial powers

35. In 1978, Congress proposed the Equal Rights Amendment, which stated that "equality of rights under the law shall not be denied or abridged by the United States or by any state on account of sex." In this case, Congress used its

   (1) constituent powers
   (2) electoral powers
   (3) executive powers
   (4) investigatory powers
   (5) judicial powers

36. In 1979, Congress divided the Department of Health, Education and Welfare into two separate departments—the Department of Education and the Department of Health and Human Services. In this case, Congress was using its

   (1) constituent powers
   (2) electoral powers
   (3) executive powers
   (4) investigatory powers
   (5) judicial powers

37. Most federal agencies are required to make annual reports to Congress, and members of Congress routinely call on agency heads for information and explanations. In so doing, Congress is using its

   (1) constituent powers
   (2) electoral powers
   (3) executive powers
   (4) investigatory powers
   (5) judicial powers

**38.** The activities of the Senate Watergate Committee—along with those of the special prosecutor, the federal judiciary, and the press—helped lead to the resignation of President Richard Nixon, who realized that his alternative would most likely be impeachment and conviction. In this example, Congress used its

    **(1)** constituent powers
    **(2)** electoral powers
    **(3)** executive powers
    **(4)** investigatory powers
    **(5)** judicial powers

*Items 39 and 40* refer to the following passage.

The United States no longer has the highest standard of living in the world. Part of the reason is that American productivity—output of goods and services per worker—has declined. The reasons for this decline are complex, some reflecting short-term or even positive developments.

Other reasons for the decline appear more basic and troubling. One analysis links the decline in American productivity, especially in sectors such as the automobile and steel industries, to an emphasis on the present, rather than the future. Emphasis on *immediate* profitability has led to a failure to invest enough in modernizing equipment and processes. For example, statistics from the Organization for Economic Cooperation and Development reveal that the United States trailed behind all other Western countries and Japan in converting its steel plants into continuous casting. The steel plants were profitable as they were, and the costs of converting them would have, in the short term, destroyed this profitability.

According to this analysis, the focus on the present is reflected not only in managerial decisions but also in consumer habits and business-government relations. Thus, in this view, the solutions to America's productivity problem will not be easy ones.

**39.** Which of the following statements best summarizes the main idea of the passage?

    **(1)** The United States no longer has the world's highest standard of living, largely because American productivity has declined.
    **(2)** Some reasons for the decline in productivity are short-term or even positive, whereas others are more basic and troubling.
    **(3)** The steel and auto industries are among the leading examples of the decline in American productivity.
    **(4)** American focus on the present has been a major contributor to the decline in productivity.
    **(5)** U.S. companies have not invested sufficient capital in industrial equipment and processes.

**40.** Which of the following statements is best supported by evidence presented in the passage?

    **(1)** The decline in productivity has been greatest in the steel and auto industries.
    **(2)** The U.S. steel industry lagged behind its counterparts in other countries in switching to continuous casting.
    **(3)** The decline in U.S. productivity is linked to an emphasis by industry decision-makers on the present rather than the future.
    **(4)** Consumer habits and business-government relations are part of America's productivity problem.
    **(5)** In the United States, productivity in the service sector has been greater than that in industry.

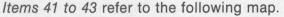

*Items 41 to 43* refer to the following map.

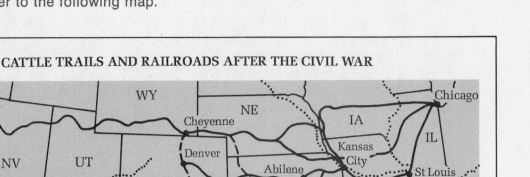

**41.** Based on the map, which of the following towns is most likely to have been one of the "cow towns"?

(1) Chicago
(2) San Francisco
(3) Kingsville
(4) Abilene
(5) St. Louis

**42.** Which of the following best explains the position of the cattle trails?

(1) They followed the deep valleys of the Great Plains.
(2) They brought cattle from the north to the ranches of Texas.
(3) They brought cattle from Texas to the railways for transportation.
(4) They linked up with the rivers for transportation.
(5) They led north to avoid Native-American territories.

**43.** Which of the following statements is supported by information provided in the map?

   **(1)** San Francisco did not become a major city until the railroads connected it to the rest of the country.
   **(2)** Ranching was not a big industry before the railroads, because there was no way to get cattle to the East.
   **(3)** After the coming of the railroads, people did not travel on the Mississippi and Missouri rivers.
   **(4)** The largest market for southern cattle was in the Midwest.
   **(5)** The West was the greatest beneficiary of the coming of the railroads.

*Items 44 and 45* refer to the following passage.

Between 1850 and 1930 more than 35 million immigrants came to the United States—anxious to escape poverty, hunger, political oppression, and religious persecution in their own countries, and drawn by the promise of America. Immigrants from the United Kingdom, Germany, and Scandinavia came in large numbers primarily during the early decades of this period. These were years of westward expansion, and many of these immigrants were lured especially by the rich lands of the prairies.

By the 1880s the immigration pattern changed somewhat. Immigrants from southern and eastern European countries (for example, Italy, Austria, Hungary, Poland, and Russia), who had initially come only in small numbers, now poured into the United States. They settled primarily in urban areas, often working in unskilled jobs in factories. Moreover, the decades between 1880 and 1930 marked the peak of immigration. In the 1930s the number of immigrants to the United States dropped sharply.

**44.** Which of the following is the most likely explanation for the change in the settlement patterns of immigrants to the United States?

   **(1)** the significant increase in the number of immigrants
   **(2)** the change in countries of origin, as there was a tendency to seek areas geographically similar to the homeland
   **(3)** the fact that the early immigrants had generally been farmers in their countries of origin, whereas the later immigrants had generally been laborers
   **(4)** the westward expansion, which opened up rich farmland
   **(5)** the industrialization of the United States

**45.** Which of the following statements about immigration to the United States from 1850 to 1930 is best supported by the passage?

   **(1)** The largest number of European immigrants came from the northern countries of Europe.
   **(2)** Prior to 1850 the United States had been an essentially homogeneous society.
   **(3)** By 1870 immigration had substantially altered the ethnic composition of the American population.
   **(4)** Immigration from northern Europe declined during the peak of immigration.
   **(5)** By the end of the period, immigration declined because problems prompting immigration had become less pressing.

*Items 46 to 49* are based on the following passage.

Although it is a little-publicized resource problem, the erosion of our soil is of great concern. Every year, soil is washed away into the sea or carried away with the wind.

Violent downpours rip the topsoil from the hillsides and carve great gulleys into the land. Windstorms blow across dry areas, turning topsoil to dust. Half of all countries suffer from severe soil-loss problems. One-third of U.S. cropland is now undergoing a marked decline in agricultural productivity because of soil erosion.

Human activity causes natural erosion rates to increase many times over. We plant on steep slopes without using the terracing method that helps save the soil. We allow animals to graze too long in the same places. We overwork the soil. Worst of all, we remove trees and don't plant new ones.

46. According to the passage, soil erosion has become a worldwide problem because of

(1) violent downpours and windstorms
(2) terracing on steep slopes
(3) overgrazing of animals
(4) a combination of natural and human activity
(5) removing trees and not replacing them

47. Based on information provided in the passage, which of the following environments is most likely to suffer from soil erosion?

(1) a meadow in the mountains
(2) a river basin with dams for flood control
(3) grazing land on an open plain
(4) a tropical rain forest
(5) a forest in a national park

48. Which one of the following statements is suggested by the passage?

(1) There is little we can do to prevent natural soil erosion.
(2) Soil erosion is less severe in the United States than in other countries.
(3) Conservation can help cut down on soil erosion.
(4) Events in nature increase the rate of soil erosion faster than human activities do.
(5) More soil is blown away than is washed away into the ocean.

**49.** Which of the following conclusions follows logically from the passage?

**(1)** Because soil erosion is such a pervasive problem, the national budget should include more money for conservation and less money for national security.

**(2)** Countries with soil-erosion management programs will not undergo steep declines in agricultural productivity.

**(3)** Soil-erosion management programs would be more effective if farmers were given better training in conservation techniques.

**(4)** Erosion is not as much of a problem now as it was in the last century, because we now know more about how to prevent severe soil loss.

**(5)** Part of the poor economic picture for today's U.S. farmers has to do with the problem of soil erosion.

*Items 50 to 52* refer to the following map.

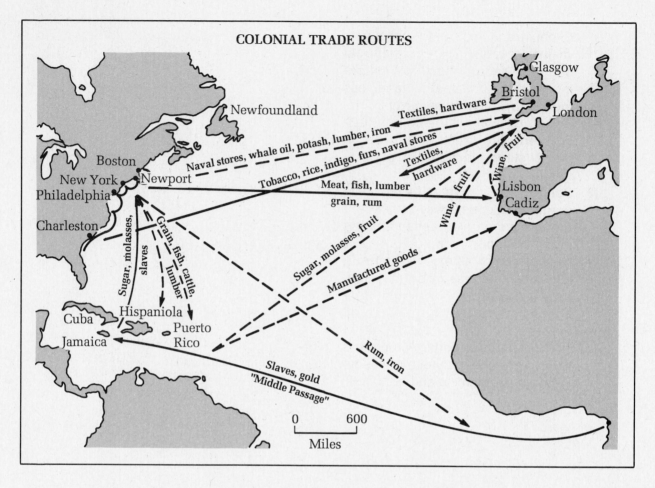

**COLONIAL TRADE ROUTES**

**50.** Based on the map, which of the following statements accurately describes an aspect of trade during the colonial period?

**(1)** The American colonies imported goods from both Great Britain and southern Europe.

**(2)** The American colonies exported lumber to both Great Britain and southern Europe.

**(3)** The American colonies imported slaves from Africa.

**(4)** The southern and northern colonies had completely different exports.

**(5)** The American colonies and the West Indies competed with each other in that their exports to Europe were similar.

**51.** Which of the following acts passed by British Parliament with regard to the American colonies can be explained on the basis of the map?

**(1)** act forbidding the colonies to establish furnaces to manufacture steel and hardware

**(2)** act forbidding gold bullion acquired from the West Indies to be minted into coin

**(3)** act imposing duties on colonial imports of luxury items

**(4)** act requiring revenue stamps to be affixed to all commercial bills and other documents

**(5)** act granting the East India Company a monopoly on all tea imported by the colonies

**52.** Which of the following statements is supported by information provided in the map?

(1) The complexity of trade routes ensured that countries which traded with one another were at peace.

(2) Great Britain imposed more restrictions on which countries the colonies could import from than on which countries they could export to.

(3) Great Britain favored a liberal trading policy with its colonies.

(4) The countries of western Europe enjoyed a profitable relationship with the British colonies in America.

(5) Repressive British trade policies ensured that the colonies would eventually revolt.

**53.** The writer [of a recent study] found that as one moves from middle-class urban centers in Britain to the rural lower-class islands, the distance between chairs at table decreases, so that in the outermost Shetland Islands actual bodily contact during meals and similar social occasions is not considered an invasion of separateness and no effort need be made to excuse it.

From E. Goffman, *Interaction Ritual,* Pantheon Books, 1982, p. 63. Used with permission.

Based on the information above, which of the following is most likely to have been the subject of the study mentioned?

(1) the history of British table manners

(2) customs and rituals in the Shetland Islands

(3) the relation between social class and table manners

(4) the relation between social class and definition of personal space

(5) food and family in Great Britain

*Item 54* refers to the following chart.

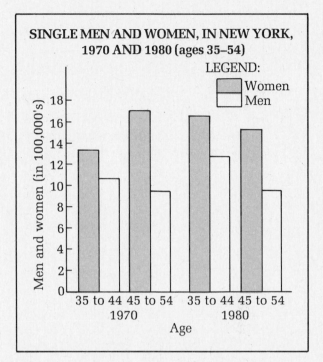

SINGLE MEN AND WOMEN, IN NEW YORK, 1970 AND 1980 (ages 35–54)

**54.** Which of the following statistics concerning New Yorkers can be determined by information provided in the chart?

(1) the percentage, in 1980, of all men and women between the ages of 35 and 54 who were single

(2) the change, in terms of percentage of total population, of single men, ages 35 to 54, from 1970 to 1980

(3) the change in the ratio between single men and single women, ages 35 to 54, from 1970 to 1980

(4) the number of single women, ages 45 to 54, who were married between 1970 and 1980

(5) the number of men, ages 35 to 54, who became single between 1970 and 1980

*Item 55* refers to the following diagram

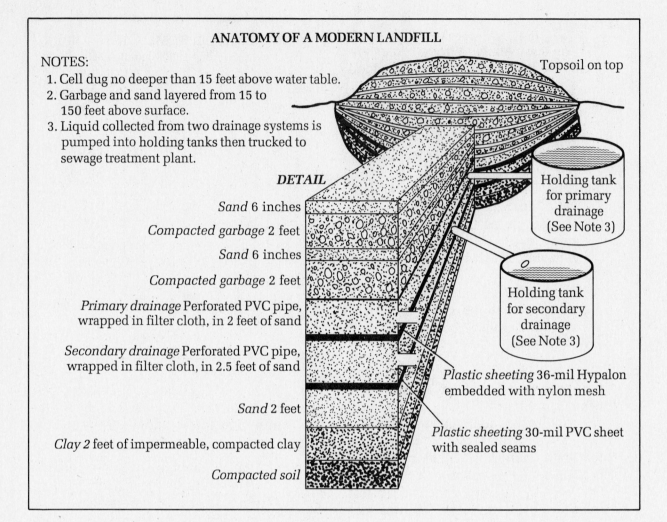

**ANATOMY OF A MODERN LANDFILL**

NOTES:
1. Cell dug no deeper than 15 feet above water table.
2. Garbage and sand layered from 15 to 150 feet above surface.
3. Liquid collected from two drainage systems is pumped into holding tanks then trucked to sewage treatment plant.

Topsoil on top

Holding tank for primary drainage (See Note 3)

Holding tank for secondary drainage (See Note 3)

*DETAIL*

*Sand* 6 inches
*Compacted garbage* 2 feet
*Sand* 6 inches
*Compacted garbage* 2 feet
*Primary drainage* Perforated PVC pipe, wrapped in filter cloth, in 2 feet of sand
*Secondary drainage* Perforated PVC pipe, wrapped in filter cloth, in 2.5 feet of sand
*Sand* 2 feet
*Clay 2* feet of impermeable, compacted clay
*Compacted soil*

*Plastic sheeting* 36-mil Hypalon embedded with nylon mesh

*Plastic sheeting* 30-mil PVC sheet with sealed seams

55. Based on the diagram above, which of the following is the best explanation for the design of a modern landfill?

(1) to appear attractive to local residents
(2) to fill dangerous holes and gulleys in the landscape
(3) to provide clean and safe fertilizer to local farmers
(4) to make the garbage safe and dry for later incineration
(5) to avoid contaminating nearby soil and water

*Items 56 and 57* are based on the following maps.

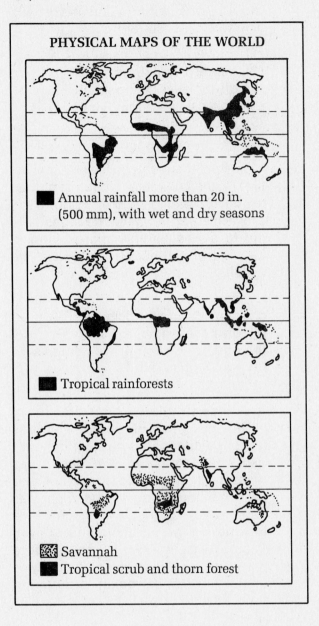

**PHYSICAL MAPS OF THE WORLD**

■ Annual rainfall more than 20 in. (500 mm), with wet and dry seasons

■ Tropical rainforests

▨ Savannah
■ Tropical scrub and thorn forest

**56.** Which of the following is information that can be gathered from the map of annual rainfall?

  **(1)** the minimum amount of rainfall in the shaded areas
  **(2)** which hemisphere receives most rain
  **(3)** which continent receives most rain
  **(4)** which continents receive less than 500 mm of rain annually
  **(5)** Which areas of the world do not have wet and dry seasons

**57.** Which of the following is information that can be gathered from all the maps?

  **(1)** Tropical rain forests require less rain annually than savannas.
  **(2)** Tropical rain forests require more rain annually than savannas.
  **(3)** Seasonal rainfall has little impact on either tropical rain forests or savannas.
  **(4)** Tropical rain forests and savannas require different climates.
  **(5)** Savannas need a cooler climate than tropical rain forests.

*Items 58 to 62* refer to the following information.

Neuroses are disorders of the mind or emotions. Listed below are five types of neuroses.

**(1) conversion neurosis:** characterized by physical symptoms, which are expressions of unconscious or unwanted desires that have been channeled into the neurotic's body

**(2) depressive neurosis:** characterized by depression, pessimism, and discouragement, in which the neurotic may withdraw from social communication and refuse to make plans for the future

**(3) dissociative neurosis:** characterized by the development of a "split" personality that acts out unconscious or unwanted desires which may otherwise be repressed by the neurotic

**(4) obsessive-compulsive neurosis:** characterized by obsessive behavior patterns, in which unconscious or unwanted desires may be channeled into irrational, repetitive activities that may be symbolically related to the problem

**(5) phobic neurosis:** characterized by abnormal, irrational fears, which may lead to the inability to engage in certain activities

Each of the following situations involves one of the types of neuroses listed above. The types may occur more than once in the set of items, but no one question has more than one best answer.

58. A man feels that his sexual desires are "unclean." He represses his desires and instead spends much of his time keeping his house spotlessly clean. He vacuums the carpets several times a day. The man is suffering from a

   (1) conversion neurosis
   (2) depressive neurosis
   (3) dissociative neurosis
   (4) obsessive-compulsive neurosis
   (5) phobic neurosis

59. A woman cannot fly in airplanes and, in general, begins to panic whenever she finds herself in a confined space. The woman is suffering from a

   (1) conversion neurosis
   (2) depressive neurosis
   (3) dissociative neurosis
   (4) obsessive-compulsive neurosis
   (5) phobic neurosis

60. A business executive feels incompetent on the job and less intelligent than his coworkers. Instead of trying to improve his performance, he stops talking to his colleagues and gives in to feelings of self-hatred. The executive is suffering from a

   (1) conversion neurosis
   (2) depressive neurosis
   (3) dissociative neurosis
   (4) obsessive-compulsive neurosis
   (5) phobic neurosis

61. A woman's children have grown up; all but one have left home. Then this last child announces he's getting married. The mother's excited. She makes plans to move to an apartment and give the house to her son. She tells her friends about how much she's looking forward to being on her own. Then suddenly, several weeks before the wedding, she develops a paralysis of the legs. The woman is suffering from a

   (1) conversion neurosis
   (2) depressive neurosis
   (3) dissociative neurosis
   (4) obsessive-compulsive neurosis
   (5) phobic neurosis

**62.** In contrast to her brothers and sisters, a woman appears not to be too upset by her mother's death. Around other people she acts as before. But when she's alone she finds herself staring out windows. She's unable to concentrate and frequently bursts into tears. Time passes, but her feelings of sadness remain. The woman is suffering from a

(1) conversion neurosis
(2) depressive neurosis
(3) dissociative neurosis
(4) obsessive-compulsive neurosis
(5) phobic neurosis

*Items 63 and 64* are based on the following passage.

The American Revolution, also known as the War for Independence, was fought to give American colonies the right to elect their own leaders, make their own laws, and conduct their own trade without interference from Great Britain's king and Parliament. The American colonists had long enjoyed a certain degree of freedom, but they didn't feel secure in that freedom, as it was often just a result of negligence or oversight. The British government could, and did, appoint colonial governors, restrict colonial trade, and impose various taxes. Taxes, the colonists thought, should be levied by colonial legislatures, not by Parliament, in which they were not represented. The American Revolution was fought to enable Americans to determine their own destiny and to fully develop their own government.

**63.** Based on the passage, which of the following actions by the British government would have been most likely to anger the colonists?

(1) repealing a tax levied on the colonies
(2) sending soldiers to help suppress Indian rebellions
(3) imposing import duties on goods entering American ports
(4) making trade agreements with other powers
(5) giving land grants to wealthy colonists

**64.** Based on the passage, which of the following statements might best reflect the feelings of many American colonists on the eve of the Revolution?

(1) They were mostly concerned about British restrictions of their economic rights and freedoms.
(2) They felt that Great Britain had too many interests worldwide and that the security of the American colonies was therefore in jeopardy.
(3) They envied the greater freedom and democracy of French and Spanish colonies.
(4) They felt their rights, needs, and freedoms could not be best served by an overseas power.
(5) They did not want to keep their link to Great Britain because so many of them had come from countries other than Great Britain.

Answers are on page 286–290.

# SIMULATED TEST
# Performance Analysis Chart

**Directions:** Circle the number of each item that you got correct on the Simulated Test. Count how many items you got correct in each row; then count how many items you got correct in each column. Write the amount correct per row and column as the numerator in the fraction in the appropriate "Total Correct" box. (The denominators represent the total number of items in the row or column.) Write the grand total correct over the denominator, **64**, at the lower right corner of the chart. (For example, if you got 54 items correct, write 54 so that the fraction reads 54/**64**.) Item numbers in color represent items based on graphic material.

| Item Type | History (page 85) | Geography (page 103) | Economics (page 112) | Political Science (page 125) | Behavioral Science (page 137) | TOTAL CORRECT |
|---|---|---|---|---|---|---|
| Comprehension (page 34) | 1, 29, 41, 50 | 25, 46, 56 | 2, 3, 6, 27, 39 | 18, 20, 23, 26 | 14, 15 | /18 |
| Application (page 43) | 63 | 47 | | 19, 34, 35, 36, 37, 38 | 8, 58, 59, 60, 61, 62 | /14 |
| Analysis (page 51) | 17, 30, 42, 44, 51 | 11, 48, 55, 57 | 4, 7, 28 | 21, 24 | 9, 53, 54 | /17 |
| Evaluation (page 61) | 31, 32, 43, 45, 52, 64 | 12, 49 | 5, 13, 33, 40 | 22 | 10, 16 | /15 |
| TOTAL CORRECT | /16 | /10 | /12 | /13 | /13 | /64 |

The page numbers in parentheses indicate where in this book you can find the beginning of specific instruction about the various fields of social studies and about the types of questions you encountered in the Simulated Test.

# Answers and Explanations

# Introduction

In the Answers and Explanations section, you will find answers to all the questions in these sections of the book.

- Lesson Exercises
- Chapter Quizzes
- Unit Tests
- The Practice Items
- The Practice Test
- The Simulated Test

You will discover that the Answers and Explanations section is a valuable study tool. It not only tells you the correct answer, but explains why each answer is correct. It also points out the reading skill that is required to answer each question successfully. Even if you get a question right, it will help to review the explanation. The explanation will reinforce your understanding of the question and the skills it tests. Because you might have guessed a correct answer or answered correctly for the wrong reason, it can't hurt to review explanations. It might help a lot.

# INSTRUCTION
## _UNIT I_ Reading Strategies

## Chapter 1
## A Strategy for Reading

### Lesson 1

**Previewing gives you an idea of how the material is organized and what it is about.**

1. _Comprehension/Reading Skills._ List of definitions. There is a list of five climatic regions in South America.
2. _Application/Reading Skills._ (1) Amazon Basin, (2) Coastlands, (3) Highlands, (4) Pampas, (5) Wastelands
3. _Comprehension/Reading Skills._ The material is easier to read, think about, and remember if you have an idea of what it is about and how it is organized before you start reading it.

### Lesson 2

**By asking questions as you read, you become more actively involved in your reading, and your comprehension improves.**

1. _Application/Reading Skills._ Sample question: What did each of these women do?
2. _Evaluation/Reading Skills._ Sample wording: "Reading to answer questions helps you to understand and remember more of what you read. In the long run, it will save you time, because you are not just reading randomly, you are reading with a purpose, which makes your reading more efficient."
3. _Application/Reading Skills._ Sample question: What is the difference between the definitions of _recession_ and _depression_?

### Lesson 3

**The four levels of questions are: comprehension, application, analysis, evaluation. By identifying the level, you can adjust your thinking and**
reading to answer the question successfully.

1. **(2)** _Comprehension/Reading Skills._ Comprehension, or understanding of the material, is required for each of the higher levels. Application items require, in addition, that you use the information in a new context. Analysis items require that you use the understanding to examine relationships between ideas. Evaluation items require that you use the understanding to determine the accuracy of the information or methods used.
2. _Application/Reading Skills._ The question is an application question. It asks you to take the information given about Louie in the passage and to apply it to a new situation. From the story about Louie going back to the restaurant after a bad experience, you are asked to draw conclusions about how Louie would handle another bad experience.
3. _Comprehension/Reading Skills._ FALSE. You will not be asked to name the level of items on the GED. However, knowing the type of thinking required by each of the different levels will help you answer items more efficiently.

## Chapter 1 Quiz

1. _Comprehension/Reading Skills._ Sample wording: . . . You should quickly look for clues such as title, labels, and organization into rows and columns, bar graph, circle graph, line graph, etc.
2. _Analysis/Reading Skills._ Sample answer: (1) You save time because you know what you are looking for. (2) You keep yourself from getting confused by wrong answers that sound right.
3. **(4)** _Comprehension/Reading Skills._ This is an example of one of the shorter types of items you will find on the GED. You will

never be expected to "pull information out of thin air," but sometimes you will be given only a small bit of information to work with.

4. _Comprehension/Reading Skills._ The question asked ("Who would be the LEAST likely to . . . ?") is an evaluation question because it asks you to assess the validity of information based on provided criteria.
5. _Application/Reading Skills._ Number of inmates. Pay attention to each of the two labels on a line graph, because they tell what two things are being compared.
6. _Comprehension/Reading Skills._ The clue words _Items 6 to 9_ tell you that you will need to answer four items based on the passage. The words are prominent because they are in italics, or slanted print.
7. _Comprehension/Reading Skills._ Make up yourself. As you read the passage, allow your curiosity to help you come up with your own questions.
8. _Application/Reading Skills._ Sample question: Are the wives also allowed to have two or more husbands? The question is answered indirectly in the second sentence. Since you are told that polyandry is more rare, you can infer that wives in these cultures usually cannot have more than one husband.
9. _Comprehension/Reading Skills._ The question asked ("Which of the following is an example of polygyny?") is a comprehension question, because it measures your ability to understand a definition.
10. _Comprehension/Reading Skills._ Predict answers to the questions (including test items). Now that you have had practice in previewing and questioning, you can sometimes skip steps or vary the order.

# Chapter 2
# Comprehension

## Lesson 1

**Restatement is an important comprehension skill because it provides a way to check whether you understand what you are reading.**

1. **(3)** *Comprehension/Reading Skills.* Choice (3) restates the last sentence in the paragraph.
2. *Comprehension/Reading Skills.* Sample wording: A republic is a way of government in which almost all people have the vote, and the authority of the state is held in check by a constitution.
3. *Comprehension/Reading Skills.* TRUE. The statement restates the third sentence in the paragraph.

## Lesson 2

**Skills used in summarizing include deleting unimportant or repetitious details, generalizing from a list of specific items, combining a list of items under a more general statement, and selecting or creating a main idea.**

1. *Comprehension/Reading Skills.* Sample wording: Among the major Swiss resources, industry and farming are in the north, whereas forests and dairying are found in the south.
2. *Comprehension/Reading Skills.* Sample wording: The Austrian economy is characterized by industry in the east; dairying in the west; farming in the north, middle, and southern sections; and forests in the middle.
3. *Comprehension/Reading Skills.* Sample answer: Listing the main place where each resource can be found.

## Lesson 3

**Strategies include asking yourself whether the implication makes sense, whether it is supported by the facts in the selection, and whether it is supported by your own background knowledge.**

1. **(4)** *Comprehension/Reading Skills.* Because sentence (1) in the paragraph states that interstate compacts are a common way to establish cooperative relations, it follows that cooperation between states is possible.
2. *Comprehension/Reading Skills.*

Sentence (1) states that cooperative relations are one result of such compacts.
3. **(4)** *Comprehension/Reading Skills.* Choice (1) is incorrect because cooperation does not necessarily imply friendship. Choice (2) may sometimes be true, but it is also possible that interstate compacts might override states' rights. Choice (3) is incorrect; if it were true, then interstate compacts would be less necessary. Choice (5) is also contradicted by the fact that interstate compacts often override state borders.

# Chapter 2    Quiz

1. *Application/Reading Skills.* Look for prominent clues to the form of the chart, such as headings and divided sections. Think about questions as you read, such as: Did citizens in 1972 differ from those in 1980 with regard to what qualities they thought a President should have?
2. *Comprehension/Reading Skills.* Summary. Typical summary questions are those that ask you to identify the main idea or best title for a passage or a graph.
3. *Application/Reading Skills.* (1) I, (2) R, (3) S. A reader must infer what the implications of a passage are. Items that refer to specific parts of a passage often require you to restate the section. Selection of the best title or caption requires summarizing of important points.
4. *Comprehension/Reading Skills.* Income. The last line refers to the income of live-alones.
5. *Comprehension/Reading Skills.* *Middle-income* earners seems to refer to those who are in the "middle" between being wealthy and earning less than $10,000.
6. *Comprehension/Reading Skills.* TRUE. The first line tells us that it is a challenge to deal with the diversity, or range, of live-alones.
7. *Comprehension/Reading Skills.* The last line. About half earn middle-sized incomes and about half earn less than $10,000.
8. *Comprehension/Reading Skills.* Sample wording: The amount that the central Federal Reserve Bank charges financial institutions when it gives them loans was

lower in 1986 than it had been in nine years.
9. *Comprehension/Reading Skills.* 1977. How high the line rises indicates how high the discount rate is. You can see that the line had not dipped this low since 1977.
10. **(2)** *Comprehension/Reading Skills.* The sentence after the star in the box tells you that the annual average for 1986 was not available.

# Chapter 3
# Application

## Lesson 1

**Comprehension items test your understanding of what a passage or graphic says. Application items require you to comprehend the material, then move a step beyond and apply what you have learned to a new situation.**

1. *Comprehension/Reading Skills.* Understand; make predictions; read. An application question requires you to understand the material so that you can apply it to a new context. It is usually helpful to have an answer in mind before reading through the choices, so that you can zero in on the correct choice rather than being confused by the many options.
2. *Application/Reading Skills.* (a) C, (b) A, (c) A. Unlike the first item, the second and third items refer to material apparently not mentioned in the original material.
3. **(2)** *Application/Reading Skills.* Since the passage states that individuals need to be motivated by rewards, it makes sense to show people in departments what the rewards of hiring minorities will be.

## Lesson 2

**The "new" type of item consists of a list of categories or definitions followed by a set of items, each containing the same five choices.**

1. **(2)** *Application/Reading Skills.* The son is banning from memory all painful experiences with his father.
2. **(4)** *Application/Reading Skills.* The child is attributing his own unacceptable actions to his baby sister.
3. **(1)** *Application/Reading Skills.* The teenager's aggression is being given an acceptable outlet—football.

## Chapter 3 *Quiz*

1. *Application/Reading Skills.* The comprehension item. Since application items require that you understand *and* use the information, they are at a higher level than comprehension items.
2. *Comprehension/Reading Skills.* FALSE. You will find all levels of items, including application items, based on both passages and graphics.
3. *Comprehension/Reading Skills.* Before the set of items. The list of definitions or categories is followed by the items themselves.
4. **(3)** *Application/Reading Skills.* By applying what you have learned about the new trend toward candidates' showing more emotion, you can see that the politician might gain votes by talking about his son's death.
5. *Application/Reading Skills.* TRUE. The point of the article is that showing emotional sensitivity is often considered a strength in candidates, whereas it used to be considered a weakness.
6. *Application/Reading Skills.* Sample answer: A politician gains the votes of Vietnam War veterans by talking about how helpless he felt after returning from his own tour of duty.
7. **(5)** *Application/Reading Skills.* Of the choices, only this one captures the idea that those affected by the plummeting oil prices cannot control the prices.
8. *Application/Reading Skills.* One of the last cars. According to the theory, the United States might eventually be affected by the fall of a country in South America just as later rollercoaster cars follow earlier ones.
9. *Application/Reading Skills.* Sample answer: The prices of many foods, such as seasonal vegetables, go up and down, with the consumer being a lot happier about the low prices than the farmer and supermarket are.
10. *Comprehension/Reading Skills.* Rollercoasters. You need to understand that both rollercoasters and oil prices go up and down and that the "ride" frightens many people.

## Chapter 4 **Analysis**

### Lesson 1

**Facts can be measured or observed; opinions involve personal interpretations that cannot be proved; hypotheses are educated guesses to explain what has happened and to predict what will happen.**

1. **(1)** *Analysis/Reading Skills.* The origins of Congressmen are facts that can be checked. Choices (2), (3), (4), and (5) all describe matters of opinion, as words like *impressed, beautiful, proud,* and *important* indicate.
2. *Application/Reading Skills.* Sample answer: "they cannot help being impressed each time they see this beautiful city again." It is only the writer's opinion that the Congressmen are impressed, and only the writer's opinion that the city is beautiful.
3. *Analysis/Reading Skills.* (1) O, (2) H, (3) O. None of the statements can be proved. Both (1) and (3) reflect opposite opinions about the clubs. Choice (2) presents a theory to explain the clubs.

### Lesson 2

**To identify an unstated assumption, ask yourself: What does the writer take for granted about the topic?**

1. **(2)** *Analysis/Reading Skills.* Choice (1) is contradicted since smaller states had fewer representatives. Choices (4), and (5) are directly stated. Choice (3) is contradicted by the material in the passage.
2. *Analysis/Reading Skills.* Sample wording: Happy. Since the cartoonist draws the consumers in the last car with smiling faces, we can tell he assumes they are happy about the drop.
3. *Analysis/Reading Skills.* Sample answer: Several of the other customers may have mentioned that the low prices made them a bit nervous and that it might be better to have moderate prices now to avoid sky-high prices later.

### Lesson 3

**A supporting statement is one of several details the author includes to lay the groundwork for the main conclusion.**

1. **(5)** *Analysis/Reading Skills.* The details about Canadian and Mexican insurance requirements lay the groundwork for the final sentence, containing the main idea: Whatever country you plan to visit, you should check first to find out about insurance requirements.
2. *Analysis/Reading Skills.* Canada requires you to show that your company will meet Canadian accident requirements. Mexico requires you to take out a special tourist policy.
3. *Analysis/Reading Skills.* The new sentence is a supporting detail. It adds support for the original conclusion, that travelers should check on insurance before they make their trips.

### Lesson 4

**To judge which of several explanations is the most likely one for a particular change, use what you are told plus any background knowledge you have on the subject and ask yourself: Would this lead to the change described or to something else?**

1. **(3)** *Analysis/Reading Skills.* We are told that New York courts have specifically protected military activities from lawsuits. Choice (1) is not correct; we are told that nuclear testing was linked to cancer and that Agent Orange was linked to health problems. No evidence is given for Choices (2), (4), or (5).
2. *Analysis/Reading Skills.* The courts' decision would probably discourage someone from making any further suits against the government for causing military-related health problems, since two such previous suits have been unsuccessful.
3. *Analysis/Reading Skills.* A reversal of the decisions, especially with huge monetary awards attached, would probably have the effect of encouraging others to bring similar suits.

## Chapter 4 **Quiz**

1. *Application/Reading Skills.* (1) b, (2) c, (3) a. (1) asks you to apply the President's broad statement to a specific new case; (2) asks you to consider how one idea (cause) might be related to another (effect); (3) simply asks if you understand a term used: *tariff.*

2. *Comprehension/Reading Skills.* Sample answer: The girl's lawyers argue that as a vegetarian, she should be protected by the First Amendment from having to do something against her beliefs just as people with religious beliefs are so protected.

3. *Analysis/Reading Skills.* (1) F, (2) F, (3) O, (4) O. Sentences (1) and (2) can be proven true. Sentences (3) and (4) are personal interpretations that cannot be proven true or false.

4. *Analysis/Reading Skills.* Sentence (4). Details about the case are included as a build-up to the general issue of whether the First Amendment protects the girl from having to dissect frogs.

5. *Comprehension/Reading Skills.* FALSE. According to the chart it is a fact that about half of those questioned *believe* that supermarkets are more efficient than Congress.

6. *Analysis/Reading Skills.* Sample answer: Since those surveyed gave Congress the lowest efficiency rating, you can conclude that they did so because they do not feel Congress does a very efficient job.

7. *Analysis/Reading Skills.* Sample answer: They have had experience with supermarkets where food can be bought quickly and inexpensively, and they hear about the time and money wasted by Congress.

8. **(3)** *Analysis/Reading Skills.* The sentence describing the split in the women's movement also mentioned that the split cost the movement some valuable allies. Since this is followed by a sentence describing the delay in passing women's suffrage, the author seems to assume that the split caused the delay. Choices (1) and (2) are directly stated. Choices (4) and (5) may be assumptions, but there is no evidence in the passage that the author holds them.

9. *Analysis/Reading Skills.* (a) is an effect and (b) is a cause. The hard work of women's organizations helped cause the Nineteenth Amendment to be passed.

10. *Analysis/Reading Skills.* (b) and (c) are supporting details that lead to (a), the conclusion. Once we know that the split cost the movement some valuable allies, and

that there was a delay in the passage of women's suffrage until 1920, we can come to the conclusion that without a split, suffrage might have been won earlier.

## Chapter 5
# Evaluation

## Lesson 1

**To judge whether there is adequate evidence to support a statement, ask yourself: Is there enough of the right kind of information to back up this statement?**

1. *Evaluation/Reading Skills.* The conclusion is not adequately supported. A large vocabulary may be typical of a successful person, but that does not mean that a large vocabulary by itself is enough to make a person successful.

2. *Evaluation/Reading Skills.* The conclusion is not supported by the evidence. The anthropologist has not presented any data about why people perform the ritual. He or she is merely speculating that there is a connection between the ritual and the early hour of the morning in which it is performed.

3. **(4)** *Evaluation/Reading Skills.* Since only Americans were polled, not people around the globe or police alone, Choices (1) and (5) are incorrect. There is no evidence in the chart to support choices (2) or (3).

## Lesson 2

**By realizing how values affect a writer's beliefs, the reader can be a more critical judge of the accuracy of information presented.**

1. **(4)** *Evaluation/Reading Skills.* If the writer believed that children should have to earn the money they are given, the writer would not be suggesting allowances.

2. *Evaluation/Reading Skills.* No. Someone who believes in teaching children that money has to be earned might say that a regular allowance should be established only if children do something to earn it.

3. *Evaluation/Reading Skills.* Sample answer: (1) It is wrong to eat a hamburger because it is made from a living creature. (2) Fast-food hamburgers are okay but not as good as barbecued hamburgers.

## Lesson 3

**To assess whether a statement is supported with documentation, ask yourself: Are statistics, observations, or measurements of some sort provided to support the idea?**

1. **(4)** *Evaluation/Reading Skills.* The Chicago school study provides documentation for Choice (4). None of the other alternatives mentioned are actually documented in the passage.

2. *Evaluation/Reading Skills.* Japanese. If the writer had proved that core curriculum accounts for Japanese student achievement, he would have made a better case for teaching Americans a core curriculum.

3. *Evaluation/Reading Skills.* Sample wording: A study could have been done comparing two groups of "low" students, with one given more words to learn than the other.

## Lesson 4

**If you can detect errors in reasoning, you will not accept faulty arguments.**

1. *Evaluation/Reading Skills.* You cannot conclude that the decrease in the number of blue-collar workers resulted in the decline in productivity. Just because two things happen at the same time does not mean that one causes the other.

2. **(5)** *Evaluation/Reading Skills.* Without further evidence, there is no reason to "blame" white-collar workers for the low output. Choices (1), (2), and (3) describe facts from the passage. Choice (4) is an accurate summary of the information.

3. *Evaluation/Reading Skills.* TRUE. Once you learn that blue-collar productivity went up while white-collar productivity declined, you have enough evidence to state that blue-collar workers put in a more "respectable showing" in terms of productivity.

## Chapter 5   **Quiz**

1. **(4)** *Comprehension/Reading Skills.* The reader can infer that if Americans are the "least sensitive to other cultures" and would do well to understand other countries' languages, they often do not learn those languages. Choice (5) is contradicted in the passage.

There is insufficient evidence to support (1), (2), and (3).

2. **(1)** *Evaluation/Reading Skills.* The author of the study states that the U.S. is losing the war because of its cultural insensitivity. It is logical to conclude that the writer suggests that U.S. residents be more sensitive. Choice (2) is contradicted by the passage. There is no evidence to support (3), (4), or (5).

3. **(2)** *Evaluation/Reading Skills.* Such a person would probably have best access to documentation—proof on paper.

4. **(1)** *Application/Reading Skills.* As with all evaluation items, this one requires that you judge the accuracy of information.

5. *Evaluation/Reading Skills.* All three. The values of the writer affect whatever that person writes, whether it is a personal journal, neutral-sounding court notes, or an objective-seeming textbook.

6. *Evaluation/Reading Skills.* Sample answer: (1) Which side of the Revolutionary War did the girl support? (2) Did her family have relatives living in England?

7. *Evaluation/Reading Skills.* TRUE. Textbooks may seem to contain "hard facts," but the very choice of which facts to present is affected by the writer's point of view. The British writer might choose to include more details sympathetic to the British side than an American author might.

8. **(b)** *Evaluation/Reading Skills.* The chart does not tell us anything about the composition of immigrants in the rest of New York's population. Statement (b), on the other hand, is documented by figures.

9. *Evaluation/Reading Skills.* The mean, or average, age is found by adding up all the ages and dividing by the number of drivers. Most drivers might be younger than 33.5, but a few who are much older would bring up the average.

10. *Evaluation/Reading Skills.* FALSE.

Just because approximately half the drivers had some college does not prove that college was necessary for the license any more than finding that half of the drivers had brown eyes would show that brown eyes are necessary for the license.

---

# *UNIT I*  **TEST**

1. *Comprehension/Reading Skills.* *Checks and balances* refers to the system designed to prevent any one branch of government from becoming too powerful. Each branch is allowed to intervene in certain decisions made by the others if those decisions seem inappropriate.

2. **(3)** *Application/Reading Skills.* Choice (3) is the only case in which the legislative branch is actually checked in its power.

3. **(2)** *Analysis/Reading Skills.* Choice (1) is not supported in the passage; each branch cannot check each of the other branches on any decision made. Choice (3) may be true, but there is no evidence to support it. Choices (4) and (5) are contradicted by the evidence.

4. *Analysis/Reading Skills.* Fact. This statement is a fact because it can be proved and is documented (by the Constitution).

5. *Evaluation/Reading Skills.* "Circular reasoning" is being used here. There is nothing in the statement to show that the system is actually effective in doing what it was created to do.

6. *Comprehension/Reading Skills.* Sample wording: Of 1,349 newspeople polled about which news organization they considered most reliable, many chose the same ten organizations, with *The New York Times*, Associated Press, United Press International, and the *Washington Post* being the "top four."

7. *Comprehension/Reading Skills.* CBS. You can probably recognize that all the other sources listed are magazines, newspapers, or wire services.

8. *Application/Reading Skills.* *Washington Post.* Make sure you understand the chart. Find 10 in the "% of vote" column and move your finger across until you find who won 10 percent of the "most reliable" vote: the *Washington Post.*

9. *Analysis/Reading Skills.* Print sources such as magazines and newspapers can provide more detailed, less sensationalized information.

10. *Evaluation/Reading Skills.* FALSE. You can conclude that many (about one-third) of the newspeople believe that *The New York Times* is the most reliable source. You have no information to show that their belief is well-grounded.

11. **(4)** *Comprehension/Reading Skills.* The passage says that economics, not slavery, was the main cause. The North wanted tariffs and the South did not.

12. **(1)** *Comprehension/Reading Skills.* Choice (2) is incorrect, since you are told that the South was primarily agricultural, not industrial. Since import taxes are paid by the consumer on goods imported from foreign countries, you can eliminate choice (3).

13. **(1)** *Application/Reading Skills.* Choice (2) is wrong, since tariffs raise the prices on imported products, thus enabling American producers to raise their prices too.

14. *Analysis/Reading Skills.* (a) S, (b) S, (c) S, (d) C. Details about the economy of the South and that of the North are included because they help the reader understand why economic factors were the main cause of the Civil War.

15. *Evaluation/Reading Skills.* The initial statement is faulty, so the argument founded on it is also faulty. Opposition to slavery was NOT the main cause of the Civil War.

# UNIT II Foundations in Social Studies

## Chapter 1
## Introduction to Social Studies

### Lesson 1

**Social studies is a complex field of study because it involves many branches of the social sciences.**

1. *Comprehension/Social Studies.* People are said to be social because they live in organized groups or communities.
2. *Application/Social Studies.* Choices (a), (b), and (d) are United States customs or beliefs. Choices (c) and (e) are traditions in other societies.
3. *Comprehension/Social Studies.* FALSE. The lesson notes that social studies is concerned with the past (history) and can help us prepare for the future.
4. *Analysis/Social Studies.* A society is a group of people who associate with one another for some common purpose. Within a large society there may be subgroups. For example, American society may be divided into any number of separate yet interdependent smaller societies based on a variety of factors: cultural, economic, religious, regional, ethnic, political, and so on.

### Lesson 2

**A social science is an area of study concerned with people and their roles in society. The physical sciences, by contrast, are concerned with natural phenomena. Social sciences are concerned with human events, systems, and beliefs.**

1. **(3)** *Comprehension/Social Studies.* The distribution of population is a concern of cultural geography.
2. *Application/Social Studies.* It would be classified as political science because it is concerned with different types of government.
3. *Application/Social Studies.* Physical geography. The map shows land elevations.
4. *Analysis/Social Studies.* A study of the physical structures of Earth includes mountains, oceans, rivers, lakes, forests, and deserts. All of these structures are found in nature, but they affect mankind.
5. *Evaluation/Social Studies.* Many industries require natural resources: shipping centers require good harbors; lumber and paper mills are located close to sources of timber; factories require a source of power, and so on. The location of a country's waterways, farmland, mineral resources, and forests plays a vital role in its economic development. Capitalist countries thrive on private ownership of business. Socialist or communist countries have little or no private ownership. The role of government greatly affects a country's economic development.

### Lesson 3

**Social scientists use graphs, maps, charts, tables, time lines, and cartoons to present their findings.**

1. *Comprehension/Social Studies.* Approximately 20,000 automobiles were sold for $10,000.
2. *Analysis/Social Studies.* According to the graph, as the price increases the number of cars sold decreases.
3. **(2)** *Evaluation/Social Studies.* The graph shows that millions of new factory jobs were created between 1870 and 1970. It follows that cities grew rapidly during that period. None of the other conclusions can be drawn and seem to be contrary to the evidence presented.
4. *Comprehension/Social Studies.* Political cartoons are usually the tool used to express opinions. The other tools mentioned typically display facts.

## Chapter 1   Quiz

1. **(3)** *Comprehension/Social Studies.* Biology is a branch of natural science, not social studies.
2. *Comprehension/Social Studies.* Answers should appear in this order: (b), (a), (d), (c), (c).
3. *Analysis/Social Studies.* (a) *Socialize* means to mingle, mix with, meet; (b) *society* (as in *Society of Engineers*) means a group formed to pursue a common interest; (c) *social* (as in *social event*) describes an event devoted to meeting people or catching up on family events.
4. *Analysis/Social Studies.* (a) economics; (b) cultural geography; (c) physical geography; (d) history; or economics.
5. *Analysis/Social Studies.* Natural resources play a major role in economic development. A map of natural resources would identify areas where major industrialization, farming, mining, or shipping could be located.
6. *Evaluation/Social Studies.* Here are six ways government can affect economics: (1) When government taxes particular goods, the price of the goods is raised. This can lead to decreased consumption. (2) Government may encourage more production of a product by providing tax incentives to an industry. (3) At certain times, particularly in time of war, government may control the distribution of certain products. (4) Government regulations concerning imports can affect both the producers and the consumers of products. (5) Government may regulate or deregulate prices in certain industries such as transportation and communication. (6) Government may enact laws regulating conditions in the work place.
7. *Evaluation/Social Studies.* Objectivity and consistency are very important in anthropology because anthropologists study cultures different from their own. If they judge those cultures, they may misunderstand them; the conclusions they come to may not be valid. It is essential for them to

consider the customs of different cultures in the context of those cultures, rather than to compare the customs to their own.

8. *Application/Social Studies.*

Hindu 85%
Christian 3%
Moslem 11%
Buddhist 1%

9. *Evaluation/Social Studies.* The idea that government gets its power from the governed was revolutionary because it meant that the people held final power and not the ruler. Therefore, the ruler was responsible to the people. The people had certain rights, including the right to change governments. Under divine right, none of this is possible.

10. *Evaluation/Social Studies.* It means that change is a part of political development and that change is a desirable thing.

# Chapter 2  American History

## Lesson 1

**The Crusades, the Renaissance, and the rise of monarchies stimulated Europeans to explore remote parts of the world. The New World was discovered by explorers seeking new trade routes to Asia. Colonies were established by monarchies seeking to increase their wealth and power.**

1. *Comprehension/History.* Spain sent Christopher Columbus in search of a new trade route to Asia. Instead, he discovered the Caribbean Islands. Later, Spanish explorers in search of gold established settlements in Mexico, South America, the Caribbean, and Florida.
2. *Analysis/History.* In town meetings each freeman cast his own vote on an issue. That form of self-government is *direct* democracy. In the House of Burgesses, indirect democracy, representatives did the voting.
3. *Application/History.* Just as in the twentieth century, scientific invention during the Renaissance made exploration of the world possible.

## Lesson 2

**In 1765 and 1767, the king imposed heavy taxes and restrictions on the colonies in order to pay England's war debts after the French and Indian War. The colonies protested and the Revolutionary War began.**

1. *Analysis/History.* Individualism led to rapid economic prosperity. England imposed taxes. The Boston Tea Party, one of many protests by the colonists, prompted King George to send troops, and in 1775 the Revolutionary War began.
2. *Evaluation/History.* The colonists had a strong belief in economic and political independence, free enterprise, and self-government.
3. *Application/History.* Most Americans pay local, state, and federal taxes. Because nearly every American of voting age may vote for representatives to all three levels of government, there is representation of those taxed.

## Lesson 3

**The colonies became one nation by ratifying the Articles of Confederation, thereby agreeing to cooperate with one another. Later, to strengthen the central government, the Constitution was written and ratified.**

1. *Analysis/History.* Each state protected its own interests and did not want the federal interference. As a consequence, there was no common currency, no laws binding all the states, and no national army to put down rebellion or to protect America from outside forces.
2. *Comprehension/History.* There were no uniform tax laws or currency, so foreign nations had to deal with each state and not with the Confederation as a whole.
3. *Evaluation/History.* Large states supported the Virginia Plan because it would have given them a larger voice in the legislature; small states supported the New Jersey Plan because it would have given them a voice equal to the larger states'.
4. *Evaluation/History.* (a) and (c) Southern states; (b) and (d) Northern states. At the time of the Constitutional Convention, slavery in the North was nearly extinct. Each side wanted to get as much representation for itself as possible in the national legislature; each state also wanted its taxes as low as possible.
5. (4) *Comprehension/History.* Only (3) and (4) established governments. Since central government

under the Articles of Confederation consisted only of one house of Congress, it must be concluded that the presidency was first established by the Constitution.

## Lesson 4

**During the first fifty years, America pursued a policy of territorial expansion at home, and a policy of nonintervention in foreign affairs. This allowed the country, for the most part, to maintain peace and stability while expanding from the East to the West Coast.**

1. *Application/History.* Today all citizens at least 18 years old are allowed to vote. In early America only white, male property owners had the right to vote.
2. *Analysis/History.* Washington endorsed the principle of neutrality in foreign affairs. Monroe incorporated that principle into the foreign policy of the Monroe Doctrine.
3. *Application/History.* The Monroe Doctrine warned foreign powers against establishing new colonies in North America. That warning applied to Russia and its southward movement from Alaska where it already had colonies.

## Lesson 5

**Most Northerners favored a strong central government that would enact laws to support American banking and trade. Southerners represented any central government interference, particularly with regard to slavery. To protect its own interests, the South withdrew from the Union and formed its own government.**

1. *Comprehension/History.* Jackson aligned himself with the "common" people of the West and the South rather than with Eastern landowners. He favored individualism, and opposed a strong central government.
2. *Analysis/History.* The Industrial Revolution made the North dependent on its ability to compete with foreign manufacturers. It wanted a strong central government to impose tariffs on imports. The South did not want the North's influence in a strong central government that might challenge slavery, on which the cotton economy depended.
3. *Comprehension/History.* Lincoln, as his popularity in the North indi-

cated, was for a strong central government. The South saw his election as a defeat since it opposed strong central government.

## Lesson 6

**The Civil War was fought on Southern territory and caused great destruction and a high death toll. However, the South's defeat did not cause major changes in the Southern way of life.**

1. (2) *Evaluation/History.* Because the Emancipation Proclamation ended slavery in only the eleven Confederate States, Choice (4) is wrong and Choice (3) is unlikely. In 1863 blacks could not vote, so Choice (5) is wrong. Choice (1) is wrong since he promised not to interfere with existing slavery.
2. *Application/History.* (a) Reconstruction; (b) carpetbaggers.
3. (4) *Evaluation/History.* The lesson does not indicate that the North's generals were better than the South's.

## Lesson 7

**With post–Civil War industrialism people moved to cities to work in factories. Immigration rates rose and cities began to experience the social problems crowded living conditions cause.**

1. *Comprehension/History.* (a) 75%; (b) 25%; (c) 50%.
2. *Analysis/History.* According to the bar graph, Chicago grew more than any other city between 1850 and 1900. Chicago's population increased by nearly 4500%. No other city's population increased that much.
3. *Evaluation/History.* Both the AF of L and the Progressive Movement tried to improve conditions for American workers.

## Lesson 8

**The abuses of business, which affected workers, consumers, and children, caused the government to take a direct role in regulating business practices and to intervene in other aspects of American life.**

1. *Application/History.* Those actions were based on antitrust laws, which prohibit monopolies.
2. *Comprehension/History.* (a) the Nineteenth Amendment to the Constitution; (b) the Department of Labor; (c) compulsory education;

(d) the Stock Market Crash.
3. (3) *Evaluation/History.* The New Deal concerned itself with workers, consumers, and farmers. Defense programs were not part of the program.

## Lesson 9

**America pursued a policy of isolationism until the 1890s, when industrialization had created a need for new markets and sources of raw materials. America became imperialistic as it aggressively sought political and economic control in other countries and territories. Later, in a spirit of internationalism, the United States entered World Wars I and II and emerged from each more powerful on the international scene.**

1. *Evaluation/History.* According to information in the lesson, the United States government's neutrality was stricter before World War I than before World War II. During World War II, the United States provided supplies to the Allies before it actually joined them in fighting the Axis nations.
2. *Comprehension/History.* (a) isolationism; (b) imperialism.
3. *Application/History.* The United Nations.

## Lesson 10

**Since World War II, the United States has taken an increasingly active role in international affairs. The United States has been a leader in organizations such as the U.N. and NATO.**

1. *Application/History.* The Soviet Union's policy has been one of imperialism. Establishment of the Soviet bloc, for example, was not the product of isolationism.
2. *Comprehension/History.* (a) the cold war; (b) the Third World; (c) détente.
3. (2) *Comprehension/History.* NATO is an alliance of Western European countries, Canada, and the United States.

## Lesson 11

**Major domestic issues since World War II have been economic and social reform. Civil rights laws and other legislation to improve the quality of life for all Americans have been hallmarks of most recent administrations.**

1. *Comprehension/History.* A Supreme Court decision that recognized segregation in schools to be unconstitutional began the process of desegregation.
2. *Analysis/History.* The civil rights acts under the Eisenhower administration affected voters' rights; those under the Johnson administration affected first voting, employment, and public accommodation, and later, private accommodation. Later acts provided further support for the rights of people in their daily lives, including the right to employment and housing without discrimination.
3. *Evaluation/History.* Eisenhower was the president most likely to support a conservative federal spending policy. Truman proposed funding for education, but a conservative group opposed him. Under Johnson, direct federal aid to schools was established. According to the lesson, Eisenhower did not address funding for education, which is evidence that his policy was most like that of the conservative coalition's.

## Lesson 12

**Problems the United States will continue to face are inflation, recession, poverty, unjust limitation of civil rights, scarcities of natural resources, world hunger, arms control, and international unrest.**

1. *Comprehension/History.* Recession.
2. (5) *Comprehension/History.* The chart in Figure 3 shows that the candidates were Reagan, Carter, Anderson, and other candidates (more than 1). Therefore, there were more than four candidates.
3. *Evaluation/History.* The 1980 election was not won by a popular vote landslide. Reagan, the winner, got only 51% of the popular vote, which is only a little more than a majority (50% + 1). A landslide popular victory would require nearly all of the popular votes.
4. *Analysis/History.* The map in Figure 3 shows which states were carried by which parties. Since it shows no states carried by the Independent Party, Anderson did not receive the majority of the popular vote in his home state.

## Chapter 2   Quiz

1. **(2)** *Application/History.* Wilson's remarks encouraged the United States to become involved with world concerns by fighting for democracy in foreign countries.
2. *Application/History.* World War I. The war lasted from 1914 to 1918; the United States entered the war in 1917.
3. *Analysis/History.* ". . . the right of those who submit to authority to have a voice in their own governments. . . ." Democracy means government by the governed.
4. **(2)** *Evaluation/History.* By imperialism, one country may seek economic control of another for gain. War to protect trade interests could be seen as imperialistic.
5. **(2)** *Application/History.* Most foreign aid spending was in Europe after World War II from 1946 to 1952. The Marshall Plan provided aid to war-torn Europe during that time.
6. **(5)** *Application/History.* Kennedy was president from 1961 to 1963. Third World countries are underdeveloped ones, all outside Europe and North America. The time of the aid and the regions affected make only the Middle East and South Asia, 1953 to 1966, correct.
7. **(1)** *Analysis/History.* The graphs split Asia into two regions: East and South. Since spending for South Asia is combined with that for the Middle East, spending for all of Asia cannot be separated.
8. *Application/History.* Civil liberties. Because the statute was a state law, it was the government, not a private group or individual, that violated freedom.
9. *Application/History.* Civil liberty. The Fifth Amendment is part of the Bill of Rights, which protects civil liberties.
10. *Application/History.* A Civil Rights Act. Violation of a freedom by a private group, such as a department store, is protected by Civil Rights Acts. (Employment is covered by the 1964 Act.)

## Chapter 3   Geography

### Lesson 1

**Geographers use four kinds of maps: political maps, physical maps, topographic maps, and special-purpose maps.**

1. *Application/Geography.* A topographic map, because it gives details about land elevation. This information tells a hiker whether the land will be flat or hilly and how steep a climb to expect. (Physical maps are not as detailed.)
2. *Application/Geography.* One inch equals 920 miles. From below the capital of Tunisia to just below the capital of South Africa is about 4140 miles (4½ inches).
3. *Application/Geography.* The degrees of longitude and latitude in order to give its position.
4. *Analysis/Geography.* According to the map, Southwest Africa is located at that position.
5. **(5)** *Comprehension/Geography.* A political map indicates human-made boundary lines and names of countries, states, and other political divisions.

### Lesson 2

**The major climates are polar, tropical, and temperate.**

1. *Comprehension/Geography.* Climate is the average condition of a place over a long period of time. Weather, on the other hand, can vary from day to day.
2. *Comprehension/Geography.* The temperate climate is the most hospitable to human life because the temperature range, seasonal changes, and adequate rainfall are good for agriculture and conducive to economic growth.
3. *Comprehension/Geography.* Marine and mediterranean are subcategories of the temperate climate.
4. *Evaluation/Geography.* (b), (c), and (f). Temperature, rainfall, and seasons are the three factors of climate. Weather (a), industry (d), and population (e) are products, not factors, of climate. Deserts (g) occur in only one of the three climates.

### Lesson 3

**Certain natural resources, such as oil, coal, and trees, lend themselves to specific industries. The presence or absence of natural resources can determine the wealth or poverty of a region.**

1. *Comprehension/Geography.* An environmental crisis occurs when a natural resource is polluted or exhausted.
2. *Comprehension/Geography.* Water in rivers provides hydroelectric power.
3. *Application/Geography.* Exhausting a natural resource, such as by mining all the tin and copper in a region, would eventually deprive workers of their source of livelihood. People would leave the region because there would be no work.

### Lesson 4

**It is important to preserve and protect the environment because a clean environment is essential for life.**

1. **(4)** *Application/Geography.* The preservation of historical sites is not a concern of the EPA. All the other choices name environmental concerns that need watching.
2. *Analysis/Geography.* Balance suggests the use of natural resources to meet economic needs, and their protection so that the environment survives. For example, a power plant could be built on a river and use the water to generate power, but the same plant should not use the river as a dumping ground for harmful chemicals.
3. **(1)** *Evaluation/Geography.* The lesson implies that pollution from certain chemicals, such as DDT, can cause diseases. The other choices contradict implications that the lesson carries.

### Lesson 5

**Cultural geography is concerned with peoples and populations. Peoples includes racial and ethnic groups. Populations are the numbers of people who are resident in or moving between areas.**

1. *Analysis/Geography.* America is called the "melting pot" because people of all races and ethnic groups have emigrated from all over the world to live there.
2. *Comprehension/Geography.* Figure 2 is a special-purpose map. It shows particular features of regions, in addition to population distribution.

3. *Analysis/Geography.* The map indicates that the largest areas of dense population are in Asia.

## Chapter 3   **Quiz**

1. *Comprehension/Geography. Physical geography* studies geographic features of a region; *cultural geography* studies the peoples and the population distribution in a region.
2. *Application/Geography.* It can enact laws to control pollution. It can protect our natural resources.
3. *Comprehension/Geography.* Contour lines are used to show the elevation of specific areas of land.
4. *Application/Geography.* England, Scotland, Northern Ireland, and Wales are all part of Great Britain. The Irish, Scottish, Welsh, and English are all ethnic groups. Therefore, any two would be correct.
5. *Analysis/Geography.* (a) political; (b) special purpose; (c) physical or topographic; (d) political; (e) special purpose.
6. *Comprehension/Geography.* The prime meridian.
7. *Application/Geography.* Cuba is situated next to the United States in the Western Hemisphere; therefore Soviet missiles would have been capable of reaching nations in the Western Hemisphere.
8. *Application/Geography.* On the Yukon or the Mackenzie river.
9. *Comprehension/Geography.* The map indicates oil deposits on the western shore of Great Bear Lake.
10. *Analysis/Geography.* FALSE. Most of Canada's mineral resources can be found in southern Canada.

## Chapter 4
# Economics

## Lesson 1

**Under communism, government controls business; under capitalism, control is private; under socialism, both types of control exist.**

1. *Comprehension/Economics. Goods* include cars, clothing, machinery, and food. *Services* include repair work, tutoring, child care, and medical care.

2. (b) *Analysis/Economics.* There are elements of capitalism and socialism in most countries espousing one or the other. The differences between capitalist and communist economic systems, however, are much more drastic.
3. *Evaluation/Economics.* The most competition would exist in a capitalist system; the least competition would exist in a communist system.
4. *Evaluation/Economics.* Economics involves the study of *people* in their ordinary business lives, earning and enjoying a living.

## Lesson 2

**Competition forces businesses to keep quality high and prices low because many businesses may produce the same product. Because consumers have a choice, businesses must do more than just produce a product to attract a buyer.**

1. *Comprehension/Economics.* To help the overproduced product reach its equilibrium point, the manufacturer could (a) reduce the product's market price and/or (b) reduce the rate of production of the product.
2. *Application/Economics.* (a) conglomerate; (b) partnership; (c) corporation.
3. **(2)** *Application/Economics.* Companies usually advertise to influence consumers to buy products. The more people want to buy, the greater the demand for a product.
4. *Application/Economics.* Professional groups that often form partnerships are doctors, lawyers, and accountants. They can share facilities and staff as well as knowledge as they provide their services.
5. *Evaluation/Economics.* A free-enterprise system stimulates competition. More and better products are made for lower prices.

## Lesson 3

**Commercial banks make loans to businesses and individuals. Savings institutions do not lend money to businesses. They make loans only to individuals and offer other consumer services as well.**

1. *Comprehension/Economics.*
   (a) FALSE (b) FALSE (c) TRUE (d) TRUE
2. *Comprehension/Economics.* (a) Checking accounts are offered by commercial banks, mutual savings banks, and savings and loans. (b) Commercial banks are most likely to offer loans to businesses. (c) Savings and loans are most likely to offer mortgage loans. (d) Credit unions are most likely to offer high-interest savings accounts.
3. *Application/Economics.* The difference between a credit card and a debit card is that when you use a credit card, you are borrowing money that you must repay with interest. When you use a debit card, the money you receive is not borrowed, but only electronically subtracted from your own bank account.
4. *Analysis/Economics.* Credit unions are owned by the people depositing their money. They are not run for profit. The interest rate they charge on loans is less than a bank's, and they give higher interest on savings accounts. They also offer draft accounts.

## Lesson 4

**An elastic currency is one in which the supply of money can be changed quickly. The powers of the Federal Reserve Board directly affect the national supply of money by controlling the cash reserves of all banks in the United States, fixing discount rates on loans to private banks, and buying or selling U.S. bond issues. These powers all make money elastic.**

1. *Comprehension/Economics.* The Federal Reserve Board (1) sets cash reserves for all banks, (2) sets the discount rate for loans to private banks, and (3) buys and sells U.S. bond issues.
2. **(1)** *Evaluation/Economics.* The Federal Reserve Act *greatly* increased government control over banking. Choice (2) is not implied because the president appoints Federal Reserve Board members. Only the Senate, not Congress as a whole, approves appointments. Choice (3) is incorrect. Since the FDIC was established to insure against banks failing, far fewer banks have failed.
3. *Analysis/Economics.* (a) nonmembers; (b) member banks; (c) national banks.

## Lesson 5

**Tax revenues pay for many programs in health care, education, and housing, among others, to improve the quality of life for many citizens.**

1. *Comprehension/Economics.* (a) The food stamp program used 65% of federal food program funds. (b) Schools were involved in 27% of federal food programs.
2. *Analysis/Economics.* A progressive tax increases as income or profit increases. Income tax is an example of such a tax. A regressive tax places the heaviest burden on individuals and groups with the lowest incomes. Sales tax and highway tolls are examples of regressive taxes.
3. (2) *Evaluation/Economics.* Government does collect taxes and regulate banking. It does not, as a matter of course, take over failing businesses.

## Lesson 6

**Inflation is most damaging to people with fixed incomes, such as retirees, because it causes the fixed amount of money they must live on to lose value. While wage earners may receive cost-of-living adjustments, retirees living on pensions do not usually receive increases to make up for inflation.**

1. *Analysis/Economics.* The creation of public works projects helps combat recession by increasing employment in a period of high unemployment.
2. (4) *Application/Economics.* While the cost of gold is an economic indicator that tells us something about the state of our economy, gold is not an essential good or service that consumers must buy.
3. *Comprehension/Economics.* The Gross National Product is the value of all goods and services produced and sold in one year.
4. *Application/Economics.* Like prices of goods, the costs of services also increase in times of inflation. Wages do not always rise quickly enough to keep up with inflation. Inflation means that it costs more to make ends meet, especially for people on fixed incomes.
5. *Analysis/Economics.* Statistics can be used to identify a problem, study it, reach an answer, and report the facts. Statistics can give us a graphic picture of a problem.

## Lesson 7

**Human resources play a vital role in the economy. Industry could not exist without labor or management. It takes people to produce products and provide services. Automation may eliminate some jobs, but it creates others. People will always be essential.**

1. (3) *Analysis/Economics.* Collective bargaining does not determine wages or working conditions for management employees.
2. (2) *Evaluation/Economics.* The chart does not show the actual number of strikes in any year, only the number of days people spent on strike times the number of people involved.
3. *Evaluation/Economics.* Reasons for calling a strike might include: (a) a contract between labor and management cannot be agreed upon; (b) wage increases are too low; (c) management does not increase any benefits or improve working conditions; (d) management tries to lower wages and benefits, or make working conditions worse.

## Lesson 8

**An embargo affects the economy of the country that is the importer and that of the country that is the exporter. The import nation loses an essential product. The export nation loses a consumer of its goods.**

1. *Comprehension/Economics.* (a) mineral fuels; (b) no; (c) beverages and tobacco.
2. *Comprehension/Economics.* All three answers are correct. Balance of trade is discussed in terms of imports and exports. Tariffs can affect rates of import.
3. *Application/Economics.* This favorable balance of trade means more money would come into that country and help the economy.
4. *Analysis/Economics.* (a) A consumer is more likely to favor a free market because it allows more choice at comparable, or even lower, prices. (b) A manufacturer might be in competition with a foreign industry and so is more likely to favor protected markets that help to limit the competition.
5. *Evaluation/Economics.* A tariff is really a tax. Since tariffs discourage imports and raise prices for goods that are imported, consumers are restricted to buying either domestic

products or foreign goods whose prices have been raised by tariffs.

## Chapter 4   Quiz

1. *Comprehension/Economics.* An economic good is an actual item that people pay for. A service is also something that people pay for, but it is not an actual item.
2. *Comprehension/Economics.* capitalism (b); communism (a); socialism (c).
3. *Evaluation/Economics.* Advertising affects supply and demand by trying to create demand by influencing consumers. If demand is created, a greater supply is needed to satisfy it.
4. *Comprehension/Economics.* (a) demand deposits; (b) thrifts; (c) draft accounts.
5. *Comprehension/Economics.* (a) true; (b) true; (c) false.
6. *Analysis/Economics.* Franklin meant that taxes are essential to run any kind of government, so there will always be taxes as certainly as there will be death.
7. *Comprehension/Economics.* (a) The most cars were produced in 1976. (b) Each symbol represents 1 million cars. (c) $6\frac{1}{2}$ million cars were produced in 1980. (d) 2 million more cars were produced in 1976 than in 1980.
8. *Analysis/Economics.* Recession means a decrease in production and employment. This is not compatible with the rise in wages and prices that occurs in a period of inflation.
9. *Analysis/Economics.* The increase in industrialization in the early twentieth century resulted in a need for greater numbers of workers and the creation of many skilled jobs. Greater numbers gave workers more power. Skilled workers were not so easy to fire since they were harder to replace. Thus they were able to make more demands.
10. *Evaluation/Economics.* (3) An embargo can greatly affect the balance of trade, depending on its extent and duration. Choices (1) and (2) are true.

## *Chapter 5* **Political Science**

### Lesson 1

**The major types of government are *monarchy,* in which one person rules; *dictatorship,* in which one person rules over all aspects of life; *fascism,* a form of dictatorship that glorifies the state; *oligarchy,* in which a small group of families rules; and *democracy,* in which all the people vote to decide how a country is to be run.**

1. *Application/Political Science.* This is an example of a dictatorship. The ruler controls all aspects of life.
2. *Comprehension/Political Science.* Direct democracy (New England town meeting); representative democracy (Senate, House of Representatives, state legislatures, or local governments).
3. *Application/Political Science.* The country was governed as a monarchy. Local government was composed of a group of noble families; therefore, it was an oligarchy.
4. *Analysis/Political Science.* FALSE. The state or country itself is all-important, even at the expense of individuals.

### Lesson 2

**The Declaration of Independence expressed a belief in individual freedom and in social and political equality. The Articles of Confederation were a plan for the new government by which the states would rule themselves.**

1. *Comprehension/Political Science.* ". . . Life, Liberty, and the Pursuit of Happiness."
2. *Evaluation/Political Science.* ". . . That whenever . . . government becomes destructive of these ends, it is the right of the people to alter or to abolish it." Since government gets its power to govern from the people, the people may reject the government if it is deemed not to serve their best interests. The people can exert power over the government.
3. *Comprehension/Political Science.* Each state had control over its own affairs. The states were not ruled by a central government, but they cooperated with one another.

4. *Evaluation/Political Science.* Yes, the lesson cites a lack of central power under the Articles. As the weaknesses of this confederation surfaced, it became apparent that a stronger document was needed.
5. *Analysis/Political Science.* The colonials feared that such a government might use its power to limit individual freedoms.

### Lesson 3

**The American Constitution distributes political power among three branches of government: executive, legislative, and judicial. So that no branch will be more powerful than the others, the Constitution also provides a system of checks and balances.**

1. *Application/Political Science.* This illustrates the system of checks and balances. The executive branch (president) may veto a bill passed by Congress. However, Congress can override the president's veto by a two-thirds majority vote.
2. *Analysis/Political Science.* The separation of powers was built into the Constitution to ensure that no branch of the federal government would become too powerful.
3. *Evaluation/Political Science.* No president can assume dictatorial powers. The president can be removed from office, his or her veto can be overridden, and presidential appointments must have congressional approval.
4. *Evaluation/Political Science.* This was done to satisfy both large and small states. There are two senators from each state, which gives small states equal representation and political power in the Senate. The number of representatives is based on population, which gives populous states proportionately greater representation and power in the House of Representatives.
5. *Application/Political Science.* Because this involves interpreting the law, it is a matter for the judicial branch.

### Lesson 4

**The Federalists, who favored a strong central government and wanted a Constitution, added the Bill of Rights to gain the support of the anti-Federalists, who believed in individual rights and were opposed to the Constitution.**

1. *Comprehension/Political Science.* The first ten amendments, also called the Bill of Rights, expressly state what our rights are. They provide for freedom of speech, press, and religion; the right to life, liberty, and private property; and the right to a speedy trial by an impartial jury.
2. *Analysis/Political Science.* The Fourteenth Amendment is referred to as the "equal protection" amendment because it extends the due process clause of the Fifth Amendment to include both due process and equal protection under the law.
3. *Application/Political Science.* Under the Fourteenth Amendment, anyone, alien or citizen, residing in any state enjoys the same rights and protection under the Constitution: "No state shall deny . . ."
4. *Evaluation/Political Science.* This is so because persons can be imprisoned, tried, or punished without any proof of guilt on the part of a totalitarian government.
5. *Comprehension/Political Science.* Amendments must also have the approval of three-fourths of the state legislatures.

### Lesson 5

**The federal system gives some powers to the states and some powers to the central government. Certain powers are also shared between the two. The Constitution stipulates which powers these are and which government has them.**

1. *Application/Political Science.* Federal. The federal government regulates interstate trade.
2. *Application/Political Science.* Fire protection—local; highway maintenance—federal and state; garbage collection—local; mail delivery—federal; snow removal—local; training the handicapped—federal and state.
3. *Evaluation/Political Science.* Local government gives people a voice in affairs that are close at hand. Local government gives people more direct control over their lives.
4. *Comprehension/Political Science.* Such a law would be contrary to the Constitution because the power over marriage laws is one reserved for the states. (See Table 2 in the lesson.)

## Lesson 6

**Individual citizens can participate in the political process by voting in federal, state, and local elections and by active membership in political parties and interest groups.**

1. *Application/Political Science.* No, only citizens 18 years of age or older may vote.
2. *Comprehension/Political Science.* The purpose of a presidential primary is to select candidates for the general election through the votes of convention delegates.
3. *Evaluation/Political Science.* All three groups participate in the political process as special interest lobbies. Their constituents are, respectively, veterans, blacks, and local businesses.
4. *Analysis/Political Science.* Yes, it is possible. If, for example, a presidential candidate received the electoral votes of only the least populous states and received one half *minus* one of the popular votes in the 25 most populous states, that candidate could get more than half the vote and less than half the electors' votes.

## Lesson 7

**Government works to improve the quality of life through programs to help people who do not have or cannot get employment, and to preserve the environment and the quality of public services.**

1. *Comprehension/Political Science.* Programs such as Social Security, Medicare, Medicaid, or Food Stamps could be listed.
2. *Application/Political Science.* Yes, because it attempted to help people acquire job skills. Working would improve the quality of their lives.
3. *Analysis/Political Science.* The Internal Revenue Service collects federal taxes. Schools (education) are under the power of states, which delegate some controls to local boards. Because federal and state governments cooperate to provide school lunches, they exercise their responsibility concurrently.

## Lesson 8

**Nations interact peacefully through international organizations, diplomatic relations, and regional, military, and economic alliances.**

1. *Comprehension/Political Science.* (2) NATO is a military organization made up of the United States, Canada, and the nations of western and southern Europe.
2. *Application/Political Science.* TRUE. The question of economic relations among western European nations is one for the Common Market.
3. *Comprehension/Political Science.* Nations join international organizations so they can settle their disputes before these disputes lead to war. They also join to benefit from international economic and social programs.
4. *Analysis/Political Science.* The goals of the United Nations are to save people from future wars, to support human rights, and to offer the means for countries to work out their problems without resorting to war.

## Chapter 5   Quiz

1. *Comprehension/Political Science.* The Declaration of Independence set forth the fundamental beliefs that all people are created equal, that government depends on the consent of the governed, and that governments should be changed if they do not protect the rights of the people.
2. *Comprehension/Political Science.* The government set up under the Articles lacked an executive branch—the presidency—and a judicial branch—the Supreme Court.
3. *Application/Political Science.* The cartoon shows that Senate approval of a Supreme Court justice is not always easy to get. Approval of the appointment of Justice Scalia was granted more easily than that of Justice Rehnquist.
4. *Application/Political Science.* It is the responsiblity of the executive branch to enforce the laws passed by Congress.
5. *Application/Political Science.* Since each state elects one representative for each 500,000 people, the two states elect 34 and 2 representatives, respectively.
6. *Analysis/Political Science.* The judicial branch. Federal judges are appointed, not elected.
7. *Comprehension/Political Science.* The chart shows that Democrats controlled both houses of Congress until the Republicans took control of the Senate in 1981.
8. *Comprehension/Political Science.* International organizations; diplomatic relations; cultural or economic groups.
9. *Analysis/Political Science.* The candidate would need 109 more electoral votes. The five largest states (California, New York, Texas, Pennsylvania, and Illinois) have 161 votes; a majority of 538—270 votes—is needed.
10. *Analysis/Political Science.* Residents of D.C. vote for presidents but have no representation in Congress. There are 3 more electoral votes (538) than seats in Congress (535). They are D.C.'s votes. Evidence that the 3 votes are D.C.'s is based on this: Each of the 50 states has 2 senators; there are 100 senators. Therefore, D.C. has no senators. It can be assumed that it also has no representatives in the House.

## Chapter 6
# Behavioral Science

## Lesson 1

**To gather data, the behavioral scientist may observe behavior and also question people about their thoughts, their feelings, and their behavior.**

1. (1) *Application/Behavioral Science.* Choice (1) is an example of observable behavior. Choice (2) would be correct if the sociologist had reported that Charles had smiled. Choices (3) and (4) are also incorrect; what we *can* observe are behaviors such as crying or yawning. Choice (4) tells us only what this sociologist thinks is observable.
2. *Application/Behavioral Science.* (a) anthropology; (b) sociology; (c) sociology; (d) psychology.
3. *Comprehension/Behavioral Science.* (a) psychology; sociology; anthropology; (b) cultures; (c) observed.
4. *Application/Behavioral Science.* (a) experimental method; (b) control; (c) the number of rats in each cage.

## Lesson 2

**Each perspective emphasizes a different way of looking at behavior and how it can be changed to help people achieve mental health.**

1. *Application/Behavioral Science.* The statement indicates the psychoanalytic approach because it focuses on repressed memories.
2. *Application/Behavioral Science.* Fantasizing works as a defense mechanism because it is used to provide relief from anxiety.
3. *Comprehension/Behavioral Science.* (a) developmental; (b) clinical; psychotherapy; (c) experimental.

## Lesson 3

**Heredity provides the potential for personality development, while the environment shapes the actual development.**

1. *Application/Behavioral Science.* Newborn infants show differences in personality from birth.
2. *Application/Behavioral Science.* Operant conditioning.
3. *Application/Behavioral Science.* Positive reinforcement.
4. *Application/Behavioral Science.* The psychologist would probably recommend rewarding students' good performance. The graph shows the psychologist thinks reward works better than punishment to encourage improvement.

## Lesson 4

**Social institutions satisfy needs that members of a society might find difficult to satisfy on their own.**

1. *Application/Behavioral Science.* A social institution. Government regulates society in a way individuals, alone, cannot.
2. *Comprehension/Behavioral Science.* (a) norms; (b) social mobility; (c) deviant.
3. **(3)** *Application/Behavioral Science.* Wearing a bikini to the supermarket is acceptable behavior under very few circumstances in American society.

## Lesson 5

**Norms provide the guidelines for role-playing. People watch others play roles to find out how to behave.**

1. *Comprehension/Behavioral Science.* In Part One, the girls played with only toys typically thought of as girls' toys. In Part Two, the girls played with both "girls' toys" and "boys' toys."
2. *Application/Behavioral Science.* Part One of the experiment shows that the girls' socialization had taught them which toys were appropriate for girls. In a group, all the girls played with only "girls' toys."
3. *Evaluation/Behavioral Science.* The experiment suggests that peer group expectations strongly influence individuals' behavior. Only when alone did any girls play with "boys' toys."

## Lesson 6

**Cultural traits are behaviors that are accepted by most members of a culture. They define a culture and distinguish one culture from another.**

1. *Analysis/Behavioral Science.* Culture C probably has the greatest influence on two of the other cultures, both B and D. Culture C is physically near both B and D. Cultural diffusion can be a by-product of the human interaction that begins with trading, for example.
2. *Evaluation/Behavioral Science.* Cultures change. Some change faster than others. Cultural diffusion produces cultural change.
3. *Evaluation/Behavioral Science.* (a) dominant culture; (b) subculture; dominant culture.
4. *Evaluation/Behavioral Science.* The members of the dominant culture might see the behavior of individuals in the counterculture as being threatening to the dominant culture.

## Lesson 7

**Objectivity is important because the anthropologist studies cultures that may be very different from his or her own. Without objectivity, the anthropologist may allow feelings to falsify the report on the behavior that has been studied.**

1. *Application/Behavioral Science.* Cultural relativity.
2. *Analysis/Behavioral Science.* A lack of cultural relativity usually means that the individual is guilty of ethnocentrism.
3. *Application/Behavioral Science.* Some rites of passage in contemporary United States culture are graduation ceremonies, weddings, retirement parties, and funerals.

## Chapter 6   **Quiz**

1. *Analysis/Behavior Science.* What is very rewarding to one person can be considered a hindrance by another. It is important to know what an individual considers rewarding so that you know how to reinforce desirable behavior.
2. *Comprehension/Behavioral Science.* (a) unconscious; (b) humanistic; (c) cognitive.
3. *Application/Behavioral Science.* Part 1—psychologist (studies behavior and thoughts of individuals);
Part 2—sociologist (studies behavior of people in groups and group dynamics);
Part 3—anthropologist (studies different cultures and compares behavior in different cultures).
4. *Comprehension/Behavioral Science.* The traditional nuclear family consists of a couple and their children.
5. *Comprehension/Behavioral Science.* (1) biological; (2) punishment; reward; (3) environment.
6. **(4)** *Comprehension/Behavioral Science.* The largest segment of the population in 2000 (39%) will be middle-aged adults (between 35 and 64 years of age).
7. *Analysis/Behavioral Science.* A primary group is more likely to have a greater influence on an individual's values because members of a primary group encourage each other to conform to the group's beliefs. Secondary groups are often short-lived, but primary groups, like the family, are characterized by long and intimate relationships.
8. *Analysis/Behavioral Science.* Role conflict occurs when an individual tries to play two roles that have conflicting behaviors.
9. *Application/Behavioral Science.* (a) acculturation (accepting the culture of a new society); (b) cultural diffusion (the spread of cultural traits from one place to another); (c) enthnocentrism (belief that their own culture is superior to others).
10. **(3)** *Evaluation/Behavioral Science.* Choices (1) and (2) are incorrect. Choice (4) contains information that is not on the graph. Choice (5) is wrong because the immigrants were members of a variety of cultures.

## Chapter 7
# Interrelationships Among the Branches of Social Studies

## Lesson 1

**When stock prices fell, people who had bought stock on credit were asked to pay the balance of the purchase price. When the buyers were unable to provide payment, the stocks had to be sold, but there were few new buyers available.**

1. *Evauation/History.* No. Even though Table 1 shows that unemployment declined from 1933 to 1939, it does not show what effect the two agencies had on that decline.
2. *Evaluation/Economics.* (1) Companies failed, so (a) goods that they produced for export were taken off the world market and (b) raw materials that they had imported lost their United States market. (2) Unemployment grew, so imported manufactured goods lost their United States consumers, who could no longer afford to pay for them. (3) The crash caused a loss of trust in the United States economy, so investors—including foreign investors—withdrew their backing. These three factors, among others, negatively affected foreign consumption, production, and investment and, therefore, foreign economies.
3. (2) *Comprehension/Economics.* Companies had surplus products because consumers could not afford to pay for them. The ratio *more than 1:1* indicates that there was more than one manufactured item for each consumer who was able to buy and who wanted to buy.

## Lesson 2

**United States involvement in two world wars contributed to the feminist movement by providing a way into the work place for women. Women took over many jobs in industry as replacements for men who were needed in the armed services.**

1. *Comprehension/History.* Political events (World War I and World War II) contributed to changes in the status of women by taking women out of the home and into the work place.
2. *Comprehension/Behavior Science.* The title suggests that the author says women's status in society is lower than men's—second, not equal.
3. *Evaluation/Economics.* As the passage indicates, industries that are involved in war-related work increase production and employment opportunities. Increased production and employment are signs of an expanding economy.

## Lesson 3

**The Supreme Court declared school segregation to be unconstitutional. Further action by the courts and by presidents resulted in the decision's enforcement in all areas of the country.**

1. *Evaluation/Political Science.* The evidence is that twice the Supreme Court ruled on whether or not required segregation is constitutional. Supreme Court rulings judge or interpret laws that exist.
2. *Application/Political Science.* The Supreme Court decides whether laws are constitutional. Because the Constitution is the foundation for all laws in all states, if a law is unconstitutional in one state, it is unconstitutional in all states.
3. *Evaluation/History.* The historian could observe that during the 335 years from 1619 to 1954, there was extremely little social change that could be recognized as combative toward racial discrimination. The period of change—since 1954—is shorter than one-tenth of the total time that discrimination against blacks has existed in the United States. Change in only 30 to 40 years, compared to nearly 400 years, could be called *rapid*.
4. *Application/Political Science.* Congress, with state legislatures' ratification, amended the Constitution. The Supreme Court interpreted the amendment in a 1954 decision. President Eisenhower enforced the law in Little Rock in 1957.

## Lesson 4

**The vast, flat areas of the Soviet Union have long made the country subject to invasion by its neighbors. To reduce the risk of invasion by land, the Soviet Union created a buffer zone of its immediate neighbors and, thus, created the Soviet bloc.**

1. *Comprehension/Political Science.* The Soviet Union has been invaded by the West many times. To protect itself from future invasion, it must have buffer states on its borders.
2. *Application/Political Science.* Cold war refers to a period of strained relationships marked by propaganda and small-scale confrontations, as opposed to large-scale military actions that are typical of war.
3. *Evaluation/Political Science.* No. Détente is a period of constructive accord. The cartoon represents mutual distrust between the Western and the Soviet blocs. Neither side believes the other's so-called peaceful intentions.
4. *Analysis/Geography.* Because Cuba is near the United States, both the Soviet Union and the United States recognized that Soviet missile bases there would be a great threat to United States security. Cuba was the pro-Soviet country that is geographically the closest to the United States.

## Lesson 5

**Starvation in Africa can be called a political issue because (a) it has been aggravated by civil war and (b) relief efforts have been hindered by political factionalism.**

1. *Analysis/Political Science.* Three ways in which Ethiopia's civil war hastened the development of food shortage were (a) fighting troops destroyed farms with the result that no food could be grown; (b) farmers fled productive land for safety and therefore could not produce food; (c) farmers—now refugees in areas that were already affected by famine—caused a greater drain on already limited food supplies.
2. *Analysis/Behavioral Science.* Famine shows that if basic survival needs are not satisfied, there can be no social organization. Without food, social organization breaks down. People who once lived in organized groups—families, towns, countries—that have values, regulations, policies, and goals are forced to abandon everything to search for food.
3. *Application/Political Science.* As an organization that is set up to ar-

bitrate international disputes, the United Nations could help to settle the conflicts between the two countries. It could also use its service organizations to assist with direct relief efforts.

## Chapter 7 **Quiz**

1. *Evaluation/Economics.* Speaker 2. Because Speaker 1 thinks that oil prices may fall, he or she probably would not encourage nuclear-plant construction because energy from fossil fuels will be less expensive in the future. Speaker 2, who thinks oil prices will rise, is more likely to advocate less-expensive, alternative energy sources such as nuclear power.
2. *Application/Economics.* A factor of supply and demand is that suppliers can charge as much for products as consumers are willing to pay. Because the United States demands and depends on oil, foreign suppliers, to serve their own economic growth, could set high prices for supplies.
3. *Application/Economics.* If financially insecure companies are forbidden to sell stock, or if disclosures suggest that investment in them is risky, investors would not invest blindly in failing companies as they did before the crash, which was one of the reasons for the crash.
4. *Evaluation/Political Science.* The Constitution is the supreme law of the land. All other laws are tested against it. If an existing or a future law allowed sex discrimination and if that law were tested against a constitutional amendment, that law could be deemed unconstitutional. In time, the effect of the amendment would be felt wherever discrimination exists.
5. **(3)** *Application/History.* The president sent troops to Little Rock in 1957 to enforce a Supreme Court decision. Choice (1) is a headline that might have been printed in 1896, and Choices (4) and (5) in 1954. Choice (2) could not have been a headline because the sending of troops is an executive power.
6. *Evaluation/Geography.* Some factors that have encouraged the United States' economic development are its abundance of natural

resources for manufacturing and energy sources; its coastlines, which provide good harbors; its river systems, which provide easy transportation; and its climate, which is conducive to productive agriculture.
7. **(4)** *Evaluation/History.* The amendment was ratified after World War I—in 1920. Women had participated in the national war effort both in the military and in civilian jobs. Their contributions helped create the climate mentioned. Choice (1) is wrong mainly because individual voters do not approve amendments; Choices (2) and (5) are incorrect mainly because the war had ended by 1920; Choice (3) is not true.
8. *Comprehension/History.* Yes, one did. New York State gave women the right to vote in 1917.
9. *Application/Political Science.* For an amendment to be added to the Constitution, two-thirds of the states' legislatures must ratify it. That requirement applied to the Nineteenth Amendment, as to any other.
10. *Evaluation/History.* Alaska and Hawaii were not states in the period from 1890–1919. Because they were not states, their positions on women's suffrage would have been irrelevant to the point of the map, which is to show states' postures on the issue just before the amendment was ratified.

## UNIT II **TEST**

1. **(4)** *Analysis/Behavioral Science.* Bolivia and Zaire both have relatively short life expectancy and high infant mortality rate statistics. All other countries from which there is complete data have long life expectancy and low infant mortality rates. Choices (1) and (2) are incorrect based on statistics for Bolivia and Taiwan; Choices (3) and (5) are wrong since birth rates are not reported.
2. **(4)** *Comprehension/History.* According to the passage, the South's economy was upset during the Civil War—mainly by damages fighting caused—and after the Civil War because Southern slaves had been freed. Choices (1) and (3) are contradicted by the

passage; Choices (2) and (5) are only two factors that contributed to the Civil War's overall effect on the South's economy.
3. **(2)** *Comprehension/History.* According to the passage, "Some plantation owners held onto their land through . . . sharecropping." Therefore, Choices (1), (4), and (5) are incorrect. Choice (3) was true of only some plantations.
4. *Analysis/History.* The first paragraph suggests three causes for shortages: (a) farms were abandoned, (b) transportation systems were destroyed, and (c) cities were seriously damaged. With little production and transportation of goods, and disorganization in urban centers, shortages of necessities resulted.
5. *Analysis/History.* Because the South's agricultural economy had depended on slavery for inexpensive labor, the *Emancipation Proclamation* forced the South to find a new way to afford to farm. Sharecropping was introduced as the solution.
6. **(2)** *Application/Behavioral Science.* Selling illegal drugs could be called a victimless crime, because seller and buyer participate willingly in an illegal activity.
7. **(1)** *Comprehension/Economics.* Because the passage states that capitalist countries with *mixed* economies have some government ownership of industry, in a *pure* capitalist economy all industry would be privately owned. Similar reasoning shows the other four alternatives to be illogical.
8. *Evaluation/Political Science.* (a) The judicial branch can declare a presidential act unconstitutional; and (b) the legislative branch may impeach and convict any federal official. That the executive branch (including the president) enforces the law does not imply that the president is above the law.
9. **(3)** *Analysis/Political Science.* The Supreme Court interprets laws and can declare laws unconstitutional. The Supreme Court has the right to consider laws passed by Congress and signed by the president, so it has the last word.
10. *Evaluation/Political Science.* The president can make treaties, but the Senate must approve them. Cases related to treaties are handled by federal courts. The pow-

ers regarding treaties make it impossible for any branch of government to act on its own: the power of each branch is checked by that of another.

11. **(4)** *Evaluation/History.* The Civil War (1861–1865) appears to have interrupted a trend of increasing immigration to the United States. In each decade from 1820 to 1859, there was a large increase in immigrants over the previous decade's. The same trend picks up in 1870–1889. The trend did not stop, therefore, but apparently slowed around the time of the Civil War.

12. *Analysis/History.* The goal was to reduce the number of immigrants. Immigration rates fell off sharply after 1929. That is the evidence that the plan's goal, since it was *exceeded* by the Depression's effects, was to reduce immigration rates.

13. *Evaluation/Political Science.* The six reasons are named in the phrases beginning with "to form . . ." and ending with ". . . our posterity." The first reason, "to form a more perfect Union," is the one that most emphasizes that the Constitution hoped to establish a nation, not a confederation of states.

14. *Evaluation/Geography.* (a) The approximate population of the world is 5 billion because one-tenth is 500 million. Questions (b), (c), and (d): Not enough information. (e) Yes. In the average diet in a developed country, three times as much food carries only twice as much protein as the average diet in a developing country.

15. **(1)** *Application/Geography.* A person who regularly eats less than the minimum critical diet is most likely to live in Asia. Of the choices, only Cambodia is an Asian country.

16. **(2)** *Evaluation/Geography.* Because people in the developed world, compared to those in the developing world, eat three times as much food and gain only twice as much protein, it is reasonable to assume they eat more meat. When people eat meat, they don't get all the protein that was in the grain fed to the animals. None of the other choices is supported by the passage.

17. **(5)** *Comprehension/Geography.*

All of the East Coast area of the United States, from Maine to Georgia, remained under British control from 1689 to 1763. The maps show no British control of the other areas named, except of more of the South in 1763.

18. *Analysis/History.* The map of North America in 1763 is the only one that shows no French territory in North America.

19. **(2)** *Analysis/History.* The maps for 1689 and 1750 show Florida under Spanish control. Georgia, in 1732, was the British king's only colony bordering Florida. It was, therefore, the outpost against the Spanish. Since the king and colonists were British, Choices (3) and (5) are wrong; Choice (1) is wrong because all of the colonies bordered French territory in 1732; Choice (4) is wrong because Indians are not a subject of the maps.

20. **(4)** *Evaluation/Political Science.* The purpose of the quoted portion of the First Amendment is to prohibit (a) the establishment of a state religion and (b) legislation restricting religious expression. Other choices are wrong because the amendment (1) neither encourages nor discourages religious expression, (2) is not a tax law, (3) does not rule out legislation affecting religious organizations (such as tax laws), and (5) is to protect people's freedom from government power, not to increase varieties and choices.

21. **(1)** *Analysis/Economics.* The passage contrasts Keynesian and conservative economic theories. Keynesians, representing the liberal side, favor public assistance to increase buying power. Choices (2) and (4) are supply-side approaches; (3) and (5) are not mentioned in the passage as favorable to the unemployed.

22. **(4)** *Application/Economics.* Supply-side economists favor limiting government influence and spending. Therefore, they would be against the influence and spending that loans to businesses are.

23. *Application/Economics.* Yes. A supply-side economist prefers to limit government involvement in the economy. This laissez-faire approach would probably favor limited government regulations for airlines.

24. **(3)** *Evaluation/Economics.* The passage indicates that supply-side

economists seek to curb inflation and balance the federal budget. The most probable reason for their rise was the increase in inflation in the 1970s.

25. **(3)** *Evaluation/Economics.* If businesses grow, it is possible that the poor could take advantage of increased employment opportunities. Because the poor are not likely to save or invest, Choices (1) and (2) are not correct. Balancing the federal budget and reducing public assistance are related: they provide no direct benefit to the poor, so Choices (4) and (5) are incorrect.

26. *Analysis/Political Science.* The Republican Party. There are 100 seats in the Senate; a majority of 51. At the time of the election, Republicans held 31 seats; Democrats, 35. To maintain a majority, the Republicans needed to win 20 state elections; the Democrats, only 16.

27. *Application/Geography.* The areas in western South America (from about 5°N to about 30°S) where there is little or no vegetation are mountainous. Elevations range as high as 13,000 feet. The cold of mountainous climates makes it difficult for vegetation to thrive.

28. *Application/Geography.* The dominant climate is similar to that in the continental United States because both areas are in temperate zones equidistant from the equator. The seasons are similar, but they occur at opposite times of the year. In southern South America, for example, summer lasts from December 21 to March 21.

29. **(3)** *Application/Behavioral Science.* Religion is an institution in most societies: it serves a variety of needs, and it influences life at almost every level. Religion includes many traits and complexes. Religion, at large, is different from individual, isolated religious groups, which are subcultures.

30. **(1)** *Application/Behavioral Science.* Like the symbol that a green traffic light is under particular circumstances, waving a chicken is a symbol in a wedding ceremony.

31. **(4)** *Application/Behavioral Science.* Within institutions there are various roles, one of which a person plays when functioning in the context of a particular institution. Steward, student, and husband

are roles in three different institutions: the economic system, education, and the family.

32. **(2)** *Application/Behavioral Science*. The family is an institution. One of the complexes within that institution is courtship and "public" engagement before marriage. Some of the traits of that complex are a ring, announcements, parties, and planning wedding events with friends and family members.

# PRACTICE

## PRACTICE ITEMS

1. **(2)** *Analysis/History*. The map shows that at the time of the Missouri Compromise, there was an equal number of free states and slave states. Slavery was a controversial issue at this time and threatened to split the country. By maintaining equal representation of both sides of the slavery controversy, the United States was able to delay legislation that a minority representation would fight.

2. **(4)** *Comprehension/History*. The first event that is mentioned in the passage that lead to an organized effort to combat racial segregation is Rosa Parks's action in 1955. Choices (1), (3), and (5) list events that happened after 1955. The passage does not state when the Supreme Court made its ruling on segregated public schools (Choice [2]).

3. **(4)** *Analysis/History*. The passage implies that the signing of the Civil Rights Bill of 1964 was a result of the march on Washington, D.C. Choices (3) and (5) describe events that helped make possible the march on Washington, D.C. Choices (1) and (2) are conclusions that are not addressed in the passage.

4. **(5)** *Evaluation/History*. The courts decided against the laws that had been established by the states on the grounds that these laws were unconstitutional. The states had, in effect, passed laws that denied rights that were given to all citizens by federal laws, thereby violating the Fourteenth Amendment. The Tenth Amendment, which is mentioned in Choice (2), could have been used as support for a court decision that upheld the state laws.

5. **(4)** *Comprehension/History*. All the choices use information that is contained in the passage, but the others tell only a part of the story. The main point of the passage is that two national authoritarian leaders, who were believed to be corrupt, left office in 1986.

6. **(4)** *Comprehension/History*. The illustration shows President Johnson feeding tax money into the Vietnam War, thus either depriving Great Society programs of funds or leaving them only what was left after the war effort was fully funded.

7. **(1)** *Evaluation/History*. Because President Johnson is shown in control of Vietnam, the Great Society, and tax dollars, the cartoon implies that he was not coerced into any decisions about how tax money should be spent, but instead freely chose to spend more money on Vietnam than on the Great Society. The representation of President Johnson as the head of all three sectors that are displayed in the cartoon supports Choice (2). The caption provides support for Choice (3). The fact that both vehicles have pulled up to the same gas pump supports Choice (4). Choice (5) is supported because the Vietnam tank is shown to be a much larger vehicle than the Great Society car; it would take much more tax money to fill up the tank than it would the car.

8. **(5)** *Analysis/History*. The construction of the Panama Canal allowed the U.S. navy to easily shift its fleet from one ocean to another and therefore to meet any threat from either east or west. Choices (2) and (4) are unlikely results because the map shows that the Panama Canal was situated in regions that were already well traveled by U.S. ships. Trade in South American countries, as mentioned in Choice (3), was most likely a result of the lack of any easy access to the Pacific Ocean except around the continent; therefore, the construction of the Panama Canal would be unlikely to increase trade. Choice (1) is also unlikely because in 1914, produce could be shipped across the country most cheaply by train; costs would be unaffected by changes in ocean routes.

9. **(3)** *Comprehension/History*. The passage states that the frontier line advanced westward quickly *after* 1800 and that in 1783, the frontier line "was still largely east of the Appalachian Mountains." Therefore, one can infer that few Americans moved west of the eastern seaboard before 1800 and that in 1800 most Americans could, in fact, be found living on the eastern seaboard.

10. **(4)** *Application/History*. The passage states that the frontier had crossed the Mississippi by 1820. Kansas is located a little west of the Mississippi, right on the frontier line. Choices (1) and (3) give locations that would be located east of the frontier in their times. In 1783, California was completely unsettled, so Choice (2) does not name a frontier as defined by the passage. Choice (5) is incorrect because there was no longer a definable frontier in 1890.

11. **(5)** *Evaluation/History*. The steel plough, an agricultural tool, made possible the settlement of the Great Plains, thereby pushing the frontier more quickly to the west.

12. **(3)** *Application/History*. Only Choice (3) describes an action that would further the American boundary toward the Pacific Ocean. Note that the annexation of Hawaii (Choice [5]) is an expansion of U.S. territory *beyond* the Pacific coast and therefore could not properly be considered a part of manifest destiny.

13. **(2)** *Analysis/History*. All the crimes that are listed in the alternatives, except for treason, are possible crimes with which Watergate participants might have been charged. Treason would involve the selling or the trading of state secrets to an enemy. The crimes that are mentioned in the passage are burglary, the use of secret funds, and wiretapping. Although obstructing justice and lying to a grand jury are not directly mentioned in the passage,

the nature of the scandal and the behavior of some White House officials implies that these are far more likely crimes to have been committed than treason.

14. **(5)** *Application/History*. President Nixon, like President Reagan, stood accused of denying prior knowledge of illegal activities that were performed by his subordinates. In none of the events that are presented by the other alternatives was a president accused in a similar manner.

15. **(5)** *Evaluation/History*. The Supreme Court decision showed that a president could not abuse the privileges of the office and get away with it. The president must still abide by the law—in this case, by yielding the tapes when ordered to. It did not, as in Choice (1), find him guilty of any crime, nor did it, as in Choice (3), suspend any of his rights as an American citizen. Choice (2) is incorrect because American citizens are not required to prove their innocence; it is up to the state, or to a plaintiff, to prove their guilt. The president does have the right to take the Fifth Amendment, but it does not apply in this instance.

16. **(4)** *Analysis/History*. The only crime of President Nixon that is mentioned in the passage is that of withholding the tapes, which is a form of obstructing justice. Thus, Choices (2) and (5) are obviously incorrect. It is not illegal to record conversations in the White House, as in Choice (1), and it is never implied that President Nixon harbored or protected criminals, as in Choice (3).

17. **(4)** *Application/History*. Being an Eastern European, the Russian is in a group of approximately 750,000 people who emigrated to the United States between 1951 and 1970. Of all the groups to which the immigrants who are mentioned in the alternatives belong, this is by far the smallest, the next-largest being the group of immigrants from the Americas between 1911 and 1930, a group of approximately 2,500,000.

18. **(4)** *Analysis/Geography*. Only the concentration of population in the lowlands is an explanation of its distribution. Each of the other statements is a description of information provided.

19. **(2)** *Comprehension/Geography*. The need for caution is the central theme of the passage. Choice (3) flatly contradicts it, while Choices (4) and (5) are opinions that are never implied. Choice (1) is an implication that the passage makes but not an adequate summary of the whole.

20. **(3)** *Evaluation/Geography*. An action that is based on Choice (3) would result in the wholesale exploitation of resources without any regard to consequences and would therefore result in the opposite of what the passage suggests should be done. Choices (1) and (2) are both in agreement with the passage's prescription, although they emphasize different aspects of it. Choices (4) and (5) raise issues that are never discussed.

21. **(2)** *Analysis/Geography*. A high population-growth rate is associated with a situation in which the birth rate is significantly higher than the death rate. This situation is found in Stage 2. Note that in Stage 1 both the birth rate and the death rate are high.

22. **(1)** *Application/Geography*. Strong health services imply a low death rate, while family planning implies a low birth rate. Both of these are prerequisites of Stage 4. Every other alternative is characterized by either a high birth or high death rate, or by both.

23. **(4)** *Analysis/Geography*. The population will grow if the birth rate exceeds the death rate, but that growth will not necessarily increase, as stated in Choice (1). The other alternatives are not supported by the data in any way.

24. **(4)** *Application/Geography*. In order to share a similar climate, cities must have equivalent distances both from the ocean and from the equator. While some alternatives share one of these factors, only Chicago and Detroit share both.

25. **(2)** *Comprehension/Geography*. In the Southwestern region all states but one fall into the two most urbanized groupings indicated in the map legend. None of the other regions has as high a proportion of states in these groupings.

26. **(3)** *Evaluation/Geography*. Only a ranking of states is possible on the basis of the information in the map. The other choices would all require numerical figures and/or other data as well.

27. **(3)** *Comprehension/Economics*. According to the graph, tariff rates fell from about 40 percent in 1910 to about 12 percent in 1920, including the years of World War I (1914–1918). Each of the other alternatives is negated by the chart.

28. **(2)** *Analysis/Economics*. Of the choices given, the best way to effect an improvement is to import less. Raising tariffs would make foreign goods more expensive and thus would reduce the demand for them. As a result, goods that are made at home would become more competitive, and a balance of trade might be achieved.

29. **(4)** *Analysis/Economics*. A strong franc would enable French importers to buy more American goods, which would become lower priced as compared to French goods. An inflated French economy would lower the value of the franc, while an inflated U.S. economy would raise the costs of production. In both cases, American goods would be more expensive and less attractive to French buyers. United States import tariffs would have no effect on French importers. While a depression might affect the value of the dollar, the passage does not discuss its effect on exports.

30. **(5)** *Comprehension/Economics*. The passage states that private ownership and government ownership exist side by side. It does not, as in Choice (4), give details as to the type of ownership allowed to each. The postal service serves only as an example of government ownership, not as a model.

31. **(2)** *Application/Economics*. According to the graph, the largest portion of the consumer's budget is spent on food. The farming of produce and livestock is administered by the Department of Agriculture.

32. **(2)** *Comprehension/Economics*. The sample family spends $1,200 a year on clothing, while the graph shows that the average family in their income group ($15,000 a year) spends only about $900. The family is therefore *not* average in terms of annual clothing expenditure. There is no way of telling from the graph what is the annual household income, only

what each household spends. A family whose income is $30,000 spends about $1,800 a year on clothing, clearly less than double the expenditure of the sample family.

33. **(4)** *Evaluation/Economics.* The line that shows the average relationship between income and clothing expenditure is straight, indicating a proportional rate that is the same (about 6 percent) regardless of income. The graph does not indicate the number of wage earners or people in a household, nor the amount that each can afford to spend. A family's annual expenditure cannot be predicted, because the graph shows that many—such as the sample family—are outside the average.

34. **(3)** *Application/Economics.* Choices (1) and (2) are examples of tax incentives. Choice (4), although a kind of subsidy, aids the welfare recipients rather than the company. Choice (5) is neither subsidy nor tax incentive.

35. **(3)** *Analysis/Economics.* Federal loan insurance means that the government would not have to provide the loan, but merely guarantee it (paying only in the rare case where the borrower defaults). Therefore, it would be far less expensive than a subsidy, which requires cash, or a tax incentive, which deprives the government of income. While Choice (4) may be true, it is not an advantage. None of the other choices are implied by the passage.

36. **(3)** *Comprehension/Economics.* The passage states that owners of proprietorships and partnerships have unlimited liability, while corporate stockholders have limited liability; they all have some sort of liability. Only the owner of a partnership can be a partner (as in Choice [4]) and must share control with the other partners (as in Choice [5]).

37. **(1)** *Application/Economics.* The six people share both ownership and labor in their business and therefore satisfy the requirements of a partnership. Choices (2) and (3) are examples of proprietorships, while Choice (5) is a corporation that is run by directors. Choice (4) is not an example of business ownership because the farmer is a tenant.

38. **(4)** *Analysis/Economics.* The passage states that the liability of a corporate stockholder is limited to the amount that a person invested in the corporation. Therefore, no matter how the company fares, a person's personal assets cannot be claimed by creditors, unlike those of owners of proprietorships or partnerships.

39. **(2)** *Evaluation/Economics.* The need to accommodate the wishes of several owners, as in a partnership or a corporation, often results in management policies that are based on a compromise of ideas. These policies may be weaker than those that are composed by single individuals, which reveals an advantage to proprietorship. Choice (1) is untrue because unlimited liability can greatly affect a person's life if he or she is called upon to pay all business debts from personal assets such as the car or the house. Choices (3) and (4) imply that there is no money to be made or risks to be taken in partnerships or corporations, which is untrue. Choice (5) is a statement of opinion, not an argument that is based on the passage.

40. **(5)** *Evaluation/Economics.* As each share gives a stockholder one vote in the corporation's affairs, it follows that many shares give the stockholder a greater influence. Choices (1) and (2) are never implied by the passage, while Choice (4) is not true because a partner has unlimited liability, regardless of the amount of money that is invested. Choice (3) may or may not be true, but it is not discussed in the passage.

41. **(4)** *Application/Political Science.* Though the case involves local taxes and local residents, the law contested is a state law. The case is therefore tried in a State Superior Court.

42. **(2)** *Application/Political Science.* The original case, being a violation of the state drinking laws, would have been tried in a State Superior Court. As the owner wishes to see the ruling overturned, it is appealed in the next highest court—the state Court of Appeals.

43. **(3)** *Application/Political Science.* Civil rights are administered and protected by the U.S. Constitution at the federal level, and infringe-

ments of them are therefore tried in a Federal District Court.

44. **(1)** *Application/Political Science.* If the reporter believes that her right of free speech has been violated, it is a federal charge and will therefore be tried in a Federal District Court. Appeals will go to the next-highest court, being a federal Court of Appeals. If the case continues to be contested, the highest court to which it can be brought—and the highest in the country—is the Federal Supreme Court.

45. **(3)** *Application/Political Science.* Although the accident occurred in Indiana, where the plaintiff lives, the driver of the other car is an Illinois resident. Therefore, the case would be settled in Federal District Court, which handles interstate matters.

46. **(1)** *Evaluation/Political Science.* Because the United States is now protected by a well-armed military establishment, it is true that armed civilians are no longer necessary for the country's safety as they may have been during the Revolutionary War.

47. **(3)** *Comprehension/Political Science.* The poll tax, which was not abolished until 1969, required citizens to pay before they could vote. The law therefore discriminated against poorer citizens for whom this tax was more burdensome than for the rich. All the other choices were qualifications for voting that had been abolished prior to 1950.

48. **(4)** *Evaluation/Political Science.* Because there are fewer qualifications for the right to vote than ever before, the proportion of voting to nonvoting citizens is greater than ever. Choice (2) cannot be determined from the time line, while Choice (3) is untrue because a major group of citizens—all those under 18—do not have the right to vote. While Choice (1) may be true, the time line makes no reference to the growing population. Choice (5) cannot be determined from the time line and is in fact untrue— constitutional amendments are the most important of *several means* by which the right to vote has been extended.

49. **(2)** *Analysis/Political Science.* Women gained the right to vote in 1920, only two years after the end

of World War I. This happened before the Depression and too long after both the Civil War and the gaining of voting rights for black males to be affected by them. The Equal Rights Amendment was not raised as an issue until 1972.

50. **(2)** *Analysis/Political Science.* The passage describes the various functions of international organizations—judiciary, military, economic, and cultural. Though each of the other alternatives is true, they are statements of fact that support the conclusion. Only Choice (2) provides a summarizing conclusion for the passage itself.

51. **(2)** *Comprehension/Political Science.* The illustration shows a law-abiding citizen who is willfully and happily breaking the law, as if he had no respect for it. The result of this disrespect would bring a "flood" of lawless anarchy behind it. There is no implication, as in Choices (1) and (4), that the law will be difficult to enforce. Choice (3) is incorrect because the law made the sale of liquor illegal. Choice (5) is incorrect because the illustration shows the citizen breaking the law, not voting against it.

52. **(4)** *Analysis/Political Science.* Big cities, industrial workers, and minorities all benefit from federally funded work programs. If the Democratic Party were to remove these, it might expect to lose a good deal of its support from these groups. Choices (3) and (5) would be beneficial to these groups and would most likely increase their support for the Party. There is no mention of the defense industry or farmers in the passage and, therefore, no implication that Choices (1) and (2) would be opposed by Democratic supporters.

53. **(3)** *Application/Behavioral Science.* Choice (3) is not an example of reinforcement because the teacher is not seeking to alter the students' behavior, but instead is altering his or her own to adapt to that of the students. Choices (1) and (5) are examples of positive reinforcement, while Choices (2) and (4) are examples of negative reinforcement.

54. **(3)** *Application/Behavioral Science.* The colonizing group is forcing the other group to do work; therefore, this is an example of coercion.

55. **(5)** *Application/Behavioral Science.* The teams are competing against each other under a set of mutually acceptable rules.

56. **(2)** *Application/Behavioral Science.* Both individuals want the same piece of land, and they are struggling against each other in order to achieve their ends.

57. **(4)** *Application/Behavioral Science.* In exchange for lending the lawn mower, the owner requires the neighbor to provide some service in return.

58. **(5)** *Application/Behavioral Science.* The new supermarket may or may not be interested in driving the other supermarket out, but, in either event, they are both striving toward the same goal— winning new customers—under the same law of economic competition.

59. **(3)** *Analysis/Behavioral Science.* If one knows the number of people who are living, one can determine from the crude death rate the number of those who have died. From this figure, one may determine the percent in real numbers of those who have died from heart disease. None of the other factors will allow this number to be determined.

60. **(4)** *Evaluation/Behavioral Science.* Unlike other causes of death, accidents do not seem to follow any sort of trend: though they are higher in 1940 than in 1900, they are lower in 1975 than in 1940. Gastroenteritis disappears after 1900, and tuberculosis after 1940, so we may assume that cures have been found and that they will not reappear. Heart disease has become steadily more common, and there is no reason to assume a reversal of this trend. Diabetes may not have been a diagnosed disease in 1900, but its appearance on the chart under the 1940 and the 1975 columns reveals that it has been steadily becoming less common.

61. **(3)** *Evaluation/Behavioral Science.* Heart disease and stroke are known to be affected by stress, and both have been increasing. Choices (1) and (5) are untrue because childhood and infectious diseases (such as flu or syphilis) have almost disappeared. Choice (2) is unsupported because the graph merely shows that the incidence of cancer is increasing but does not show how effective treatment has become for all those who have contracted cancer. Choice (4) is unsupported because there is no data provided in the graph that relates to the age of the reported deaths.

62. **(1)** *Comprehension/Behavioral Science.* The passage states that education is considered to be a sexually neutral field and that such articles, when written anonymously, were taken by most subjects to be written by a man. Choice (2) might be true only *after* the subjects had decided that the article was written by a man.

63. **(3)** *Analysis/Behavioral Science.* The passage specifically states that the role of men and, therefore, their behavior is thought to have more value in society than that of women. While Choices (1), (2) and (5) may or may not be true, they do not explain the study's findings but rather are factors that support them. Choice (4) does not explain the findings in the study but implies that contradictory results should have been found.

64. **(2)** *Evaluation/Behavioral Science.* Only the statement in Choice (2) is directly supported by the study. The study did not test any of the factors that are mentioned in Choices (1), (3), and (5). The statement in Choice (4)— that the role of the male is more highly valued than the role of the female—is not directly shown by the research, but is instead an opinion that is given to explain the results of the research.

# PRACTICE TEST

1. **(4)** *Evaluation/Behavioral Science.* The chart shows that younger children tend to worry more than older children do about such problems as hunger and poverty, violence in the United States, and nuclear destruction, which are all societal problems. The chart also shows that 60% of ninth graders worry about school performance, and that 57% of them worry about their looks, which eliminates Choice (1) and Choice (5). There is no indication that children worry less as they mature, as in Choice (2). Although more younger children worry about suicide than do older children, this does not mean that they are actually more likely to kill themselves.

2. **(4)** *Application/Behavioral Science.* Each of the titles refers to a named priority on the chart. In this case, the highest priority referred to is the third, "How well other kids like me."

3. **(2)** *Evaluation/History.* California and Texas entered the Union during the nineteenth century, while Arizona and New Mexico were not admitted until the twentieth. The other choices are hypotheses that cannot be determined by the information provided.

4. **(1)** *Comprehension/Economics.* The passage states that failure to repay one's loan will result in losing one's insurance. Because the borrower loses the policy in place of the money that has been borrowed against it, the cash amount of the loan will not be forfeit. The passage makes no statement about a default being the cause of a change in interest rates. In fact, defaulting on a loan does not have any effect on its interest rate.

5. **(4)** *Application/Political Science.* Only Choice (4) satisfies all the requirements based on the chart.

6. **(5)** *Analysis/Political Science.* Because the president can expect opposition from the Democratic majority, his best chance of passing a bill would come with the congressional elections, when a Republican majority might come to power. Elections for the entire House and for one-third of the Senate occur every two years in November, but elected officials only take their seats in January. Therefore, the greatest possible change in effective representation would occur at the beginning of the President's third year in office.

7. **(2)** *Evaluation/Political Science.* With sufficient growth, a population increase will necessarily result in an increase of House representation. Because Senate representation is limited to two senators per state, the Senate will not change. There is no information to suggest any decrease in representation, as in Choice (3), while the regularly spaced increase implied in Choice (4) would be very improbable.

8. **(1)** *Comprehension/Behavioral Science.* Each of the other choices specifically contradicts statements made in the passage.

9. **(4)** *Application/Behavioral Science.* Type A persons enjoy high-pressure situations; they experience the most stress in situations, such as a traffic jam, that are beyond their control.

10. **(4)** *Application/Behavioral Science.* Smoking, lack of exercise, and stress are all factors that contribute to the chances of a heart attack. Only Choice (4) is the type of person who is free of all these factors.

11. **(2)** *Evaluation/Behavioral Science.* The passage makes no reference to the relationship of personality type to smoking. It mentions exercise as only one factor, not the best, in preventing heart attacks. It does claim our ability to identify potential victims. Therefore, only Choice (2) can be correct.

12. **(5)** *Analysis/Behavioral Science.* The entire passage is devoted to the effect of life-style on a person's chances of heart attack, which is discussed in each of the three paragraphs. There is nothing to suggest, as in Choice (3), that personality traits are the *primary* factor in this determination. Each of the other choices is discussed in only one section of the passage and are facts that contribute to the overall conclusion that life-style is a factor in determining the risks of a heart attack.

13. **(4)** *Application/Geography.* If latitude indicates distances north of the equator, the only way to determine the answer is to compare one latitude to the other.

14. **(2)** *Evaluation/Political Science.* The central theme of the Fourteenth Amendment is the inability of a state to infringe upon the Constitutional rights of its citizens. Of the five choices, that of desegregation refers to a civil-rights inequality that a state is ordered to correct.

15. **(3)** *Analysis/Political Science.* The most immediate effect of the Fourteenth Amendment would be to establish federal laws concerning citizens' rights as the preeminent authority in the United States. The amendment does not imply that federal authorization was needed by a state to pass a law (Choice [4]), merely that no state laws could contradict federal laws. Note that slavery was abolished by the Thirteenth Amendment in 1865.

16. **(1)** *Evaluation/History.* The passage states that ministers led the colonies, implying a strong connection between church and state. Choices (2), (3), and (4) are untrue; no mention is made of what the ministry was like before Harvard was built, and no discussion is given about college education in general. While choice (5) is true, it is nowhere suggested by the passage.

17. (1) *Application/Behavioral Science.* If she applied for the job, she must have wanted it. Therefore, she is giving a false explanation to hide her embarrassment.

18. (2) *Application/Behavioral Science.* The person is denying the existence of his illness.

19. (4) *Application/Behavioral Science.* The younger child's hostility is masked beneath an opposite reaction to the one that is truly felt.

20. (3) *Application/Behavioral Science.* The person is projecting his hatred of others onto their own personalities.

21. (1) *Comprehension/Economics.* A balanced budget implies no increase or decrease in the public debt. Of the choices given, this situation occurred only between the Civil War and World War I (1870–1910). Since 1910, the debt has risen almost continuously.

22. (2) *Analysis/Economics.* The decrease occurred from 1920 to 1930, before the Depression but too distant from the Civil War to be affected by it (as Choice [1] implies). A decrease in expensive federally funded programs would allow more federal revenues to be spent on the debt, which would drop as a consequence. Lowering federal taxes, as in Choice (4), would increase the public debt because less money would be coming in to cover government expenses. State taxes, as mentioned in Choice (5), would have no effect on federal revenues.

23. (4) *Evaluation/Economics.* The debt rose by approximately $100 billion during the 1960s, implying that increased federal spending was NOT covered by a raise in income taxes. Each of the other choices is supported.

24. (4) *Application/Political Science.* Only the Iranian hostage crisis meets the passage's definition of terrorism. The events in Choices (1) and (2) were not intended to effect political change by frightening governments; Choices (3) and (5) did not involve political demands at all.

25. (1) *Evaluation/Geography.* The passage gives an example of direct pollution of water (factories pouring wastes into rivers and lakes) and another of indirect pollution (fertilizers and pesticides being washed from soils). Therefore,

Choice (1) is the correct answer. None of the other choices are supported by the passage.

26. (5) *Analysis/History.* The passage states that the incident had its beginnings in a protest by labor unionists and others. All the other statements are stated or implied in the passage as *opinions*, not as facts.

27. (4) *Analysis/History.* The passage states that the Knights, a reform-unionist organization, gave way to the A.F. of L., a trade-unionist organization. It also says that trade unionists, in contrast to reform unionists, favored strikes and a focus on working conditions. Therefore, Choice (4) is the most likely result.

28. (1) *Evaluation/History.* The passage describes differences between reform unionists and trade unionists as to the goals to be pursued and the methods to be used in pursuing those goals. The other choices may or may not be true; they are not suggested by the passage.

29. (4) *Analysis/Political Science.* A member of Congress is a public servant whose presence when Congress is in session is deemed too important to disturb except in cases when major crimes or acts of treason have been committed. A member is not, however, above the law and will still be charged for all minor crimes.

30. (4) *Comprehension/Economics.* In every other country, the industrial sector is smaller than either the agricultural or the service sectors, or both.

31. (4) *Analysis/Economics.* A smaller number of farmers who produce the same amount of crops suggests that one farmer is doing the work of many. Therefore, farming in the United States must have increased in efficiency. The other choices, although they may be true, in no way explain the ability of few people to grow large amounts of food.

32. (3) *Application/History.* The Monroe Doctrine specifically disclaims United States rights in the colonies owned by European countries, such as Algeria. The other choices are all examples either of neutrality or of defense of the American continents. Choice (5) is equally an example of self-defense, though outside of the Western Hemisphere.

33. (5) *Comprehension/History.* Choices (2), (3), and (4) are all either untrue or not mentioned in the passage. While Choice (1) is a valid statement, it does not adequately define the overall change in the nation.

34. (2) *Evaluation/History.* The passage does not imply that food shortages (Choice [4]) were a problem or that the Revolutionary War was the only cause of isolationism (Choice [5]). Choice (1) is untrue because the United States fought naval wars in Cuba, Guam, and so on. Note that United States belligerence (Choice [3]) was directed at Spain, not at Cuba.

35. (1) *Analysis/History.* In order to maintain needed trade without being able to dock at foreign ports, United States merchants must have relied on an increase in the docking at domestic ports by foreign merchants.

36. (4) *Analysis/Political Science.* Choice (1) is an opinion. Choice (2) is incorrect because checks and balances were not designed to safeguard against control by a political party. Choices (3) and (5) are faulty statements. Choice (4) contains the only stated fact that pertains to the illustration, since the lawmaking procedure gives some power to the legislative branch and some power to the executive branch of the government.

37. (2) *Comprehension/Political Science.* The only information that is contained in the illustration is found in Choice (2). Choices (3), (4), and (5) are contradicted by information in the illustration. Although Congress can override a President's veto, it by no means has to; so Choice (1) is incorrect because the President may successfully veto a bill.

38. (3) *Evaluation/Political Science.* Choice (3) is the only statement that is accurate and embodies a fundamental principle of democracy (government of, by, and for the people).

39. (3) *Evaluation/Economics.* Choice (1) is conjecture, and Choice (5) is a statement of fact. Choices (2) and (4), though they might be argued as true, are not conclusions that are supported by this passage. Choice (3) is the only conclusion that is supported by the passage.

40. **(2)** *Application/Behavioral Science.* Although Choice (2) describes a situation in which a common language is spoken, no common culture is shared. Note that Choice (3) describes a situation in which *two* languages are shared by the nation, which is still defined as a society.

41. **(5)** *Evaluation/History.* The table shows that, in some cases, more people have immigrated from small countries (such as the Philippines) than from large ones (such as India). Choice (4) is not correct because the table shows that nearly all Koreans and Indochinese immigrated after 1950. The other choices are incorrect because the table does not give any information about why or when specific immigration took place.

42. **(1)** *Analysis/History.* The table states that most Korean and Indochinese immigration occurred after 1950, the period of time coinciding with the Korean and the Vietnam wars.

43. **(3)** *Comprehension/Political Science.* As the cabinet is not an official body, it can make no decisions or decrees by itself that are constitutionally binding. It can only act in an advisory or an unofficial capacity, as is stated in Choice (3).

44. **(4)** *Application/Political Science.* The secretary of the treasury is not authorized to devalue the dollar; only the president may do so. Every other choice refers to changes or actions that are only proposed, not executed.

45. **(4)** *Application/Geography.* A climatic map includes such conditions as rainfall averages, which are important factors in the determination of types of agricultural crops.

46. **(1)** *Application/Geography.* The Continental Divide is a physical feature in the Rocky Mountains. A topographical map would show this feature.

47. **(2)** *Application/Geography.* A contour map gives specific information about elevation. It would detail the slopes and the valleys of a given terrain, thus allowing one to determine a flood pattern.

48. **(5)** *Application/Geography.* Potential investors would be interested in the location of natural re-

sources on which to build an industry. A geological map is one source of such information.

49. **(3)** *Application/Geography.* The border between the United States and Canada would be shown on a political map.

50. **(3)** *Application/Behavioral Science.* A self-made, self-educated millionaire would exemplify status *inconsistency* because the person has a high income status but a low education (and possibly family-background) status. The restaurant worker who has a modest income is an example of status *consistency* (occupation/income), as is the lawyer whose parents are doctors (occupation/family background). Neither a woman truck driver nor a working retiree involve any inconsistency in status, although they may not reflect the traditional notion of roles assigned to them by society.

51. **(3)** *Comprehension/History.* The fact that congressional authority was wielded against the tribes indicates that they posed a threat. Choices (1) and (5) are therefore untrue, while Choices (2) and (4) are specifically negated by the passage.

52. **(4)** *Analysis/History.* The acquisition of citizenship entails the acquisition of the right to vote, thus enabling citizens to take power in their government. Nothing else is implied in the description of the Indian Citizenship Act.

53. **(5)** *Application/Behavioral Science.* An unemployed couple who have children is categorized in the table as a no-wage-earner nuclear family, the smallest type of household (1%).

54. **(5)** *Comprehension/Behavioral Science.* The table shows that no type of household is dominant in United States society. (The largest type of household, child-free or post-child-rearing marriages, accounts for only 23%.) Choices (2), (3), and (4) describe comparisons that are specifically contradicted by information in the table.

55. **(4)** *Analysis/Behavioral Science.* An increased divorce rate would lower the percentage of married couples, not increase it as in Choices (2) and (5). Single-parent families would possibly increase in percentage, while cohabited households would not be affected.

56. **(1)** *Analysis/Geography.* Only region A has the high temperatures and the lack of rainfall that would make it a desert. Note that while region C also has no rainfall, it has extremely cold temperatures throughout the year.

57. **(3)** *Analysis/Geography.* Region C is peculiar because it is colder during the summer months and hotter during the winter months, a phenomenon found only in the southern hemisphere.

58. **(2)** *Comprehension/History.* The passage states that skilled workers had more power than unskilled workers in dealing with employers. The fact that skilled workers were more difficult to replace gave them this power.

59. **(4)** *Comprehension/Economics.* The passage states that the government generally intervenes only at times of war or severe shortage, or when domestic industry needs special protection from foreign competition.

60. **(4)** *Application/Economics.* The passage defines quotas and taxes as indirect government influence, while a survey does not qualify as any form of interference. A wage-and-price freeze, however, is a direct order from the government to manufacturers and employers, similar to the method of controlling prices through a price ceiling.

61. **(3)** *Analysis/Economics.* Repealing tariffs would allow competitively priced foreign cars to enter the domestic market, thus forcing American companies to lower their own prices in order to remain competitive.

62. **(4)** *Analysis/Economics.* Inexpensive imported shoes might undercut United States manufacturers, whose production costs are significantly higher than those of their competitors. A low tariff would slightly raise the retail price of imported shoes, allowing domestic shoes to compete with them. The tariff would not affect the price of domestic shoes.

63. **(4)** *Evaluation/Economics.* High tariffs make it prohibitively expensive for foreign manufacturers to export their goods to the United States. The government would want to prohibit importing in order to give United States industry time to catch up in the development of similar products or

to reduce unemployment. Therefore, Choice (1) would provide a
situation that might lead to a repeal of tariffs, while Choice (4) is
the only alternative offered in
which the government would
want to establish high tariffs.
Choices (2), (3), and (5) would not
directly affect a decision to impose high tariffs.

64. **(3)** *Comprehension/History.* The
passage implies that the growth of
cities and factory work was a new
development of the Industrial
Revolution. Previous to this development, therefore, most work
was done in nonfactory settings in
small workshops or at home.

# SIMULATION
## SIMULATED TEST

1. **(3)** *Comprehension/History.* The cartoon depicts President Johnson struggling to hold up a crumbling world. Lacking solutions for the problems of the nation and the world, he's trying to prevent a total collapse. While Nixon is eager to assume the burden, Johnson, knowing the magnitude of the problems, is giving him fair warning. Choice (5) is incorrect precisely because Nixon was taking over the presidency from Johnson, not sharing it. And there is no evidence in the cartoon to support choice (1), choice (2), or choice (4).

2. **(4)** *Comprehension/Economics.* The passage states that mass-produced goods have almost entirely replaced handmade goods. This implies that handmade goods may be hard to find. Though they may be more expensive than mass-produced goods, this does not mean, as in choice (3), that only the rich can afford them. Though choice (1) may be true, it is nowhere suggested in the passage. Choice (2) and choice (5) are also alternatives that are not suggested in the passage.

3. **(4)** *Comprehension/Economics.* The graph of New York City expenses shows that at 22 percent education is the city's second largest expense, after human resources. School maintenance and teachers' salaries would be paid from money allocated to education.

4. **(5)** *Analysis/Economics.* New York City home owners pay property taxes, which account for 23 percent, or the largest single source, of the city's revenues. And all residents who work must pay city income tax. Income tax can be assumed to make up an important part of the "other taxes and local revenues" category, which altogether represents 44 percent of the city's revenues. Corporations, in choice (4), also pay a tax, which in the graph would again be included in the "other taxes" category. It can safely be assumed, however, that their contribution to the 44 percent will be less than residents' and home owners' share of the 44 percent plus the 23 percent represented by property taxes. Choice (1) is incorrect because the federal contribution to New York City revenues is only 11 percent. Choice (2) is incorrect because the New York State contribution is only 22 percent. Choice (3) is incorrect for the same reason, since state sales tax would become part of the New York State contribution to the budget.

5. **(3)** *Evaluation/Economics.* The graph shows that New York City must receive aid from the state and federal government in order to pay its expenses. Choice (4) and choice (5) are incorrect because they are based on opinion rather than on evidence provided in the graph. Choice (2) is incorrect because the graph does not show what other cities contribute to their own budget. Choice (1) is not supported by any evidence in the graph.

6. **(2)** *Comprehension/Economics.* The passage indicates that numerous new, higher-status jobs have become available since the United States began its shift to a service economy. Choice (3) is not supported by the passage. Though the passage states that education is the most important factor in upward mobility, it also says that race and sex are important too, so choice (5) is incorrect. Choice (1) and choice (4) contradict information in the passage.

7. **(3)** *Analysis/Economics.* Because lack of education may be a factor limiting upward job mobility, providing grants to minority scholarship funds would likely help increase mobility. All the other choices either are not supported by the information in the passage or are contradicted by it.

8. **(4)** *Application/Behavioral Science.* The passage states that neurotic symptoms are inadvertent behaviors that express unconscious troubles. A person who is dieting to lose weight is engaging in a deliberate behavior to resolve a problem that he or she is very much aware of. In contrast, the other choices involve behaviors that are not deliberate and that might well express troubles that the individual is not aware of.

9. **(3)** *Analysis/Behavioral Science.* The passage specifically discusses physical manifestations of the unconscious mind. Of all the choices, only dreaming is not a physical expression, but a mental expression of unconscious stress.

10. **(4)** *Evaluation/Behavioral Science.* The entire passage is devoted to showing how different symptoms are associated with different kinds of neuroses. Therefore, a person's neurosis can, at least in some cases, be diagnosed by examining symptoms. Though choice (2) and choice (5) may well be true, they are not discussed in the passage. Choice (3) is incorrect because, although asthma may be a neurotic symptom, it is by no means necessarily so. Choice (1) is contradicted by the passage, which states that early studies of neurosis were made before the beginning of this century.

11. **(1)** *Analysis/Geography.* The passage states that Third-World nations cannot afford the modern agricultural technology that would help make their soil more fertile and increase the amount of food grown. Thus, low-interest loans earmarked for agricultural technology might contribute to a long-term solution to the problem of hunger in the Third World. Choice (2) and choice (5) are incorrect because the passage states that shipping food overseas is costly, wasteful, and creates long-term dependencies. Choice (3) and choice (4) are not logical, because those people who were relocated would still have to be fed.

12. **(3)** *Evaluation/Geography.* The passage specifically states that there is enough food in the world to feed everyone. It is therefore true that if the world's food were distributed evenly, no one would starve. Choice (4) is incorrect, since the passage talks in terms of the poor nations as being unable—not unwilling—to spend the money. Choice (2) and choice (5) are nowhere implied in the passage, while choice (1) is contradicted by it.

13. **(2)** *Evaluation/Economics.* The passage states that though the debt is rising, it is declining in terms of percentage of annual output. This can only mean that the national output is rising faster than the debt. Though choice (1) and choice (3) may or may not be true, government loans would have little effect on national output, which depends primarily on private industry. Choice (4) and choice (5) are both untrue statements, and have little or no bearing on the issue.

14. **(2)** *Comprehension/Behavioral Science.* The passage discusses the various social factors that may have contributed to the declining fertility rate in the United States through the greater part of its history. Choice (1) is incorrect because current fertility rates are not discussed. Choice (3) and choice (4) are incorrect because they do not address the passage's central issue of fertility. Choice (5) only addresses a small section of the social issues discussed in the passage.

15. **(5)** *Comprehension/Behavioral Science.* The passage states that one of the reasons for the decline in the fertility rate was that women were beginning to find opportunities outside the home which were alternatives to childbearing. This implies that childbearing and child-raising had been the main socially acceptable activities for women before the decline in fertility. Choice (3) may or may not be true; the U.S. fertility rate before 1800 is not discussed nor are any comparisons made. The passage does not imply, as in choice (1), that no family planning or contraception was available, or, as in choice (2), that only the rich could afford leisure time. Choice (4) is contradicted by

the passage, which implies industrial workers were associated with the period *after* 1800 and with cramped, not spacious, housing conditions.

16. **(3)** *Evaluation/Behavioral Science.* The decline continued through the 1930s, thus including and ending with the Great Depression, during which many people could not afford children even if they wanted them. It is logical to assume, therefore, that the fertility rate rose with economic recovery, as people who had postponed having children during the Depression were now in a better financial position. Choice (1) and choice (2) don't fit with the passage, which implies that joblessness and financial hardship lead to *lower* fertility rates. Choice (4) could be expected to further reduce fertility rates. Choice (5) is incorrect, since such a change would have come in the mid- to late forties and the numbers involved would have been too small to have a significant effect on the overall fertility rate.

17. **(4)** *Analysis/History.* The graph shows an overall decline in farm income from 1919 to 1930. Only choice (4) could affect farm income in this way. Choice (1) and choice (3) would raise farm income. Choice (2) would probably have little effect on farm income, especially as the soldiers returned by 1919, the first year of the graph. Choice (5) is incorrect because the graph shows only the very beginning of the Depression, which would not have affected most of the 1920s at all.

18. **(2)** *Comprehension/Political Science.* The passage states that a copyright is valid even without being registered. All the other choices are contradicted by information in the passage.

19. **(4)** *Application/Political Science.* According to the passage, the publisher may publish the book without any permissions, because the copyright expired in 1941, 50 years after Melville's death. The other choices are all contradicted by information in the passage.

20. **(1)** *Comprehension/Political Science.* Trademarks are used to distinguish a product from similar products offered by the manufacturer's competitors. Therefore,

choice (2) and choice (5) are automatically incorrect. Choice (3) fails to offer an explanation. Choice (4) is nowhere implied in the passage.

21. **(3)** *Analysis/Political Science.* Nowhere in the passage is it implied that intellectual property laws are intended for the benefit of anyone except creators. Though maintaining a government record of ideas and creations may be a useful side effect of these laws, it was not a motivation for their being passed. All the other choices are stated or implied in the passage.

22. **(2)** *Evaluation/Political Science.* Copyrights last 50 years after their owners' death, patents are valid for 17 years, and trademarks are valid for 20 years. Thus, they all may easily outlive the people who established them. Nowhere does the passage discuss renewal of these registrations, as in choice (1), or the intellectual property laws of other countries, as in choice (5). Choice (3) is incorrect because computer software requires, and receives, protection from exploitation in the same way as other original creations or ideas. Choice (4) is a statement of opinion, not of fact.

23. **(1)** *Comprehension/Political Science.* In the 1980 elections, 59 percent of the population—well over half—voted, and a far larger percentage of people aged 65 to 74 voted than did those between 18 and 20. Choice (4) and choice (5) are incorrect, since over half the population voted. Choice (2) and choice (3) are incorrect because, in order to determine whether they are true, we would have to know the number of people who voted, and the passage only provides their percentages.

24. **(3)** *Analysis/Political Science.* Because nearly two-thirds of the older group voted, while only about one-third of the younger group did, the old can be said to be a more reliable voting group than the young. Choice (1) cannot be determined without knowing both the number of people involved and whether the old in fact vote as a group. Unless the old tend to vote along similar lines, they will not be a particularly powerful voting group. Choice (2) is contradicted by the passage. Choice (4) is a statement

of opinion. Choice (5) cannot be supported by the passage.

25. **(3)** *Comprehension/Geography.* The passage describes how poor people in developing countries are caught between the poverty and unemployment characteristic of the rural areas and the often undesirable living conditions characteristic of the cities. Natural resources, division of labor, and real estate development are not mentioned in the passage, while health services are only one area of discussion in it.

26. **(2)** *Comprehension/Political Science.* The Constitution allows the legislature to raise an army, navy, and air force. Nothing is said about the National Guard. Further, the power to raise troops is distinct from the power to activate them. The other choices are all supported by the passage.

27. **(1)** *Comprehension/Economics.* The chart shows that from 1970 to 1975 the number of unemployed increased by nearly 4 million. This is by far the largest change shown on the chart.

28. **(3)** *Analysis/Economics.* Because the unemployment rate is based on the percentage of people in the labor force who do not have jobs, it is affected by the total number of people in the labor force. Therefore, though more people may have been unemployed in 1983 than in 1982, they still represented a smaller percentage of the labor force because the number of employed increased even more. Choice (1) and choice (2) may or may not be true, but they cannot be determined by information provided in the chart. Choice (4) is contradicted by the chart. Choice (5) would have no effect on the rates of years prior to 1984.

29. **(5)** *Comprehension/History.* The cotton gin helped to make cotton a very profitable crop, which it had not been before. Choice (1) is incorrect because the cotton gin was invented at the very end of the eighteenth century. Choice (3) is incorrect because the cotton industry was not a once-vital industry that was now ailing; for all practical purposes, it hadn't existed. Choice (4) is incorrect because the slave-trading industry existed long before the cotton gin. Choice (2) is contradicted by the passage.

30. **(1)** *Analysis/History.* The big plantation owners had the land on which they could grow the large quantities of cotton that could now be processed with the cotton gin. They could afford the slaves to pick this cotton. In this way, the cotton boom had the effect of further concentrating wealth. Thus, choice (2) is incorrect. Choice (3) is incorrect because tobacco continued to be grown, as it is today, in many Southern states. Choice (4) is incorrect because carpetbaggers did not arrive until after the Civil War. Choice (5) is highly unlikely because Southerners lived among slaves and therefore were well aware of their suffering.

31. **(2)** *Evaluation/History.* The passage states that the cotton gin helped to make slave-keeping profitable, and increased support for slavery in the South. Choices (1), (3), and (5) are therefore incorrect. Choice (4) is not logical.

32. **(2)** *Evaluation/History.* The graph shows great increases in union membership during the Depression and during wars, and very slow increases during times of prosperity such as the twenties or the decade between the Korean and Vietnam Wars. Choice (3) and choice (5) are thus contradicted by the evidence. There is no way to determine whether choice (1) is true without having additional information. The sharp rises at several points in the graph contradict choice (4).

33. **(4)** *Evaluation/Economics.* Since the percentage of children living in poverty rose from 1979 to 1984, it is reasonable to assume that public policies and private policies designed to curb poverty among children did not succeed. There is nothing in the passage to support choices (1), (2), or (5). Choice (3) is incorrect, because the passage is implicitly treating teenage pregnancy as an *effect* of poverty, not a cause.

34. **(5)** *Application/Political Science.* Impeachment proceedings are an example of the judicial powers of Congress.

35. **(1)** *Application/Political Science.* In proposing the Equal Rights Amendment, Congress was using its constituent powers, which enable it to change the Constitution.

36. **(3)** *Application/Political Science.*

In splitting a federal agency into two separate agencies, Congress used its executive powers.

37. **(3)** *Application/Political Science.* The ongoing information-gathering process described here is in an important part of congressional supervision over agencies.

38. **(4)** *Application/Political Science.* In conducting investigations of the Watergate cover-up, Congress was using its investigatory powers. Choice (5) is ruled out because, as indicated, Nixon's resignation made it unnecessary for Congress to use its judicial powers.

39. **(4)** *Comprehension/Economics.* The main idea of the passage is that American productivity has declined and that this decline is, at least according to one analysis, explained by a tendency to focus on the present. The other statements listed either support this statement, as in choice (3) and choice (5), or are more general ideas leading up to it.

40. **(2)** *Evaluation/Economics.* The passage mentions that there are data showing that U.S. plants lagged behind in conversion to continuous casting. The statements in choice (3) and choice (4) are given as part of the analysis discussed in the passage, rather than as facts; the statements in choice (1) and choice (5) are not mentioned in the passage.

41. **(4)** *Comprehension/History.* The map shows Abilene as being at the end of the Chisholm Trail. None of the other towns are near any of the cattle trails.

42. **(3)** *Analysis/History.* The map shows that all the cattle trails end at a junction with a railroad line. It is thus reasonable to assume that the cows were being brought from the Texas ranges to the railroads, where, as the map shows, they would be shipped to major cities.

43. **(2)** *Evaluation/History.* The great distances that needed to be crossed to deliver meat to the major markets of the East prevented ranching, such as in Texas, to become profitable until a cheap way was found to transport cattle. None of the other choices are supported by information provided in the map.

44. **(5)** *Analysis/History.* The end of the nineteenth century and the early twentieth century were marked by explosive growth of cities as a con-

sequence of industrialization, which had begun after the Civil War. By working in the factories, later immigrants helped meet the supply needs occasioned by rapid industrialization.

45. **(4)** *Evaluation/History.* The passage states that the period beginning around 1880 marked the peak of immigration. It also states that immigrants from northern Europe (that is, from the United Kingdom, Germany, and Scandinavia) for the most part came prior to this period. None of the other choices are supported by the passage.

46. **(4)** *Comprehension/Geography.* The passage discusses both natural and human activity as causing soil erosion. Thus, choice (4) is correct. The other choices all list *specific* factors, each of which contributes to erosion but cannot be termed its cause.

47. **(3)** *Application/Geography.* Grazing land on an open plain is vulnerable to soil erosion by both natural and human activity. The environments in the other choices either are not vulnerable to human activity or are protected by it, and, in some cases, may also be less vulnerable to soil erosion through natural processes.

48. **(3)** *Analysis/Geography.* The passage indicates that at the very least conservation measures could cut down on soil erosion that occurs because of human activity. Terracing and planting trees are mentioned as measures that can reduce soil erosion. There is no evidence in the passage to support choices (1), (2), or (5). Choice (4) is contradicted by the passage.

49. **(5)** *Evaluation/Geography.* The passage says that soil erosion is causing a marked decline in the productivity of U.S. cropland. Such a large decline would logically affect U.S. farmers. The other conclusions are either opinions or false statements, but in any case they do not follow from the passage.

50. **(2)** *Comprehension/History.* The map shows American lumber going both to Great Britain and to Portugal. Every other choice is contradicted by information provided in the map.

51. **(1)** *Analysis/History.* The map shows that the American colonies exported their raw iron to Great Britain and imported their hardware from Great Britain. To preserve this lucrative trade arrangement, Great Britain passed the act forbidding colonial manufacture of steel and hardware.

52. **(2)** *Evaluation/History.* The map shows that colonial exports went to southern Europe and to Spanish colonies in the West Indies, as well as to the British West Indies and Great Britain. In contrast, all imports shown on the map are from Great Britain or the British West Indies. This pattern resulted from British restrictions on trade. Choice (3) and choice (4) are contradicted by information in the map. Choice (1) is both untrue and unsupported by the map, while choice (5) is an opinion, not a fact.

53. **(4)** *Analysis/Behavioral Science.* The emphasis in the passage is not on the table, but on people's acceptance of closeness in social situations. Therefore, choices (1), (3), and (5) are not as appropriate as choice (4). Choice (2) is incorrect because the article is about all of Great Britain, not just the Shetland Islands.

54. **(3)** *Analysis/Behavioral Science.* The ratio between single men and single women can be determined because we know the precise number of each and can compare them. For this reason, choice (1) and choice (2) are incorrect; choice (1) requires that we know the size of the total population between the ages of 35 and 54, choice (2) that we know the size of the total population. Choice (4) and choice (5) are incorrect because we cannot know that the numbers changed only through marriage or divorce.

55. **(5)** *Analysis/Geography.* The diagram emphasizes the aspects of a landfill that have to do with draining the liquid from the landfill into tanks. The detail shows the many precautions taken so that none of this liquid will leak into the surrounding land. This can only be interpreted as an attempt to avoid contamination of nearby soil and water. No other choice is supported by any evidence in the diagram.

56. **(1)** *Comprehension/Geography.* This map reports only about areas of the world with wet and dry seasons as well as a minimum of 20 inches of rainfall. No other information about seasons or rainfall is conveyed.

57. **(4)** *Analysis/Geography.* The maps show that savannas have climates with an annual rainfall of more than 500 mm and with wet and dry seasons, whereas tropical rain forests do not. The other choices are incorrect because the maps do not report the rainfall in tropical forests or temperature.

58. **(4)** *Application/Behavioral Science.* The man's housecleaning is an example of an irrational, repetitive activity that is symbolically related to his problem.

59. **(5)** *Application/Behavioral Science.* The woman has an excessive and irrational fear, which may interfere with daily activities.

60. **(2)** *Application/Behavioral Science.* Instead of confronting his problem, the man allows it to take over, becoming deeply depressed and antisocial.

61. **(1)** *Application/Behavioral Science.* The woman's paralysis is an example of a physical symptom that is expressing an unconscious and unwanted desire. Although consciously the woman is happy about the upcoming marriage and move, unconsciously she doesn't want her life to change.

62. **(2)** *Application/Behavioral Science.* The woman, even if she disguises her feelings from others, is suffering from a depressive neurosis.

63. **(3)** *Application/History.* The passage indicates that colonists resented British measures that restricted their political and economic freedoms. Duties passed by Great Britain raised the prices of consumer goods and infringed on colonial self-government. Choice (4) does not involve the colonies; the other choices would be unlikely to anger the colonists.

64. **(4)** *Evaluation/History.* Because Britain didn't allow the colonists representation in Parliament, and because it was an overseas power, it could make economic and political decisions that didn't serve the colonists' interests.

# GLOSSARY

**Allied Powers** in World War I, the alliance formed by Great Britain, France, Russia, Japan, the United States, and other countries; in World War II, the alliance formed by countries including Great Britain, Russia, and the United States

**American Federation of Labor** one of the first labor unions, formed in 1886

**American Revolution** the war fought from 1775 to 1783 that won independence for the American colonies from Great Britain

**Anti-Federalists** those who, in the debate over whether to adopt the Constitution, opposed the Constitution and considered the rights of states more important than national government

**antitrust legislation** laws breaking up existing monopolies and preventing the formation of new ones

**armistice** an agreement ending a war, especially the agreement to end World War I

**Articles of Confederation** document adopted in 1781 that provided for a "league of friendship" among the states but essentially let each state govern itself

**Axis nations** the alliance of Germany, Italy, and Japan in World War II

**balance of trade** the difference in value between a country's exports and imports

**benefit** service and monetary reimbursement, other than salary, that a company provides for its workers

**binding arbitration** agreement between management and labor before negotiations begin to accept whatever compromises the mediator deems fit

**blue-collar workers** people who work primarily with their hands, directly providing goods and services

**Boston Tea Party** incident in which, in angry response to taxes on imports such as tea, American colonists dumped tea from English ships into Boston Harbor

**capitalism** economic system that allows individuals to produce whatever they want and charge as much as they like for it

**carpetbagger** person from the North who migrated to the South after the Civil War for economic gain

**Caucasian** relating to the white race of people as classified by physical features

**Central Powers** the alliance formed by Germany, Austria-Hungary, Turkey, and Bulgaria in World War I

**checking account** a bank account against which checks can be written to pay for goods and services

**Civil Rights Act of 1866** legislation that granted blacks equal rights with whites

**Civil Rights Act of 1957** legislation passed to protect voting rights

**Civil Rights Act of 1964** legislation that prohibited discrimination in voting, employment, and public accommodations

**Civil Rights Act of 1968** legislation that banned discrimination in most housing sales and rentals

**Civilian Conservative Corps** a New Deal program that employed out-of-work men to maintain and upgrade America's forests

**classless society** the ideal of communism whereby all people are equal in status because all wealth is shared

**climate** the typical weather pattern in a geographic area

**cold war** the military and political stand-off between the Western nations and the Soviet Union and its satellites

**collective bargaining** the process that unions use to negotiate contracts with management

**communism** economic system in which the government owns and controls the means of production

**community** a group of people bonded together for mutual benefit

**compulsory education** legislation that requires children to attend school through a specified grade

**Confederate States of America** the political organization formed by eleven Southern states after they seceded from the United States in 1860

**conglomerate** a large corporation that controls companies in many different industries

**Connecticut Compromise** the compromise during the writing of the Constitution that gave power to large and small states by creating two houses of Congress

**Constitution** the document, created in 1787 to replace the Articles of Confederation, that provides the present structure of the government

**Consumer Price Index** the average price of essential goods and services

**consumption** the using up of goods and services

**continental climate** climate that is found in inland regions and is characterized by hot summers and cold winters

**contour lines** lines that join points of equal elevation on a topographic map

**cooperative society** belief that the best society results from the cooperation of individuals working together for the benefit of all

**corporation** a business that is licensed by the state or local government and in which private citizens are part-owners

**credit union** a non-profit savings association formed and owned by workers from a company

**Crusades** a series of expeditions in which European Christians tried to recover Palestine from the Moslems in Medieval times

**cultural geography** the branch of geography that studies the makeup and distribution of populations

**debit card** a card that allows people to pay for goods and services at stores through electronic transfer of funds

**Declaration of Independence** document issued by the American colonies in 1776 that declared them independent of British rule

**demand** the amount of a good or service that people are willing and able to purchase

**Department of Labor** the government department that seeks to improve the working conditions of the wage earner

**desert climate** a hot and dry climate with very little rainfall

**détente** a relaxing of tension between nations, especially with reference to the United States and the Soviet Union

**discount rate** a lowered rate on loans made to private banks by the Federal Reserve Banks

**distribution** the process by which a product or good is delivered to those who need or want it

**draft account** the credit union equivalent of a checking account

**elastic currency** the means by which the Federal Reserve Board regulates the amount of money in circulation

**elevation** a geographical measure of distance above sea level

**Emancipation Proclamation** President Lincoln's decree, issued in 1863, that freed the slaves

**embargo** the prohibition of trade with a particular country, usually in response to a conflict

**emigration** the movement of people out of a region

**environmental crisis** the rapid depletion of natural resources

**equator** an imaginary line that runs in an east-west direction around the middle of the earth, dividing it into Northern and Southern hemispheres

**equilibrium point** the point at which consumers will buy exactly the amount of goods supplied by the producer

**ethnic group** people of the same race or nationality who share certain cultural characteristics

**excise tax** tax paid on non-essential items

**Fair Deal** President Truman's proposed extension of the New Deal that addressed civil rights, federal aid to education, and national health insurance

**Federal Deposit Insurance Corporation** and **Federal Savings and Loan Insurance Corporation** created in 1933 by the Banking Act, these organizations insure individual accounts in member banks up to maximum allowed

**Federal Reserve Act** 1913 legislation that divided the United States into twelve financial districts and established a Federal Reserve Bank for each

**Federal Reserve Board** the organization that administers the Federal Reserve banks and national banks

**Federal Reserve System** the network of national banks administered by the Federal Reserve Board; half of all banks are members

**Federalists** those who supported the Constitution in the debate over its ratification, placing the concerns of a national government over the interests of each state

**Fifteenth Amendment** the constitutional amendment that gave blacks the right to vote

**fossil fuels** fuels such as coal and oil that were formed by the compression of plants over thousands of years

**Fourteenth Amendment** the constitutional amendment that guaranteed blacks full citizenship and equal protection under the law

**free-enterprise system** economic philosophy that says a country's economy works best when the government does not interfere in business

**free markets** trade between countries with no tariffs or restrictions

**Great Depression** a period of business failures, bank closings, and unemployment that crippled America following the Stock Market Crash of 1929

**Great Society** ideal of a society with no war, poverty, or prejudice proposed by President Johnson

**Gross National Product** total value of all goods and services produced by a country during a specific period such as a year

**hemisphere** a half of the globe determined by the equator, which divides the Earth into Northern and Southern Hemispheres, or the prime meridian, which divides the globe into Eastern and Western hemispheres

**immigration** the movement of people into a region

**imperialism** foreign policy emphasizing political and economic control over other nations or territories; characteristic of the United States at various points in its history, especially the late 19th century

**individualism**   the belief that society should exist for the benefit of the individual; the emphasis on individual initiative

**Industrial Revolution**   era of rapid developments in industry, agriculture, and transportation

**inflation**   an economic situation in which prices rise and the real value of the dollar falls

**interest**   money paid by the bank to the depositor that is a percentage of money on deposit

**internationalism**   foreign policy emphasizing active involvement and cooperation with other nations

**isolationism**   foreign policy emphasizing avoidance of alliances and international relations in general; characteristic of the United States in the 1800s

**Jim Crow laws**   state laws passed after the Civil War that legalized segregation in many Southern states

**labor**   people who do the actual work it takes to produce goods and provide services

**labor union**   an organization of workers that attempts to promote and protect the interests of members and of labor in general

**League of Nations**   an organization of countries formed after World War I to settle international disputes

**legend**   part of a map that tells what each of the symbols represents

**Limited Nuclear Test Ban Treaty** 1963 treaty signed by the United States and the Soviet Union and 100 other countries to limit nuclear weapons testing

**lines of latitude**   imaginary lines that run parallel to the equator to the north and south

**lines of longitude**   imaginary lines that run parallel to the prime meridian to the east and west

**loan**   money provided by a bank that must be paid back with interest

**management**   people who supervise and make major decisions about how a business is run

**manufactured goods**   the finished products of an industrial process

**manual laborers**   see blue-collar workers

**marine climate**   climate that is found near the sea and tends to be humid and mild

**Marshall Plan**   economic assistance offered by the United States to countries recovering from the devastation of World War II

**Mayflower Compact**   agreement by the Pilgrims of the Mayflower to govern themselves by direct democracy

**mediator**   important third party who helps labor and management settle disputes

**Medicare Act**   act by Congress that provides hospital and health insurance for all Americans over age 65

**Middle Colonies**   New York, New Jersey, Pennsylvania, and Delaware

**migration**   the movement of people from one region to another

**Mongoloid**   relating to the race of people that originated in Asia

**monopoly**   control of all the business in a certain field by one company

**Monroe Doctrine**   policy first stated by President Monroe that other countries were not to further colonize or otherwise interfere in the Americas

**mortgage**   a long-term loan for the purchase of a house

**mountain climate**   climate that is found at higher altitude and tends to be cool

**mutual savings bank**   a bank owned and run for a profit by the people who deposit their money there

**natural resources**   anything in the environment that people make use of, such as water, minerals, soil, and forests

**negotiate**   to work out terms of agreement, as in a contract between labor and management

**Negroid**   relating to the race of people that originated in Africa

**New Deal**   the name given to a number of programs introduced by President Franklin D. Roosevelt that were designed to bring the United States out of the Great Depression

**New England colonies**   Massachusetts, New Hampshire, Rhode Island, and Connecticut

**New World**   the name given to North and South America by the European explorers of the 16th century

**Nineteenth Amendment** Constitutional amendment that gave women the right to vote

**North Atlantic Treaty Organization (NATO)**   an alliance of western nations created in response to the formation of the Soviet Bloc

**Peace Corps**   organization formed under President Kennedy to provide educational and technical assistance to underdeveloped nations

**Pearl Harbor**   United States Naval installation in Hawaii that was attacked by the Japanese in 1941 forcing the United States to enter World War II

**personal income tax**   a percentage of each paycheck, based on salary, that is paid to the federal government

**physical maps**   maps that show lakes, rivers, mountains, and other physical features

**polar climate**   climate found in the very cold regions around the North and South poles

**political map** map that shows boundaries between countries, states, counties, etc., and locations of cities and bodies of water

**population** the number of people who live in a specified area

**population density** the average number of people in a specified unit of land, such as a square mile

**prime meridian** an imaginary line that runs north-south and divides the Earth into Eastern and Western Hemispheres

**profit** money over and above production costs gained by selling goods and services

**Progressive Movement** movement in the early 20th century to improve American life by expanding democracy and achieving economic and social justice

**progressive tax** a tax in which the amount to be paid increases as income increases, such as income tax

**property tax** a tax based on the value of real estate a person owns

**proprietor** the owner of a business

**protected market** a region or a country in which certain industries are protected from foreign competition

**race** a group of people with similar physical characteristics that are passed from one generation to the next

**raw material** material such as wood, coal, or stone that is used to make or is fashioned into a finished product

**recession** an economic situation that is characterized by decreased production and increased unemployment

**Reconstruction** the rebuilding and readmission into the Union of the Southern states following the Civil War

**regressive tax** a tax that has one rate for all and therefore weighs more heavily on people with lower incomes than on the wealthy, such as sales taxes

**Renaissance** a reawakening in Europe of an interest in science and the arts between the 14th and 17th centuries

**reserve limit** the amount of money the Federal Reserve Board requires banks to keep on hand; lowering the reserve limit makes more money available for loans

**revenue** income, especially income received by the government from taxes, etc.

**sales tax** tax collected by states that is a percentage of the selling price for goods and services

**salutary neglect** policy of Great Britain in the first half of the 18th century that in effect allowed the American colonies to virtually govern themselves

**savings and loan association** savings institution set up mainly to provide loans for the purchase of homes

**school tax** a proportional tax that helps pay for the costs of local schools

**sea level** the position of the sea's surface between high and low tide, used to measure land elevation

**sectionalism** giving loyalty to one's region rather than the nation, especially the division between the North and South over slavery and economic issues that led to the Civil War

**share** the part of a corporation owned by a private citizen who invests in that corporation

**sharecroppers** farmers who work other people's land and give a share of the crop as rent, especially blacks in the South after the Civil War

**Shays' Rebellion** an uprising of debtor farmers in Massachusetts that revealed the weakness of the Articles of Confederation

**Social Security tax** a proportional tax taken out of each paycheck that helps pay for Social Security benefits

**social welfare programs** programs, generally funded by taxes, that aim to improve the quality of life

**socialism** economic philosophy that states that wealth should be equally shared by all

**society** group of people who live within a certain geographical area and share traditions and institutions

**Southern Colonies** Maryland, North Carolina, South Carolina, Virginia, and Georgia

**Spanish-American War** war the United States fought against Spain in 1898 to free Cuba from Spanish rule and protect U.S. economic interests

**special purpose map** map that shows particular features of a region such as natural resources, climate, land use, or population

**Stamp Act** tax imposed by Great Britain in 1765 on legal documents and newspapers in the American colonies

**stock** see share

**Stock Market Crash** in 1929, the sudden plunge of stock values on the New York Stock exchange

**strike** the stopping of production by workers seeking higher wages or improved conditions

**supply** the amount of a good or service that is available for people to purchase

**Taft-Hartley Act** 1947 legislation that placed restrictions on labor unions

**tariff** a tax on imports

**tax bracket** tax division that is determined by amount of personal income and is used to calculate how much tax a person owes

temperate climate   relatively moderate climate characterized by four distinct seasons, including a period during which crops can be grown

Third World   the underdeveloped and in some cases impoverished countries of Africa, Asia, and Latin America

Three-Fifths Compromise   the compromise between Northern and Southern states during the writing of the Constitution that determined for the purposes of taxation and representation five slaves and three free persons counted equally

Thirteenth Amendment   the constitutional amendment that ended slavery throughout the country

topographic map   a physical map that uses special contour lines to show the elevation of various features

town meetings   town gatherings in colonial New England at which men voted on the town laws and elected representatives to colonial assemblies

toxic   poisonous

Treasury Department   the department of government concerned with the management of revenue, including the minting and circulation of money

Treaty of Paris (1783)   agreement between Great Britain and the American colonies that ended the Revolutionary War and granted American independence

Treaty of Paris (1898)   treaty that ended the Spanish-American War, freed Cuba of Spain's control and gave Guam, Puerto Rico, and the Philippines to the United States

tropical climate   hot and humid climate found near the equator

Truman Doctrine   President Truman's policy that provided military and economic aid to countries threatened by communist expansion

U.S. bond issues   securities sold by the government to private citizens in order to raise money, especially in war time

United Nations (U.N.)   organization of nations set up after World War II to encourage international peace and cooperation

Union   the 19 Northern states that opposed the Confederacy in the Civil War

War on Poverty   attempt by President Johnson in the 1960s to eliminate poverty; part of his Great Society

weather   the way the climate changes from day to day

white-collar workers   people who work primarily at desk jobs in offices

World War I   the war waged in Europe from 1914 to 1918 that involved 30 countries, with the United States entering the war in 1917

World War II   the war that pitted the Axis nations of Germany, Italy, and Japan against the Allied nations including Great Britain, Russia, and the United States